AMILIES OF THE WORLD

Historical Linguistics: an Introduction

Historical

Linguistics: an Introduction

Winfred P. Lehmann
The University of Texas

HOLT, RINEHART, AND WINSTON
New York · Chicago · San Francisco
Toronto · London

Library of Congress Catalog Card Number 62-12987

25204—0512

Printed in the United States of America

January, 1966

To

R. P. L.

Preface

An Introduction, the subtitle of *Historical Linguistics,* has determined the scope of this book. My aim throughout is to provide an introduction to general principles. The methods used in historical linguistic study and the types of change found in language may have been dealt with compactly, but the space devoted to each reflects its importance and its contribution to the field. Through this presentation students should become acquainted with the various techniques used in historical linguistics, while instructors may pursue in greater depth principles or methods that are of interest at the moment. Examples from a variety of languages can be confusing in a general handbook presenting linguistic principles, for the system of even one language is complex. Accordingly, the discussion in this introductory text centers around the Indo-European languages, primarily English. The workbook provides additional assistance in achieving an understanding of the English system with its principal changes from Proto-Germanic to Modern English.

Though a feeling of breadth would be obtained by citations from other language groups which are becoming well explored, aside from the possible confusion of diversity, our understanding of language and change in language persuades us to avoid random examples. Without dwelling on adverse instances in publications of the past, we know that it is pointless to deal with items of language outside a system.

Bibliography has been kept to a minimum. The works cited at the end of each chapter have been selected because of their pertinence to general principles. After these have been mastered, journals and monographs are the proper sources for contemporary views on method and for attempts to modify the principles of our discipline; the *Linguistic Bibliography* is a good source for locating these, especially since it also indicates reviews.

Any handbook is successful to the extent it relies on its predecessors and on contemporary scholars. Besides acknowledging my debt to other historical linguists, I should like to thank particularly Bagby Atwood and Hans Kurath for their kindness in permitting use of linguistic maps they have prepared, T. Doebbler for designing these and the other maps for the purposes here, and Robert A. Hall, Jr. for permission to use some of his Melanesian pidgin materials. I also owe thanks to Henry Hoenigswald, Ruth Lehmann, Edgard Polomé, and Werner Winter for suggestions made on the book when it was in manuscript. It is a further pleasure to express my appreciation for academic surroundings, due in great part to a vigorous administration at the University of Texas, which made this book possible.

W. P. L.

Austin, Texas
May, 1962

CONTENTS

LANGUAGE SYMBOLS PRECEDING CHAPTER TITLES

End-paper Map: A composite map drawn by T. Doebbler under direction of the author.

Historical Linguistics: an Introduction

1 – Introduction

1.1 Languages change constantly, a fact that becomes most noticeable when we read texts a few centuries old. For instance, various kinds of change are apparent in almost any passage of Shakespeare, such as in these four lines from his Sonnet XI:

> As fast as thou shalt wane, so fast thou grow'st
> In one of thine, from that which thou departest;
> And that fresh blood which youngly thou bestow'st
> Thou mayst call thine when thou from youth convertest.

When these lines are read today, lines two and four do not rime. We may suspect that they did for Shakespeare, and our suspicion is confirmed when we find that such a word as the proper name *Clark* is in origin the word *clerk,* that *parson* is in origin the word *person,* and so on. Shakespeare's rimes also give us information about his pronunciation. We find additional evidence in the puns he uses in his plays, which we with our different pronunciation would not make. From these forms of evidence, including spellings which reflect actual pronunciation, we can pretty well determine the sound of Shakespeare's speech. From such evidence we also know that English has been changing in its sounds. This change in sound is now termed **phonological change** (see Chapter 10, pages 147–175). In comparing earlier and later forms of any language we find various types of phonological change.

The passage just quoted from Shakespeare also shows changes of form. In contemporary conversation, or even when writing poetry, we no longer use the pronouns *thou, thine,* or the accompanying verb forms ending in *-st.* There is enough material in Shakespeare's plays to determine the system of forms which he used, and to note the differences between them and the system of forms used in current English. From a comparison of the two systems we can note various changes in form. These are called **morphological changes.** Materials in other languages also give data on morphological change and lead to the conclusion that all languages change in their system of forms.

The selection from Shakespeare's sonnet also illustrates alterations in syntax. We no longer use *depart* as a transitive verb, except in archaic religious language; *convert* on the other hand is generally used as a transitive. Further examples demonstrate other **syntactic changes** between Shakespeare's English and ours. Since syntactic and morphological changes have much in common we treat them together as **grammatical change** (see Chapter 11, pages 177–192). We might also be led to suspect, noticing fewer changes in grammar than in phonology, that languages alter more readily in sounds than in forms and syntax, and this suspicion is confirmed when we study the history of various languages.

When we have dealt with changes in phonology and grammar, we have exhausted the segment of language that linguists regard as their chief concern. But we have not yet dealt with meaning, in its usual sense. Elements like *-st* have meaning, of course, for they indicate that the subject is the second person *thou* in words such as *growest* versus *grows*. Such meaning, known as grammatical in contrast to the lexical meaning of words, is of great concern to descriptive linguists, who have left study of the use of linguistic elements like *grow* and *convert* to lexicographers or students of semantics. Changes in meaning, in the usual sense of the word, are termed **semantic changes** (see Chapter 12, pages 193–210). In studying the history of any language we must deal with changes in the meanings of both forms and words, the loss of some, the introduction of others. The word *convert* in Shakespeare's Sonnet XI meant to 'undergo a change'; for us it means to 'produce a change, often from one belief to another.' Since the time of Shakespeare it has been modified in scope, as well as changed in its syntactic use. The word *wane* has almost been lost from the language, except in fixed expressions like *the waning of the moon*. Whole realms of words have been added to English since Shakespeare's day; the large vocabulary of science is an example.

1.2 In historical linguistics we study differences in languages between two points of time. As we investigate languages we also find differences between two or more points in space. The pronunciation of *depart* varies considerably in England and America, and in various sections of each country. From indications in texts over several centuries we know that in England the *r* has been lost, with lengthening of the preceding vowel; in many sections of America an *r* remains. Subdivisions of a language are referred to as **dialects.** The study of variations among dialects of a language is termed **dialect geography** (see Chapter 8, pages 115–135).

Study of variations in languages from place to place are of great concern to historical linguistics for changes may be introduced into languages as speakers of one language adopt elements of another, or as speakers of one dialect take on forms of another. The word *depart,* for example, is French in origin. When speakers of English and French were in daily contact, many words were **borrowed** by English speakers from the French vocabulary. The English *depart* may be traced back to Old French *departir,* and ultimately to Latin *dis-* 'away from each other' and *partīrī* 'to divide.' On the other hand the word *grow* can be traced back to Old English *grōwan,* and as far as we can determine to earlier stages preceding English, which are referred to as Proto-Germanic and Proto-Indo-European. For we find the equivalent of English *grow* in Old High German *gruoen* and in Old Norse *grōa.* These words are related to Modern English *green* and *grass,* and to their equivalents in the other Germanic languages. They are also related to Latin *grāmen* 'grass,' so that we must assume forms of this group of words for the language from which Old English and Latin developed; accordingly we classify *grow, green,* and *grass* as native English words. In studying any language we must distinguish carefully between native forms like *grow* and borrowed forms like *depart.* Investigations of the borrowings in languages, of the interplay between dialects and languages, and of the effect of one language on another is an important task of historical linguistics (see Chapter 13, pages 211–231).

1.3 The comparison of various languages led to the assumption that some languages are **related,** that they developed from a common source. This assumption came to be confirmed in large part through the linguistic situation in western Europe. For common words in French, Italian, Spanish, Rumanian, and several other languages show consistent similarities and differences. Compare for example the words for *hay* and *fork:*

'hay'	Fr. *foin*	Ital. *fieno*	Span. *heno*	Rum. *fîn*
'fork'	Fr. *fourche*	Ital. *forca*	Span. *horca*	Rum. *furcă*

The Spanish *h* in these words, now lost in standard Spanish, corresponds consistently with the *f* in the words of French,

Italian and Rumanian. From this consistent correspondence we assume that at least some Spanish *h* developed from earlier *f* through phonological change. This assumption is supported by other examples, such as,

'son' Span. *hijo* cf. Fr. *fils* Ital. *figlio* Rum. *fiu* Lat. *fīlius*
'iron' Span. *hierro* cf. Fr. *fer* Ital. *ferro* Rum. *fier* Lat. *ferrum*

It leads us to the conclusion that French, Italian, Spanish and Rumanian are members of one **linguistic group** or **language family.** The reason for their similarity is their common descent from one earlier language, Latin. Through such comparison we can relate other languages, assume that they developed from an earlier language, and classify them as belonging to a specific language family. Various techniques developed to understand such relationships are discussed in Chapter 9, pages 137–146.

It is of extreme importance to note from the first that such relationships must be assumed from observation of systematic differences as well as systematic similarities. Further, the system is essential, for it is difficult to define what is similar, what different, until we analyze the system of any language. The Spanish *h,* unpronounced in present Spanish and therefore the systematic absence of an initial consonant, is in some ways a more trustworthy indication of relationship than are the unchanged sounds of French, Italian and Rumanian, for it can be systematically related to the *f-* of these languages. In establishing relationships, we in this way look for recurrences, whether between similar or different segments of the two or more systems. Our conclusions may be wrong if we base relationships merely on similar words, for we may find them in languages that are totally unrelated, such as Turkish *futbol* and Japanese *futobōru,* which are borrowed from English *football,* or Japanese *bai* and English *buy,* which are chance similarities. Historical linguistics developed only after linguists abandoned the comparison of random words that looked alike from language to language, and when they began instead to determine recurrent similarities and differences in the phonological and grammatical systems, as well as in the vocabularies of the languages they assumed to be related.

Further words from French, Italian and Spanish will illustrate in greater detail the use of systematic comparison, the **comparative method** (see Chapter 5, pages 83–97). If we compare the words for 'eight':

Fr. *huit* Ital. *otto* Span. *ocho*

it would seem difficult to derive them from a common source. By assembling additional examples, we can however derive them from a specific Latin word and explain the differing development in each of these languages. Compare:

'milk'	Fr. *lait*	Ital. *latte*	Span. *leche*
'fact'	Fr. *fait*	Ital. *fatto*	Span. *hecho*

Noting the Latin sources for these three sets of words: *octō,* 'eight,' *lactem* (accusative singular after the Classical period of 'milk'), *factum,* 'fact,' we can understand the changes in these three languages and also see their essential regularity. In French the Latin [k] has been vocalized; in Italian it has been assimilated to the following [t]; in Spanish it has been changed to an affricate with loss of the following [t]. In three different geographical areas a sequence originally the same developed into three different sequences. Through use of the comparative method, knowledge of possible phonetic changes and of the earlier forms, we can determine the history of the cited forms and of most forms in French, Italian and Spanish.

1.4 The languages which developed from Latin, commonly known as the **Romance languages,** are of great importance to historical linguists, because they furnish both the materials for comparison and the earlier language from which the Romance languages developed. In them, problems are available for solution, and in Latin the solution can be verified.

Through this happy chance the essential techniques and procedures of historical linguistics may be tested. They were refined, especially through work with the language family to which the Romance languages and Latin in turn belong, the **Indo-European** group.

Shortly before 1800, Sir William Jones, an English jurist in India, observed that the ancient, learned language of India, **Sanskrit,** was systematically similar to Greek and Latin, to his native language, and to earlier forms of it. This observation had been made before, without widespread effect; after Jones' statement scholars in Europe began systematic comparison of older forms of English and German with Latin, Greek, Sanskrit and other languages. Their work in the nineteenth century led to the classification of these languages into the Indo-European family, and to the development of historical linguistics as a discipline.

Comparison of the numerals from one to ten in some of the Indo-European languages will demonstrate the relationship, especially if we also compare words for these numerals in the unrelated languages, Chinese and Japanese. (Instead of citing Old English forms, we will cite forms from Gothic, which is also a Germanic language, but one attested to be several centuries earlier than Old English.)

We cite the forms in a contemporary transliteration, not the alphabets used for Gothic or Greek, nor the characters used for Sanskrit, nor those for Chinese and Japanese. Yet without knowledge of the writing system used for each language we would have inadequate means for its interpretation. We can, for example, draw only partial conclusions from Gothic, for it was transmitted in a writing system based on that of Greek of the fourth century A.D. At this time Greek *ai* was pronounced approximately like the vowel in English *men*. We cannot however be sure that this was its only value in Gothic. Many linguists have held that the vowel of the Gothic word for 'one' was actually a diphthong, similar to that of English *mine*. For

Gothic and for any language attested in written texts, historical linguists must be able to deal with the written records which have come down to us or their conclusions may be naive. The problems involved in dealing with written records are discussed in Chapter 4, pages 63–82.

Yet for practical purposes, especially in an elementary handbook, we cite forms in a transliteration—which, like that for Mandarin Chinese, often presents problems of its own. The Mandarin forms are given here in a system named after its originator, Wade, with numerals marking tones: 1 = level tone, 2 = rising, 3 = falling–rising, 4 = falling.

Although a complete account of the similarities and differences between the words of the first six columns of Table 1 would require considerable space, we can readily note a few examples such as the *t*- in columns one and two of the words for 'two' and 'ten' corresponding to *d*- in columns three through six. By comparison, the Chinese and Japanese words permit no assumption of correspondences with any of the columns. We also note the systematic difference in vowel between Sanskrit *a* and Latin and Greek *e* in the first syllables of the words for 'six,' 'seven' and 'ten.' Analysis of all the systematic similarities and differences between the Indo-European languages required the work of many linguists during the nineteenth and twentieth centuries, and is still not complete. But even with as little material as the numerals from 'one' to 'ten' we can assume with confidence that English, Gothic, Latin, Greek, Old Church Slavic, and Sanskrit belong to one language family, and that they developed from a common source.

1.5 The comparative method, as just illustrated, is the most common procedure used in determining older patterns of a language. By examining the Japanese numerals cited in the table we can note another procedure, one especially valuable when we have no large number of related languages. Without using forms other than those of Japanese listed above we can

TABLE 1

English	Gothic	Latin	Greek	Old Church Slavic	Sanskrit	Chinese	Japanese
one	ains	ūnus	heîs	jedinŭ	ekas	i^1	hitotsu
two	twai	duo	dúō	dŭva	dvā	erh^4	futatsu
three	þrija acc.	trēs	treîs	trije	trayas	san^1	mittsu
four	fidwor	quattuor	téttares	četyre	catvāras	ssu^4	yottsu
five	fimf	quīnque	pénte	pętĭ	pañca	wu^3	itsutsu
six	saihs	sex	héks	šestĭ	ṣaṭ	liu^4	muttsu
seven	sibun	septem	heptá	sedmĭ	sapta	$ch'i^1$	nanatsu
eight	ahtau	octō	oktṓ	osmĭ	aṣṭā	pa^1	yattsu
nine	niun	novem	ennéa	devętĭ	nava	$chiu^3$	kokonotsu
ten	taihun	decem	déka	desętĭ	daśa	$shih^2$	tō

note a pattern in these numerals; the double of the lower numerals begins with the same consonant as does its half, that is, *mi* 'three' and *mu* 'six,' *yo* 'four' and *ya* 'eight.' Even though the initial consonant of the Japanese word for 'one' *hi* is now a laryngeal fricative, from such analysis, supported by other evidence in the language, we can suggest that it was once a labial. This procedure is referred to as **internal reconstruction** (see Chapter 6, pages 99–106). While we use it of necessity in a language like Japanese which seems to have no proven related languages, we may also apply it to problems in families like the Indo-European which are widely attested.

Unfortunately the common source of the Indo-European languages was spoken before writing was in use in its geographical area and we have no attested forms of it. With the methodology developed partly in the study of the Romance languages, linguists have reconstructed the "original" Indo-European language as far as our data permit. To indicate, however, that it is not attested we label it with the prefix **Proto-** and refer to it as **Proto-Indo-European (PIE).** (To indicate reconstructed or nonattested forms we place an asterisk (*) before them; since, however, a form identified as belonging to a proto-language is by definition unattested, when we use P- before a language abbreviation we may omit the asterisk.) Even reconstructed forms we like to deal with as we do contemporary, attested forms, positing their phonemic structure, as for PIE /dekm/ 'ten,' and their phonetic structure, e.g. PIE [dékm̩].

By comparing the words for 'ten' in all of the Indo-European languages we can reconstruct PIE /dekm/ [dékm̩]. We can reconstruct other words, such as PIE /g^{w}ōws/ 'cow' on the basis of Old English *cū,* Old Irish *bō,* Latin *bōs, bovis,* Greek *boûs,* Lettish *guovs,* Sanskrit *gaus,* and so on. We can also reconstruct morphological elements, such as the ending PIE /-ty/ [-ti] from forms like that for 'he is' in Greek *esti,* Sanskrit *asti,* and many others. When we reconstruct Proto-Indo-European we are dealing with a language spoken before 3000 B.C. and we obviously do not have the amount of data which are available for Latin. But we can determine the essential elements of the Proto-Indo-European phonological and grammatical systems, and even draw some inferences about their vocabularies.

1.6 It has been suggested recently that the everyday segments of the vocabulary are replaced at a definite rate, and that the words which have been maintained in related languages may be used for dating in much the same way as radioactive decay has been used in dating the age of the earth. This procedure is referred to as **glottochronology** or **lexicostatistics.** In the use of glottochronology, discussed in Chapter 7, pages 107–113, lists of one or two hundred words are gathered from related languages and the proportion of related words is determined, with no closer attention to their similarities. English *cow* and German *Kuh* would be adequately similar, but not *dog* and *Hund*. Many problems remain to be solved in the use of lexicostatistics. It has been of especial interest in attempts to solve questions on the interrelationships between languages attested only in recent times, such as the American Indian languages. As in the development of the comparative method, it is being tested with materials from the Romance and Indo-European languages, whose changes have been carefully studied, and largely accounted for.

1.7 The difference between PIE /dekm/ and NE *ten* can be accounted for by positing various types of change, at the phonological level. PIE /d/ became PGmc /t/, as in *ten,* cf. Latin *decem, two,* cf. Lat. *duo;* PIE /k/ became PGmc /χ/, later /h/, as in *hundred,* cf. Lat. *centum, hound,* cf. Lat. *canis;* in early Old English /h/ was lost between vowels. Other changes permit us to relate the two forms exactly.

We cannot however account in this way for the ending of the Modern English form *ships* as compared with the Old English nominative/accusative plural *scipu*. Here we find the plural ending remodeled after that in such Old English nouns as *stānas* 'stones' from sg. *stān* 'stone.' Study of even a small segment of a language leads to the observation that forms similarly used may influence or modify one another. When we compare the Old Church Slavic word for 'nine,' for example, with its cognates in the other Indo-European languages, we may assume that, like them, it should have begun with *n*. The simplest explanation for the initial *d* of *devętĭ* is that it was taken over from *desętĭ* 'ten.' Such influence is called **analogical;** we say that the Proto-Slavic word for 'nine' was modified by **analogy** with that for 'ten,' and that the *-s* marking the plural of *ship* was spread by analogy. Modification of this sort can be exemplified in sets of forms from any language; in contemporary Japanese, for example, 'seven' is often pronounced *hichi* rather than *shichi,* probably by analogy with *hachi* 'eight.'

Elements of a structure so closely interconnected as language undergo various types of mutual influence. Changes may be induced by the influence of one element on another, as we noted for Old Church Slavic *devętĭ;* they may be blocked; the changes may be comprehensive or only partial. The modifications induced by elements within the language are as complex as are sound changes. Similarly complex are the modifications resulting from interplay of dialects and languages.

1.8 If for example we compare the forms of numerals in another Indo-European language, Albanian, we would not be able to explain them as we have briefly the forms of English *ten;* for they embody differences that can neither be explained through regular phonological change nor analogical modification. The Albanian for 'four' is *katër*. Since this form does not agree with the form we should expect through regular development in Albanian, and since we know that Albanian was strongly influenced by Latin, we account for *katër* by assuming it was borrowed from Latin. Change resulting from interplay of languages is especially prominent in the area of vocabulary, much more so than in grammar or phonology.

Vocabulary innovations were made extensively in English, and can be illustrated as in Albanian from even such a fundamental segment of the language as the lower numerals. In examining the English ordinal numerals, we conclude that they are based on the cardinals plus a suffix, for example, *third* versus *three, fourth* versus *four,* and so on. This explanation will not do for *second* versus *two.* We can only account for it by deriving it from Old French *second,* which in turn is derived from Latin *secundus* 'next following,' an adjective related to the verb *sequor* 'I follow.'

1.9 By investigating languages for phenomena like these, with the changes they have undergone, we can determine their history and their interrelationships with other languages. After a century and a half of investigation, the development of most of the languages in the Indo-European family is well known. Other language families have not been so fully described in their development, partly because data were lacking, especially from earlier historical periods. Furthermore, linguists were primarily interested in determining the background of their own native languages, which with few exceptions were Indo-European.

The success of historical linguistic study depends on the state of descriptive linguistics. Indo-European historical linguistics developed rapidly in the nineteenth century because thorough descriptions were available for Latin, Greek and Sanskrit; on the pattern of these descriptions, grammars were produced for other early Indo-European languages, such as Gothic, Old Church Slavic, Old Irish, and subsequently for the remaining Indo-European languages, such as Armenian and Albanian. Since equally detailed descriptions were not produced for the languages of other families, even the Finno-Ugric and Afro-Asiatic, historical grammar of these families is less advanced than that of Indo-European. Where materials for descriptions are lacking, or limited in extent, or confined to recent times, historical grammar will never reach the state that it has for the Indo-European languages.

Even for the Indo-European languages historical work has been limited, for it has been confined by the state of descriptive linguistics to segments of the language. Until recently descriptive linguists have dealt primarily with segmental elements, disregarding almost entirely suprasegmentals. Accordingly, we find relatively little about stress and pitch in our historical grammars. As descriptive grammars present fuller information on these elements, historical linguists will be able to round out their accounts of the development of specific languages and language families.

More complete accounts will in turn lead to improvement of the techniques employed in historical linguistics. In discussing these we draw in large measure from data in the Indo-European language family. To illustrate the procedures of setting up language families and describing genetic relationships, we shall present in some detail the Indo-European language group.

SELECTED FURTHER READINGS

For an introduction to the problems and methods of historical linguistics see Holger Pedersen, *Linguistic Science in the Nineteenth Century,* translated by John Spargo (Cambridge, 1931). This book provides a readable, if limited, discussion of the principles of historical linguistics as they were evolved in the course of the nineteenth century.

Otto Jespersen, *Language, Its Nature, Development and Origin* (London, 1922), also discusses the history of linguistics in his Book I, pages 19–99, without however confining himself to historical linguistics.

Carl Darling Buck, *Comparative Grammar of Greek and Latin* (Chicago, 1933) [subsequently reprinted with few changes], provides a brief, though clear, introduction to historical linguistics, pages 30–67, and may be used generally with profit.

Another concise but excellent statement on the development and principles of historical linguistics may be found in A. Meillet's *Introduction à l'étude comparative des langues indo-européennes* (Paris, 1937) [8th edition], Chapter I and Appendix I.

A survey of the study of language concentrating on bibliography may be found in Chapter XIII of Louis H. Gray, *Foundations of Language* (New York, 1939).

2 – Genealogical Classification of Languages

2.1 In the previous chapter we noted evidence that many of the languages of Europe and Asia are interrelated. The evidence may be found at all levels of these languages. Most apparent is similarity of basic vocabulary: words for lower numerals, kinship, domestic animals, everyday activities. But even more convincing are the similarities one can find in various systems of the grammar. From the phonological system we may cite initial *d-* in words of the same meaning in Sanskrit, Greek, Latin, Slavic, as in the words for 'two' and 'ten.' From the inflection we may cite formal elements filling the same role in these languages, as the ending in the third person singular indicative /ty/. From derivation we may cite similar constructions, such as the *Bluebeard* type of compound in English; as we examine older forms of Indic and Greek, we find large numbers of these compounds. In syntax, too, we find similar patterns, such as the favoring of the second position in clauses for particles which relate clauses. Some of the evidence was apparent to linguists a century and a half ago. They examined the interrelationships to the extent their evidence permitted and proposed the large linguistic group known today as the **Indo-European family.**

Detailed study of the Indo-European family is important for understanding of historical linguistic method as well as for knowledge of the interrelationships of some of the world's most widely spoken languages. For the methods applied in dealing with the Indo-European languages may also be applied to other language groups. Moreover, because of the political and economic role of the speakers using languages belonging to it, the Indo-European family is probably the most important and the most widely used today. (For its distribution, and the location of other language families, see the map inside the cover.)

In attempting to set up any language family the oldest known forms of a language are of great importance, as is their time of origin. Accordingly for any historical study, we attempt to date the materials with which we are dealing. Approximate dates at which the oldest Indo-European materials are attested will therefore be given here.

An understanding of linguistic development also requires that we determine the interrelationships of language subgroups and languages within a family. The data involved in establishing such classifications are often complex. Details will generally be omitted here but can be found in grammars devoted to individual languages, such as Old English, or to individual subgroups, such as Germanic, the group to which Old English belongs. Moreover, to the present, successive stages of any language have been only approximately determined. Most of them are based on nonlinguistic evidence. The division between Middle High German and New High German, for example, has often been dated at the time of the Reformation. Other criteria used have been the introduction of printing or political developments, as for the terminal date of Middle English, or simply the turn of a century. Though external forces on the language may have been important in spreading or giving prestige to one form of it, we can use only linguistic criteria for linguistic classifications. Since this has rarely been done, the dates given here and in handbooks for stages of a language are often provisional. Even when true linguistic dating is possible, students must note that languages never change abruptly: for the Germans or English of periods like the fifteenth and sixteenth centuries, when we demarcate Middle from New German or English, there were no more apparent differences between their speech and that of their children or parents than for speakers at apparently serene linguistic times like the nineteenth century.

2.2 A part of the energy with which historical linguistic study was pursued in the nineteenth century derived from the discovery that the ancient and modern languages of much of India were related to the Germanic languages and to the classical languages as well. When this discovery was made, scholars were greatly concerned with the origins and the early institutions of mankind. The Indic materials, which were even more archaic than were those of Greece, excited the Grimm brothers, Rasmus Rask, Franz Bopp and others to devote tremendous energy and time to the understanding of the interrelationships between their own languages and those of Greece, Italy and India in which materials had been preserved for several millennia.

The name given to the family was a compound composed of one unit representing the most easterly area, India, and the most westerly area, Europe, in which the family had been located. Such hyphenated compounds have subsequently been devised for many other language families: Sino-Tibetan, Malayo-Polynesian, Afro-Asiatic, and so on. Since the Germanic family was located farthest to the north, in Iceland, many scholars, particularly in Germany, label the family **Indo-Germanic.** Others, using a term which the early Indic and Celtic authors applied to their own people, called the family **Aryan;** this name is now in disrepute because of a misuse of it for devious political purposes.

Even other names have been proposed, but the one used most widely today is Indo-European.

We will first examine, roughly in accordance with their distribution from east to west, the various subgroups of the Indo-European family of which representatives are spoken today.

2.3 Indo-Iranian, formerly also called **Aryan** or **Indo-Aryan,** is the name of the subgroup which was carried to the area of Iran and India in migrations more than three millennia ago. It consists of two subgroups, of which **Indic** is the more important; for materials in **Iranian** date from a considerably later period and are less abundant.

The earliest Indic material is contained in the *Rigveda,* a collection of hymns which is as large as the *Iliad* and *Odyssey* combined. The oldest hymns are cosmological poems, composed somewhat before 1000 B.C. Writing materials disintegrate in the Indian climate and we have no early records. But since the poems of the *Rigveda* and the other *Vedas* were considered sacred, they were memorized and transmitted orally for many generations. We can vouch for the accuracy of the transmission, for most lines of the poems still conform to the metrical forms in which they were composed.

The veneration accorded the *Vedas* which led to their careful preservation yielded other results of importance to linguistics. As the language of the *Vedas* became obsolete and difficult to interpret, their devotees prepared commentaries. Among these were grammars which informed later generations of priests how to interpret the hymns, even how to pronounce them. For a faulty pronunciation would scarcely achieve the intended aim of a hymn. The result of such linguistic analysis was a standardized language, so completely described and regulated [saṃskr̥ta] that it underwent few further changes. This saṃskr̥ta is known to us as **Sanskrit.** We date it from several centuries before 400 B.C., the putative time of its greatest grammarian, Pāṇini. A grammar attributed to him described the language with such authority and completeness that ever after it has been learned by Indian scholars with no essential deviations. To this day Sanskrit is in daily use, because of its religious associations, and in this way is comparable to Latin, Old Church Slavic, and Classical Arabic.

Beside the saṃskr̥ta "regulated, cultivated, correct" there existed spoken languages called prākr̥ta, **Prakrits.** We are much better informed on Sanskrit than on the Prakrits for a tremendous amount of learned material has been produced in India. Many of the learned texts are religious writings: the *Brahmanas* are interpretative tracts in Sanskrit, as are the *Upanishads*. Moreover, the classical works of Indian literature were composed in Sanskrit: the *Mahabharata* and the *Ramayana,* epics which are much longer than any composed in Europe. Fortunately the dramas include female characters. Since they were not permitted to speak the purified language, we have in their lines, and those of characters of lower castes, examples of Prakrits. Examples also appear in other materials. Literary Prakrit is dated from about the beginning of our era. In the period before Christ we accordingly have three stages of Indic: **Vedic** or **Vedic Sanskrit,** the language of approximately 1200–800 B.C.; **Classical Sanskrit,** succeeding it and standardized approximately 400 B.C.; and the Prakrits.

Vedic and Classical Sanskrit are often referred to as **Old Indic,** the Prakrits as **Middle Indic,** which we may date from about 400 B.C. to A.D. 1000. The Middle Indic dialect on which we have most information is **Pali;** it is the language in which the Buddhist canon is preserved. We may place it shortly before Christ, though Indic dates are highly uncertain, for the Indians were quite unconcerned about history. Fortunately contacts with the Greeks permit us to date a great Buddhist ruler, Asoka, around 250 B.C. His many inscriptions may then be used to determine the state of the Indic dialects shortly before the beginning of our era. At the end of the Middle Indic period, before A.D. 1000, we have materials known as

Apabhraṃsas 'off-branchings.' From the Apabhraṃsas developed the modern Indic dialects. Most widely spoken of these is **Hindi,** the official language of the Republic of India; Hindi is also known as **Hindustani,** and in Pakistan as **Urdu.** Others are **Bengali, Gujerati, Marathi, Panjabi** and numerous less widely spoken languages, such as **Singhalese** in Ceylon, and **Romany,** the language of the Gypsies.

Iranian materials are referred to as **Old Iranian** if from before 300 B.C. and are handed down to us in two dialects, **Avestan** and **Old Persian.** The *Avesta* is the sacred book of the Zoroastrian religion; its oldest poems, the *Gāθās,* are dated approximately 600 B.C. and are as archaic in language as those of the Rigveda, though much more troubled in transmission and accordingly very difficult to interpret. Old Persian is preserved in the inscriptions of Darius, 521–486 B.C., and Xerxes, 486–465 B.C. The inscription of greatest importance is a long trilingual text in Old Persian, Akkadian and Elamite, which was chiseled on a stone cliff at Behistan, Iran. The Behistan inscription recounts the feats of Darius. Written in the cuneiform writing system, it not only preserved for us, until recently, the oldest body of Indo-European texts surviving from the time they were written down, but it also provided the avenue to the understanding of cuneiform. To illustrate the close relationship between Old Persian, Avestan and Sanskrit we may cite words like that for 'spear': OPers. and Av. *aršti-,* Skt. *r̥ṣṭi-* or OPers. *daiva-,* Av. *daēva-* 'devil,' Skt. *deva-* 'god.'

We may date Middle Iranian from approximately 300 B.C. to A.D. 900. Various representatives of it are attested. **Pahlavi** or **Middle Persian** was the language of the Persian Empire, flourishing from about A.D. 300 to 900. Further east, **Sogdian** and to the north **Saka** or **Scythian** were spoken and to this day are not completely described, partly because many of their texts were discovered only recently.

At present various Iranian languages are still in use,

Balochi of West Pakistan, **Pashtu (Paštō)** or **Afghan,** the official language of Afghanistan, **Persian,** the language of Iran, **Kurdish,** spoken by various groups in western Iran and Turkey, **Ossetic** in the northern Caucasus, and many others. Though still spoken by millions of speakers, the Iranian languages have been displaced in many areas by Turkic dialects and have a much smaller number of speakers than do the Indian dialects. Since dialects of the two groups are spoken in much of southern Asia, Indo-Iranian has remained one of the most prominent subgroups in the Indo-European family.

2.4 Of **Armenian,** located in the southern Caucasus and western Turkey, we have no materials until the fifth century A.D. We assume from Akkadian and Greek accounts that the Armenians migrated to Armenia some centuries before the beginning of our era. Yet the oldest materials we have were presumably composed in the fifth century A.D. and are almost exclusively translations of Christian writings. A considerable number of Armenian texts have survived; some Christian writers have had their materials preserved only in Armenian. The language of these texts is referred to as **Old** or **Classical Armenian.** It was maintained with few changes as the written language until the nineteenth century. Modern Armenian exists in two branches: the **Eastern,** spoken in the Union of Soviet Socialist Republics and Iran, and the **Western,** spoken in Turkey. Some speakers of Armenian have settled elsewhere, in Lebanon, parts of Europe, and the United States.

Armenian has been heavily influenced by other languages, notably Iranian. Until late in the nineteenth century there was doubt whether it should not be classed as an Iranian dialect. Meillet, *Linguistique historique et linguistique générale,* 1.95, cited the Gypsy dialect of Armenian as an example of a language that may contain almost no native vocabulary but have its phonological and grammatical structure. The grammatical structure of Armenian then is Indo-European and exact correspondences can be set up for the basic vocabulary, such as *hayr* 'father' = Latin *pater,* and so on. Yet in spite of our certainty of its situation as a language separate from Indo-Iranian, the precise position of Armenian is not yet agreed on. It has occasionally been related to the poorly attested **Phrygian.**

2.5 The early history of **Albanian** is even more inadequately known. Our earliest records are translations of the book of Matthew from the fourteenth century A.D. We have few further materials until 1685, when a Latin–Albanian dictionary was produced, followed by religious translations, and collections of folk tales in the nineteenth century. There are two dialects: **Geg** in the north and **Tosk** in the south, extending into Greece and Italy.

Like Armenian, Albanian has undergone many changes in its vocabulary, influenced successively by Latin, Greek, Slavic and Turkish. Its origins are difficult to determine. It has been considered by some scholars a modern representative of **Illyrian,** of **Thracian** by others. To determine its early position we must either have thorough reconstruction of its early stages, on the basis of descriptive work now being carried on, or we will need new early texts. Reconstruction is hampered by the small proportion of native material in the language; discovery of early texts is a matter of chance. Without one of these aids, however, Albanian of only the past few centuries can be described.

2.6 The **Baltic** and **Slavic** groups are attested only during the past millennium, yet languages in each contain relatively archaic characteristics. Such characteristics are the large number of case forms in the noun declension of Lithuanian; it lacks only one of the cases of Sanskrit, the ablative. In its accentual system Lithuanian preserves for words a pitch accent, which Classical Sanskrit had already given up. Yet our oldest Lithuanian texts date only from the sixteenth century A.D. Our oldest Slavic texts date from the ninth century A.D. The lateness of texts from both groups has made it difficult to determine precisely their interrelationship. Some scholars class both of them in one subgroup of Indo-European, **Balto-Slavic.** Others maintain that the similarities between the Baltic and the Slavic languages are due to mutual influences exerted during a long period of contact. These scholars set up two independent subgroups of Indo-European, **Baltic** and **Slavic.** A choice between the two depends on the interpretation of minute characteristics in materials that have come down to us. We can scarcely state with assurance whether one subgroup or two are to be posited, given only recent materials.

Speakers of Slavic dialects apparently were located in southeast Poland and western Russia at the time of the Romans. Expanding, they spread out from this area and in the sixth and seventh centuries came into contact with the eastern Roman Empire in Bulgaria. The earliest Slavic documents we have date from the advent of Christianization. Shortly after 850 two missionaries, Cyril (Constantinus) and Methodius, carried Christianity to Slavic speakers and translated the Bible into their language. The language of the translation is known either as **Old Church Slavic** or **Old Bulgarian.** The Russian church has maintained it as its official language, and accordingly it occupied a position in eastern Europe similar to that of Latin in the Roman church.

The Slavic languages spoken today are classified in three groups: **South, West** and **East Slavic. South Slavic** comprises: **Bulgarian, Serbo-Croatian** and **Slovenian; West Slavic** comprises **Czech, Slovak, Polish** and **Wendish; East Slavic** comprises **Great Russian, White Russian** or **Byelorussian** and **Ukrainian.** Through the political expansion of the Russian Empire (Great) Russian was spread south into the Caucasus and east to Siberia; it has continued its expansion and today is one of the most widely spoken languages of the world.

The differences between the various Slavic languages are relatively slight, much smaller than those between the Germanic languages. One may assume therefore that there has been no long period of separation; this assumption is supported when we reconstruct Proto-Slavic, for we find it similar to Old Church Slavic.

2.7 The **Baltic** group consists of two languages still in use, plus **Old Prussian** which is known from translations of the sixteenth century and became extinct around A.D. 1700. Old Prussian is important for Indo-European studies because of its conservatism, especially in the vowel system. (Prussian was replaced partly by Lithuanian, partly by German; the name was then applied to German speakers of the area in which the Old Prussian language was spoken.) Like Old Prussian, **Lithuanian** was first recorded in a translation of Luther's catechism, dating from 1547. Modern Lithuanian is remarkable for its conservatism of pitch accent, inflection and retention of formal distinctions, especially in the substantive. The word for 'son' *sūnùs* is like that in Sanskrit, *sūnús; eĩti* 'he goes' has undergone fewer changes than has Latin *it*. Lithuanian is accordingly one of the most important Indo-European languages for comparative study. The other surviving Baltic language, **Latvian** or **Lettish,** has undergone many more changes. It, too, is known from the sixteenth century, but it no longer has a pitch accent; further, many of its inflectional endings have been lost. Several dialects are attested for both Lithuanian and Lettish. During the short extent of the two republics of Lithuania and Latvia, standard languages were established. Even today neither language has more than several million speakers.

2.8 In dealing with earlier stages of the Indo-European languages the groups which we have so far discussed are often classed together as one of the two large subdivisions of Proto-Indo-European. The chief basis for this classification is a contrast of sibilants versus velars in the remaining branches. For example, in the word for 'ten' we find:

Skt. *daśa* Av. *dasa* Arm. *tasn* OCS *desętĭ* Lith. *dẽšimt*
Gk. *déka* Lat. *decem* OIr. *deich* Goth. *taihun*

In the word for 'hundred' we find:

Skt. *śatam*	Av. *satəm*	OCS *sŭto*	Lith. *šim̃tas*
Gk. *hekatón*	Lat. *centum*	OIr. *cēt*	Goth. *hund*

The eastern languages are labeled **satem** after the Avestan form for 'hundred'; the western are labeled **centum.** When this classification was first proposed, scholars assumed that the speakers of Proto-Indo-European had split into two groups, and that in the eastern group a sound change took place which differentiated the eastern from the western dialects.

Questions have been raised concerning the division, largely as a result of observations about dialect classification. If there had been a fundamental split between Eastern Indo-European and Western Indo-European, we should expect it to be reflected in a number of differing characteristics for each group. Accordingly, we do not hold today that there was once a single predecessor of the satem languages. We interpret the distribution of velars in centum languages and sibilants in satem by assuming that by a sound change some velars became sibilants in the eastern section of the Indo-European speech community. Results of the change spread, through Indo-Iranian, Armenian, dialects poorly known, Slavic, and into Baltic; but in Baltic not all velars which show up as sibilants elsewhere were changed. The satem situation is therefore typical in a speech community after a sound change has taken place and the effects have spread. It did not affect the Anatolian languages or Tocharian, possibly because they had left the Indo-European speech community before the sound change took place, possibly because they were on its periphery. We may continue to speak of **satem** languages because the change of velars to sibilants provides one of the foremost

Indo-European isoglosses, but we no longer assume that the Indo-European speech community early split into two parts.

2.9 Though there are relatively few speakers today, **Greek** or **Hellenic** is extremely important historically. Its spread into its current area, its further expansion and contraction, is also highly interesting for general historical linguistics.

We assume from Greek history, supported by deductions based on linguistic evidence, that the present region of Greece was inhabited by non-Indo-European speakers before 2000 B.C. Place names like that of *Corinth,* with an element consisting of *n* plus dental stop, are found also in Asia Minor; they are pre-Greek, and were maintained by Greek speakers as were Indian place names in this country. Around 2000 B.C. Greeks, or Hellenes, began a southward invasion and in successive migrations gradually occupied the present area of Greece, the islands and adjoining areas in the Mediterranean, and the west coast of Asia Minor. Greek historians tell about the last of these waves, the Doric migration of around 1200 B.C. From the introduction of Greek speech we can suggest how Indo-European languages may have been spread also in areas of which we have less knowledge, such as India and Italy.

The gradual increase of our knowledge of early Greek is also of great interest for historical linguistics. Until a short time ago the earliest datable Greek material was from the seventh century B.C. Vase inscriptions and poetry—the *Iliad* and the *Odyssey*—were older but uncertain in date. (Though the fall of Troy was dated roughly at 1200 B.C., there has been little agreement on the date of the Homeric poems.) During the past half-century tablets have been found on Crete and the mainland, which for some time could not be deciphered; they were classified by their scripts as **Linear A** and **Linear B.** A number of scholars worked on Linear B after World War II, employing the methods of cryptography toward its decipherment. In 1952, one of these, Michael Ventris, published his conclusions, which demonstrated that the language used in the Linear B tablets was Greek, now called **Mycenaean Greek.** The tablets date from 1450 to 1200 B.C. Accordingly, we now have very early materials for Greek, materials even earlier than those for India. With the new material our views of the dialect situation of Greek have been modified, as well as those on the development of Greek from Proto-Indo-European and the importance of Greek in the second millennium B.C.

We have a diversity of dialect materials subdivided into two large groups: **West Greek** and **East Greek.** West Greek is further subdivided into **Northwest Greek** and **Doric.** To East Greek belongs **Attic–Ionic,** the language of Attica and much of Asia Minor. A second subdialect is **Aeolic,** spoken in Boeotia, Thessaly and carried over to Lesbos. A third subgroup is **Arcado–Cyprian,** with representatives in the inner Peloponnese and on Cyprus. It is to this group that Mycenaean Greek seems most closely related.

A reason for our hesitancy in locating Mycenaean is the imperfect script in which it was written. Linear B is syllabic. Consonant groups are either broken up, or simplified. Only the cumulative weight of evidence persuades us that Ventris' decipherment must be accepted. A Greek word for king, *basileús* is spelled in Mycenaean by syllabic symbols which we transliterate *pa-si-re-u.* These look remote from each other, but when we find 'priest' *hiereús* represented as *i-je-re-u,* 'fuller' *knapheús* as *ka-na-pe-u,* we accept the interpretation in spite of the inadequacy of the Linear B writing system for Greek.

Historically, the most important dialect is that of Athens, **Attic Greek.** Because of the intellectual domination of Athens, its dialect came to be that used throughout Greek-speaking areas, and was called the common language, *koinē,* or Hellenistic Greek. This is the dialect spread by Alexander the Great throughout his empire, and maintained as the general language far outside the Hellenic peninsula. It is the basis of the Greek used in the New Testament.

With the decline of Greek political power, the area over which the Greek language was used also shrank. Today it is largely confined to the areas governed by Greece, though there are still some speakers in other countries, notably Cyprus, Turkey and the United States. Except for **Tsaconian,** a dialect spoken in old Doric territory, the Peloponnese, modern dialects are descendants of the *koinē*. Although we cannot pursue it in detail, the diminution of Greek, like its spread, is instructive for the study of language.

2.10 **Italic** was brought into the Italian peninsula in successive waves during the second millennium B.C., like Greek into the Hellenic peninsula, though probably somewhat later. We know relatively little about the language situation in Italy before about 600 B.C., and can speak with assurance about it only from 250 B.C. We divide the Italic languages attested into two groups, **Oscan-Umbrian** and **Latin-Faliscan.** The subsequent history of the Italic languages provides a dramatic example of language spread and displacement. Latin gradually displaced all the other Italic languages, and was spread via the Roman Empire. A number of dialects developed from it in the various sections of the Empire, and in Italy itself, where the dialect of Florence was eventually selected as the basis for the standard language.

Oscan has come down to us in approximately two hundred inscriptions, from the last two centuries B.C. **Umbrian** is attested primarily through the Iguvine tablets, dated in the first century B.C. Other related dialects are poorly attested. Oscan is important for Indo-European linguistics because it is conservative in vocalism. Formerly it was assumed without question that Oscan-Umbrian belonged with Latin-Faliscan in the Italic subgroup. Recently differences have been pointed out, largely in vocabulary, in which Oscan-Umbrian is greatly different from Latin-Faliscan. In structure, however, the two are sufficiently alike to suggest their retention in the Italic subgroup of the Indo-European family.

Only a few Faliscan materials have come down to us. Another Italic dialect surviving only in inscriptions is **Venetic,** spoken in Northeast Italy before the beginning of our era. **Latin** is attested in an early inscription from Praeneste of approximately 600 B.C. which is instructive because of its archaic language and its content.

MANIOS	MED FHE	FHACED	NUMASIOI
Manius	me	fecit	Numerio.

'Manius made me for Numerius.'

Inscriptions of this sort, labeling maker and recipient, are found on artifacts in other Indo-European dialect areas and give us a great deal of information about changes in the language, as the comparison above with classical Latin indicates.

For a large body of Latin materials we must wait until shortly before 200 B.C. Subsequently we have a tremendous amount of material, much of it literary but also inscriptions giving us information on the spoken language. The spoken, or **Vulgar Latin** was spread throughout the Roman Empire and was the basis from which the Romance languages developed. Since Vulgar Latin is not as completely attested as we might like, recent work has been devoted to reconstruction of Proto-Romance from modern dialects.

Classical Latin was long maintained as a written language. Accordingly we have evidence for the emerging Romance languages only much after the collapse of the western Roman Empire: **Italian** from the tenth century; **Provençal** from the eleventh; **French** from 842, in the Oaths of Strassburg; **Spanish, Catalan** and **Portuguese** from the twelfth century; **Rumanian** from the sixteenth. Besides these seven important languages, three minor ones are attested from modern times: **Sardinian; Rhaeto-Romance, Romansch** or **Ladin,** spoken by approximately one hundred thousand speakers in Switzerland and Italy; **Dalmatian,** of which the last speaker died in 1898.

Through its spread to Central and South America, Spanish has become one of the most widely spoken languages; forms of it, differing from area to area, are used throughout this huge area except for Brazil, where Portuguese is the national language.

2.11 **Celtic** has many characteristics in common with Italic. We cannot be certain of their relationship, for no Celtic materials of any extent have been preserved from before our era. From place names, like Bohemia, we assume that Celts early inhabited central Europe. We know that they expanded tremendously in the second half of the first millennium B.C.; they established themselves in Spain, in northern Italy, and almost captured Rome; they penetrated into Asia Minor, as far as the present-day city of Ankara, were still referred to as Galatians at the time of Saint Paul's missionary journeys, and were reported by Saint Jerome to have maintained their Celtic speech to his day, in the fourth century. During their expansion they became predominant in France, England and Ireland. Since the beginning of our era, however, the Celtic languages have been steadily receding.

The Celtic languages are classified into two groups, one in which PIE /k^w/ has become *p,* the **p-Celts** or **Brythonic,** the other in which it is a velar, the **q-Celts** or **Goidelic.**

Gaulish, attested in names and inscriptions from before our era, is a continental Brythonic dialect, eventually eliminated. The remaining Brythonic dialects, **Welsh, Cornish** and **Breton** were spoken in England before the Roman invasion. Our earliest manuscript materials are *glosses,* words written in manuscripts to translate difficult words in the original, much as language students do today. We have glosses from around 800 for Welsh and Breton. Literary materials in Welsh survive in considerable quantity from the twelfth century. Today Welsh may be the Celtic language with the greatest number of speakers. Breton, which was taken to the continent in the fifth and sixth centuries A.D., probably as a result of the Germanic invasion of England, is still maintained in Brittany. Cornish became extinct in the eighteenth century.

Of Goidelic two languages are attested, **Irish** and **Manx,** of the Isle of Man, now virtually extinct. We have Irish materials in ogam inscriptions from around the fifth century A.D., followed by glosses written by Irish monks on the continent in the eighth century. From the eleventh century a large amount of literary material is attested. Irish was taken to Scotland from the fifth century; the language there is generally referred to as **Scots Gaelic.** In Ireland itself several dialects developed, which are being gradually replaced by English. With the establishment of Eire an attempt was made to establish one of these, Munster, as the national language, but the attractiveness and usefulness of English seems to offset the government's efforts. Celtic, an important subgroup several millennia ago, seems destined soon to be entirely replaced.

2.12 Much of the displacement of Celtic has been brought about by **Germanic** languages. Speakers of Germanic languages began their migrations in the last centuries before our era, and continued them more than a millennium, with penetration westward to Iceland, Greenland and America, eastward into former Baltic and Slavic territory, and southward as far as Africa. In a second expansion from the sixteenth century Germanic languages were again carried westward to North America, southward to South Africa, India, and Australia, and to lesser land masses of the world. The tremendous expansion of the Germanic languages, occasioned in the centuries around the beginning of our era by the Völkerwanderung [migration of peoples], may illustrate how various less thoroughly documented languages were spread, such as Chinese and Semitic in the centuries before the beginning of our era.

Our first information about Germanic comes from classical

writers; Caesar and Tacitus have given us especially valuable reports. The Romans seem to have confused Germans and Celts. The name, German, may have been taken over from that of a small Celtic tribe; many fanciful explanations of the past on its origin reflect more romantic speculation than linguistic competence. Apart from Germanic place and personal names we have no data until the fourth century; accordingly our attempts to determine the early history of Germanic must be based entirely on reconstruction. For this reason the classification of the Germanic dialects has until recently indicated their distribution several centuries after Christ rather than their earlier development. Handbooks generally speak of three subdivisions: **East, West** and **North Germanic.** Linguistic indications suggest that we should rather speak of two: a *ggw* group, including the so-called East and North Germanic dialects, in which *ggw* developed from *ww, ddj* or *ggj* from *jj;* a *ww* group, corresponding to the West Germanic dialects, in which *ww* and *jj* were maintained. In the past decades attempts have been made to distinguish subgroups in the *ww* group, often with greater reliance on cultural than on linguistic data. We no longer believe that there was little intercommunication among Germanic subgroups in England, Scandinavia and northern Europe. Accordingly late mutual influences may have effaced earlier relationships. Such intercommunication is especially clear in the Scandinavian area.

Materials from the fourth century A.D. have come down to us in Norway and Denmark, in the so-called Runic inscriptions. They are composed in a formalized, archaic language in which vowels of unstressed syllables are still maintained. Among the best known is that on one of the golden horns of Gallehus, Denmark:

Ek HlewagastiR HoltijaR	horna tawido.
'I Hlewagastir of Holt	made the horn.'

Early Runic inscriptions are attested from the various Scandinavian areas, especially Norway, before the eighth century, with little dialect differentiation, probably in part because the inscriptions were composed in a conservative language of priests. From the time of Scandinavian expansion we speak of two groups: **East Norse,** composed of **Swedish, Danish** and **Gutnish,** and **West Norse,** composed of **Norwegian, Faroese** and **Icelandic.**

Icelandic has a particularly rich and interesting literature from the thirteenth century. Moreover, several grammatical treatises on medieval Icelandic have come down to us, thanks to which Icelandic is thoroughly known from the medieval period on.

Although the other Scandinavian languages are labeled as separate languages, they have continued to influence each other, so that to this day Norwegian and Swedish are mutually intelligible; Danes can readily understand Norwegian and Swedish, though their own speech may cause Norwegians and Swedes difficulties. Technically such mutually intelligible forms of speech are known as dialects. For national forms of speech the term is apparently undignified. The Scandinavian languages are therefore excellent examples of the nonlinguistic designation "language" for forms of speech used by a nation rather than for forms of speech which are unintelligible to native speakers of other languages.

The most extensive early Germanic materials are from a **Gothic** translation of the Bible. The translation, comprising the bulk of our Gothic texts, is ascribed to a Visigoth, Wulfila (311–83). It has been transmitted to us by Ostrogoths, in manuscripts of the late fifth and early sixth centuries. Gothic is relatively archaic, and transparent in grammatical structure; accordingly it is important for comparative Indo-European studies. The Visigoths in Spain and the Ostrogoths in Italy were absorbed by subsequent ethnic groups, and their languages became extinct. Between 1560 and 1562, however, Busbecq, a Flemish ambassador of Charles V to Turkey, took down in Istanbul about sixty words from two natives of the Crimea.

Language characteristics, especially the *d* in *ada* 'egg' make it unmistakable that their speech was Gothic. It is referred to as **Crimean Gothic.** Before more material than Busbecq's was collected, it passed out of use.

The *ww* group comprises five dialects: **High German, Franconian, Low German, Frisian,** and **English.** For all of them we speak of Old, Middle, and Modern (New) periods. These designations are imprecise, and will remain so until historical linguists define language stages by linguistic criteria. For reference to existing handbooks, however, it is well to know that "Old" generally refers to Germanic languages before the twelfth century, "Middle" from the twelfth to the fifteenth century, and "New" to the subsequent period.

High German is attested first in proper names from the end of the seventh century, in glosses from the eighth, and primarily in religious texts of the ninth. From the earliest times there are distinct dialects. **Alemannic** in the west and **Bavarian** in the east are generally referred to as **Upper German.** Through the thirteenth century the cultural center of Germany was in the south; accordingly our medieval literary materials are chiefly in Upper German. During the fourteenth century the political center moved farther to the north. The language spread by the increasingly powerful political units of Middle Germany was also used by the Reformers of the sixteenth century, particularly Martin Luther; it is the basis of standard contemporary German. Many dialects are still in everyday use. One of these, **Yiddish,** also called **Jewish,** split off from the main body of German in the late medieval period. Lacking the speech of a long-established political center like Paris or Florence, the accepted standard was fixed only at the end of the nineteenth century. The pronunciation was based on that of the stage (Bühnenaussprache).

Low Franconian is known from fewer documents in the old period. At present it is represented by **Dutch,** and its dialect **Flemish,** attested copiously in the medieval period. **Afrikaans** is the form of Dutch which has been established in South Africa.

Before the eighth century there was close association between the dialects on the coasts of England and those of northern Germany. As a result these dialects share common innovations, and are often given a special label, **Ingvaeonic** or North Sea Germanic. From the eighth century, however, High German exerted a progressively stronger influence on the dialects of northern Germany, so that we note a break between the earliest materials handed down to us from the lowlands of Germany, labeled **Old Saxon,** and the later **Low German.** Old Saxon is attested from approximately the same time as is Old High German. Middle Low German and Modern Low German have been constantly receding before High German, especially since the political centralization of Germany in the nineteenth century.

Frisian, spoken on the coast and islands off the Netherlands and western Germany, is attested from the thirteenth century. Not a national language, it is used in various dialects by comparatively few speakers.

English is attested first in names from the seventh century. Literary remains, such as Caedmon's *Hymn* and the *Beowulf,* are generally dated somewhat before 750. The early literature was produced in the north, but virtually all materials have come down to us in the dominant dialect at the end of the ninth century, **West Saxon.** In Old English there were three distinct dialects, **Kentish, Saxon** and **Northern** or **Anglian,** further subdivided into **Northumbrian** and **Mercian.** Because of its two predominant dialects, Old English was formerly referred to as **Anglo-Saxon;** this designation is now passing out of use.

In Middle English the dialect situation is even more complex, though we may follow a classification into four subgroups, **Northern, West Midland, East Midland** and **Southern.** The dialect of London, on the border between Southern and Midland, came to be the model for standard English. Like New High German, Modern English is therefore not a direct continuation of the prominent language of the older period. The history of both languages is accordingly more complex than handbooks may suggest.

Since approximately 1600, English has expanded continually. It is now the language used most widely as a second language and as an auxiliary language for international communication; as first language, however, Mandarin Chinese probably has more speakers.

2.13 At the close of the nineteenth century these were assumed to be the only members of the Indo-European family from which materials of any extent survived. Unexpectedly there were discovered in Chinese Turkestan Buddhist writings, dating from the sixth to the eighth centuries, which are clearly Indo-European. The language was given the name **Tocharian,** as the result of a mistaken identification. There are two dialects, labeled A and B. Specialists who have been unhappy with these colorless classifications of a misapplied name have attempted with little success to introduce other labels, **Agnean** or **East Tocharian** for **Tocharian A, Kuchean** or **West Tocharian** for **Tocharian B.** One of the remarkable features of Tocharian is the preservation of palatals as *k* before back vowels, which in other Indo-European languages of the east had become sibilants. This finding gave a severe blow to the traditional classification of Indo-European into satem dialects in the east and centum in the west. We know nothing about the provenience of the speakers of Tocharian, and nothing certain about their disappearance. Since most of the basic research on Tocharian has been undertaken only recently, it has contributed little to our knowledge of Proto-Indo-European.

2.14 The second language of which abundant materials were discovered in this century has also been mislabeled with a name that has been fixed—Hittite. Excavations near the Turkish village of Boğaz Köy uncovered in 1905–1907 the archives of the Hittite Empire, which flourished from approximately 1700 to 1200 B.C. Many texts from this period were found, and more have been found since. They are written in cuneiform and could be read at once; moreover, many contain Akkadian and Sumerian, so that the meaning of the texts, and of most Hittite words, can be determined. In 1915 Hittite was identified as Indo-European by B. Hrozný. Twelve years later J. Kurylowicz identified sounds transcribed ḫ with reconstructions that Saussure had proposed in 1879, solely on the basis of reasoning from internal evidence. The publication of Saussure thus has been proved to be one of the most remarkable in linguistics. Kurylowicz' identification helped add to the great interest in Hittite, and in the early history of the Indo-European languages. Some Indo-Europeanists also proposed a reclassification of the family, because of the ḫ, other archaisms, and the early time of the records. They suggested that Hittite was a sister language, rather than a daughter language, of Indo-European, and proposed the new label for the family, **Indo-Hittite.**

The subsequently deciphered Greek texts written in Linear B have now given us Greek materials contemporary with Hittite. With arguments from linguistic evidence they have led Indo-Europeanists of today to retain the old label. One may explain the archaic features of Hittite by assuming that Hittite speakers made up the first group to leave the Indo-European community. Assumption of a considerable period of separation would also help to account for the innovations in Hittite.

Among the Hittite texts are found materials in two other related languages, **Luwian** and **Palaic.** Related texts in a different script dating from approximately 1400 to 500 B.C. have been given the name **Hieroglyphic (Hittite).** The little known languages, **Lycian** and **Lydian,** are also now assumed to be related to Hittite, with Lycian the continuation of Luwian. The entire group is referred to as **Anatolian,** and is considered a separate branch of the Indo-European family.

The discoveries in Asia Minor have broadened and deepened our knowledge of Indo-European. Hittite has preserved Indo-European velars, possibly because the change of velars to sibilants took place after the Hittites left the Indo-European community. Hittite also has a grammatical system much simpler than that of Indo-Iranian and Greek, which earlier were taken as patterns for reconstructing the Indo-European grammatical system. Adequate studies have not yet been completed to modify this view; some Indo-Europeanists, however, have suggested that the complex verb systems of Indo-Iranian and Greek represent later developments, rather than a retention from the parent language.

2.15 With Hittite we are in a position to reconstruct Proto-Indo-European of a period before 3000 B.C. This date nullifies older attempts to relate Indo-European with other language groups, and requires us to construct forms of Proto-Indo-European different from those in the standard handbooks of the late nineteenth-century Indo-Europeanists. A century and a half of work therefore has not solved all problems concerning Indo-European. On the other hand it has contributed excellent information on the development of the languages used by at least half the people living today. It has also provided the methods for determining and classifying other language families.

One of the most important tools in historical linguistics developed for genealogical classification is reconstruction of prior, unattested forms, particularly in the parent language. Yet reconstructions must not be misused. They are merely concise statements of our information on the earliest stage of a language family. As a tour de force one may attempt, as did Schleicher, to write a tale in Proto-Indo-European. One must then expect to have the tale rewritten as more information is assembled. Hirt rewrote Schleicher's tale in accordance with his views of Proto-Indo-European. Today we no longer agree with many of Hirt's reconstructions. Discovery of unexpected early materials, like those in Hittite and Mycenaean Greek, has demonstrated to be sure the basic accuracy of our reconstructions; but reconstructions smell of the lamp even more than do most scholarly products and are best kept for their proper function of serving as concise summaries of our current information.

2.16 Further language families can merely be outlined here. Genealogical classification has become so complex, and is in such flux, that a general handbook can only aim at a characterization of the state of research.

Some languages have not yet been related to other groups, and for lack of information may never be. One such is **Sumerian,** the language of southern Mesopotamia from about 4000 B.C. until it was replaced by Semitic languages. **Etruscan,** spoken in Italy until it was replaced by Latin, cannot yet be fully interpreted, let alone classified. **Basque,** of northern Spain, has no known relatives. Languages related to these either have died out without leaving materials, or they are so remotely connected that genealogical relationship is yet to be discovered. Unfortunately charlatans sometimes use this lack of information to propose unsupportable relationships.

The classification of other languages is uncertain because of the lack of descriptive studies, for example those of Australia and Papua. Classification of the languages of South America is not much further advanced. Adequate descriptive materials are beginning to be made available, and accordingly genealogical classification may soon be undertaken with profit. Classification of the languages in other areas requiring considerable descriptive study, for example those of Africa and Southeast Asia, is being pursued. For current views one must consult monographs, articles, and reviews, which can be located through bibliographies.

2.17 The language family which has been most widely studied, after the Indo-European, is the **Hamito-Semitic,** expanded by Greenberg and renamed **Afro-Asiatic.**

The Afro-Asiatic family comprises five branches: **Egyptian** (1), one of the earliest languages attested, with records from the fourth millennium B.C. Its descendant known as **Coptic** after about the fourth century A.D. survives today as a religious language. **Berber** (2), **Cushitic** (3), **Chad** (4) are known only from recent times. To **Semitic** (5) belong some of the most important cultural languages of the past and present. **Akkadian,** the only representative of **East Semitic,** has been preserved in numerous cuneiform writings from about 2800 B.C. to the beginning of our era. **West Semitic** consists of two groups, **Aramaic–Canaanite** and **Arabic–Ethiopic.** One of the most important Canaanite languages was **Phoenician,** spoken in the area of Lebanon. It was carried to Carthage, and continued in use there as late as the sixth century A.D. Known as **Punic,** it is poorly attested in a few inscriptions and some lines of Plautus. A second Canaanite language, **Hebrew,** is attested from about 1100 B.C. The account of its introduction into Palestine, given in *Genesis,* informs us of the spread of a language by a small group of nomads, who under the leadership of Abraham wandered from the north into Palestine. The recent revival of Hebrew as a spoken language is one of the strangest linguistic endeavors attested. Though it remained a highly important religious and literary language, Hebrew was largely replaced from the sixth century B.C. by **Aramaic,** which is attested in numerous dialects. In one of these, utterances of Jesus are cited in the *New Testament.* **Arabic** is the last of the Semitic languages to be widely extended, with the spread of the Moslem religion and civilization. Its dialects are spoken today throughout much of the Middle East and the north of Africa. Like **Ethiopic,** of which several forms are spoken in Ethiopia, it is attested only after the beginning of our era.

Classification of the other language families of Africa has been the subject of much recent discussion. Greater assurance will require much careful, detailed work, such as that completed on the Indo-European family.

A large family to the south of the Afro-Asiatic is the **Chari–Nile.** Apart from small or poorly defined groups most of the other languages of Africa, including the **Bantu,** are classed in the **Niger–Congo** family. One of these, **Swahili,** a trade language, is used for communication through much of eastern Africa by speakers of a great variety of languages. The **Khoisan** family, including **Bushman** and **Hottentot,** is located on the southern borders of the Niger–Congo family.

2.18 The third large language family of Asia is the **Dravidian,** whose principal languages are spoken in south India. One of them, **Telugu,** has the second largest number of speakers in India. **Tamil,** with almost as many speakers, **Kanarese** and **Malayalam,** are also important. Since some Dravidian languages are still found in the north of India, and **Brahui** in eastern Baluchistan, it is suggested that Dravidian was the most widely distributed indigenous language family in India when Indo-European speakers invaded it near the end of the second millennium B.C.

A language completely isolated, with no known cognates, is **Burushaski,** spoken in the northwest of India.

In eastern India and areas further to the east are spoken languages whose further classification is uncertain: **Munda, Mon-Khmer** and **Annam-Muong.** The leading investigator to concern himself with these languages, Father W. Schmidt, grouped them together in an **Austroasiatic** family, which he combined further with **Malayo-Polynesian** into **Austric.** The further classification, especially, is based on very little evidence.

The **Malayo-Polynesian** languages themselves require considerable further study. Largely on the basis of geographical location, they are divided into four groups, each with many dialects: **Indonesian, Melanesian, Micronesian** and **Polynesian.**

The language which is being developed into the national language of Indonesia, **Bahasa Indonesia,** often known simply as **Indonesian,** is based essentially on **Malayan,** a trade language which was formerly used especially in Malaya and Sumatra.

Since the Malayo-Polynesian family extends from Madagascar to Easter Island, and from Hawaii to New Zealand, it probably had the widest distribution of any language family, until the recent tremendous expansion of the Indo-European.

2.19 Returning to western Asia to survey the languages of the north, we find the Caucasian languages again inadequately analyzed in spite of considerable recent work. There are two families, **North Caucasian** and **South Caucasian,** of which **Georgian** is the most important member. The North Caucasian family includes languages of great phonological interest because of their many consonants and few vowels.

The **Finno-Ugric** group, with an island of **Hungarian** speakers in Europe, nomadic speakers of **Lappish** in Scandinavia, extends eastward from Estonia through Russia far into Siberia, with **Cheremiss, Mordvine** and other subbranches. **Samoyede,** spoken in far-eastern Siberia, may be one of these. The term **Uralic** is used for the combined Finno-Ugric and Samoyede group. The large number of languages in this family, with the exception of **Finnish** with four million and **Hungarian** or **Magyar** with thirteen million, is spoken by small numbers of speakers. Finno-Ugric has been receding before other languages, notably Russian; many of its languages survive in some of the more rugged inhabited areas of the world. With Indo-European and Hamito-Semitic it was one of the first families described. Subsequently it has been studied in detail and its interrelationships are well known.

Far to the east in Siberia the **Palaeo-Asiatic** or **Hyperborean** languages are spoken. Inadequately described, they may merely be a geographical group. We cannot determine whether any of them are related to **Ainu,** apparently the indigenous language of Japan.

In the central belt of Asia the **Turkic** languages are spoken. Turkic speakers made numerous incursions from this area after the beginning of our era; through one of them **Osmanli,** generally known as **Turkish,** was established in Turkey and is today the most widely used Turkic language. Approximately twenty further Turkic languages, spoken chiefly in southern Siberia, have been receding before Russian.

The Turkic languages are often classified with the **Mongol** and **Manchu-Tungus** languages in the **Altaic** family. With the exception of Turkic inscriptions from the eighth century, languages of these groups are attested from the last millennium. The classification of these three groups into one large family is made in part on the basis of typological criteria. A further hypothesis is sometimes proposed that the Finno-Ugric languages are to be related to Altaic, and the combined group is referred to as **Ural–Altaic.** This hypothesis is highly speculative.

To the hypothetical Ural-Altaic group two isolated languages are sometimes joined, **Korean** and with greater diffidence **Japanese.** Material to demonstrate further relationship, however, is so scanty that they cannot be interrelated with each other, let alone to the broader group. To illustrate the difficulties, we may review that portion of the Japanese numerals remaining after the classifier has been removed; we then are left with:

1	hi	4	yo	7	nana	10	tō
2	fu	5	i	8	ya		
3	mi	6	mu	9	koko		

It is scarcely remarkable that such short and simple forms would be difficult to relate further, especially since as we noted above *mi mu, yo ya, hi fu* are made up of two morphemes. If one of their consonants or vowels were changed or lost, the basis of comparison would be weakened. Only the **Luchuan** dialects, which are not far removed from the Japanese, can be related to Japanese. The complexity of syllabic structure which the Indo-European languages exhibit has greatly helped linguists to verify their interrelationships and to assemble the detailed information we have on their history today.

2.20 The remaining languages in Asia belong to one of the linguistic families which is of great importance for its present distribution and for the antiquity of its documents, the **Sino-**

Tibetan. It consists of three groups: **Yenisei-Ostyak, Tibeto-Burman, (Thai-) Chinese.** Yenisei-Ostyak, spoken in northern Siberia, helps support other evidence that the two other groups spread southward to the large territory they now occupy. Tibeto-Burman comprises the languages of Burma and **Tibetan,** which is attested from the seventh century A.D. (Thai-) Chinese includes various languages in Thailand and the area to the east of it, as well as the dialects of China.

Since one writing system is used throughout China, the assumption is sometimes made that **Chinese** comprises one language. It actually consists of nine, possibly seven, mutually unintelligible languages, each with subdialects. The writing system which enables their speakers to intercommunicate on paper was adapted for the totally unrelated Japanese; it could be used more widely, but contemporary demands on time seem to make retention of a system of thousands of symbols difficult even for the traditionally patient Chinese, who have taken steps towards use of an alphabetic system. If one is established, the Chinese will need to select for intercommunication one of their languages, probably a Mandarin dialect.

Starting from the south, the nine Chinese languages are: **Cantonese, Kan-Hakka, Amoy-Swatow, Foochow, Wu** (spoken around Shanghai), **Hsiang** and three subgroups of **Mandarin: Yellow River Basin and Manchurian, Southern,** and **Southwestern.** With the expansion of the Chinese population it is difficult to know the number of speakers of these languages; Mandarin is probably used as first language by more speakers than is any other language.

Chinese has been preserved in inscriptions on bone and bronzes from the second millennium B.C.; literary documents of some length, such as the works of Confucius and Laotse, have come down to us from the first millennium B.C. The materials before the sixth century A.D. are generally referred to as **Archaic Chinese. Old** or **Ancient Chinese** is dated from the sixth to the tenth centuries, **Middle Chinese** from the tenth to the thirteenth, and **New Chinese** from then to the present. Since Chinese has always been written in characters, even in earliest times, there are problems in determining the spoken form of the languages. These are solved partly with the help of borrowings into Japanese and Korean, partly with riming dictionaries. Borrowings inform us about the beginnings of morphs, riming dictionaries about their ends. In this way it is possible to reconstruct the pronunciation of Archaic Chinese and to use it for comparison with other languages of the family. From the work which has been done we can suggest that the monosyllabism of present Chinese morphs is the result of losses of final elements. Earlier stages of the language were inflected; when the inflections were lost, some differentiation was maintained through tones.

In spite of the wealth of material, many problems in (Thai-)Chinese studies have scarcely been touched. There is even doubt about the relation of Thai with Chinese. Among suggestions is classification of Thai with **Laotian** and **Shan** into a separate family, labeled **Kadai,** and related further to Malayo-Polynesian. The resemblances between Thai and Chinese are then ascribed to borrowing. Further study will lead to numerous interesting contributions on historical linguistics, and possibly also in the interrelationship of literate peoples in the second millennium B.C.

2.21 Few of the native languages of America are known from earlier than the nineteenth century. Spanish invaders preserved some Mayan materials, North American missionaries translated the Bible into Alkonkin languages, preserving somewhat earlier forms than those of today. Unfortunately, few advocated study of the indigenous languages of America; one of these few was Thomas Jefferson. In the absence of early texts we must attempt to classify the families of American Indian languages almost entirely with contemporary materials, which themselves are often inadequate.

Two types of classification have been produced. Under the leadership of J. W. Powell fifty-four language families were proposed in 1891 on the basis of relatively careful classification by the principles worked out in comparative linguistics.

A different type of classification was proposed by E. Sapir in 1929. Believing that bolder methods of determining relationship should be used, Sapir attempted to determine linguistic *stocks,* on the basis of broad structural similarity. He, in this way, reduced Powell's fifty-four families to six stocks: **Eskimo–Aleut, Na–Dene, Algonkin–Wakashan** (for Trager **Algonkian–Mosan**), **Hokan–Siouan, Penutian, Aztec–Tanoan.** Trager now classes together Penutian and Aztec–Tanoan into **Macro-Penutian.** Such classification is also being attempted for the twenty-three language families of Mexico and Central America. Until recently these have been very inadequately known. Even more poorly known are the languages of South America, of which seventy-five families or more have been proposed. One of these, **Kechuan,** is widely used today in Peru, where it is spoken as generally as Spanish. The other native languages of South America are undergoing the fate of those elsewhere in the hemisphere. If descriptive work now being undertaken is completed, we shall be able to verify previous classifications and proceed to broader classifications of the type proposed by Sapir for the North American languages.

2.22 Though we welcome it, classification of the type proposed by Sapir must not be equated with that made on the basis of reconstructions and other techniques relied on by the great historical linguists of the past. Besides reconstructions, Meillet laid great weight on features found only in segments of a system. One such is the alternation between *-r-* and *-n-* in the inflection of some Indo-European nouns; a trace of this survives in the *r* of English *water* versus the *n* of Norwegian *vatn.* Another example is the alternation between the stem vowel *o* in the Indo-European perfect singular and no vowel in the plural; again a trace survives in English, in the alternation of vowels in *was* versus *were*. Vocabulary to Meillet was one of the least characteristic features of language. General structural features he assumed could be transferred from language to language. By contrast with his views, for the gross classifications used on Indian and African languages today, vocabulary and general structure are the chief criteria. There is, accordingly, a great difference between the methods; the results must also be viewed differently.

It is doubtful whether genealogical classification like that practiced by Meillet can ever be demonstrated for languages attested only today which separated five or more millennia ago. If one compares contemporary Hindi with contemporary English, or contemporary Irish with contemporary Russian, evidence for relationship, and bases for genealogical classification are not great. Genealogical classification was admirably suited to determine the interrelationships of languages such as the Indo-European for which we have many records from several millennia. For languages attested only today we may be limited to classification based on typology.

SELECTED FURTHER READINGS

The most recent comprehensive compilation on language families is *Les langues du monde,* prepared in a second edition by a group of linguists under the direction of Marcel Cohen [though the names A. Meillet and M. Cohen have been maintained from the first edition] (Paris, 1952). There is a set of accompanying maps, and also, pages xvii–xlii, a useful bibliography.

Foundations of Language by Louis Gray (New York, 1939) contains the last large scholarly treatment made available in English, with bibliographies, pages 295–418.

Pater W. Schmidt's *Die Sprachfamilien und Sprachenkreise der Erde* (Heidelberg, 1926) is notable for a fine atlas.

For current views on genealogical classifications one will have to consult special handbooks, monographs and articles dealing with individual language families or even individual languages. Encyclopedias should not be neglected. Sapir's article reclassifying the Indian languages of North America appeared in Volume 5, pages 138–41 of the fourteenth edition of the *Encyclopaedia Britannica* (1929). The new edition has commissioned articles on language families by leading linguists. As an example of a comprehensive attempt at reclassification, J. Greenberg's *Studies in African Linguistic Classification* (New Haven, 1955) will remain fundamental for some time, though for current views on the languages of Africa subsequent reviews and restatements must be consulted. Because of the great amount of work underway on poorly described languages, because of efforts to classify them genealogically, and because of the introduction of more rigorous classifications based on linguistic criteria, current views on any language family must be determined from recent special books or reports and from the journals.

3–Typological Classification of Languages

3.1 From the beginnings of historical linguistics attempts were made to classify languages by their types rather than by their origins and relationships. In 1818, the year before J. Grimm began the publication of his grammar, which did much to develop the principles of historical linguistics, August von Schlegel proposed a typological classification which was widely followed and elaborated through the nineteenth century. It still has great popular currency.

According to this classification, languages may be **analytic (isolating** or **root)** languages (Chinese, with no inflection, is the generally used example), or they may be **synthetic, inflectional,** like Latin and Greek. A transitional class is **agglutinative** or **affixing,** like Turkish or Swahili; agglutinative languages are differentiated from inflectional languages because they maintain bases and affixes distinct from each other. Contrast the Turkish with the Latin inflections of "water":

Nom.	su	aqua
Gen.	sunun	aquae
Acc.	suyu	aquam
Abl.	sudan	aquā

The Turkish endings can be neatly separated from the stem; in Latin the ending of the genitive and that of the ablative have merged with the stem vowel, and can only be determined by historical methods. Comparing Proto-Indo-European we can determine the endings almost as if they were affixed as in Turkish. This transparency suggested to early nineteenth-century scholars that inflectional languages developed from agglutinative.

Many proponents of typological classification associated excellence as well as extent of evolution with their classes. Inflectional languages were held to represent the highest stage of evolution, and the most perfect form of human communication yet devised. The Marrist aberration in the USSR, further relating linguistic to economic development, is the latest and possibly last instance. Such absurdities have helped contribute to the lack of enthusiasm maintained about linguistic typology. In spite of its advantages in not requiring a long series of texts, and in spite of the efforts of a highly respected linguist like Sapir to propose a rigorous classification according to types, few linguists have approached languages from this point of view. Moreover, no such broad classification has been produced. Here we will discuss two which have been developed rather fully, and indicate procedures which hold promise for adequately classifying languages.

Typological classification will ultimately be based on all the systems of language, the phonological as well as the grammatical and semantic. Only recently, however, has an approach been made available for combining these systems under one classification. Before examining this approach, we shall survey one produced at the beginning of this century.

3.2 The most complete typology based on grammatical-semantic criteria is that of Finck. It is instructive to review it in order to understand the achievements of earlier typological studies, and their shortcomings.

Finck viewed man's use of speech as consisting of two essential processes:

1. Analyzing a real situation into its components.
2. Restoring it to a whole via the words of language.

As an illustrative situation we might choose that of a man approaching; this would be analyzed into two components: an actor and an action. In reporting this situation a Chinese speaker matches each component with a word: *t'a*¹ 'he' *lai*² 'come.' A Turkish speaker would use only one word: *geliyor,* combining the two situational elements. An English speaker would use three, *he is coming,* introducing more words than there are components in the situation.

According to the analysis of the situation, Finck assumed eight types. On one side stood the languages like Turkish in which a word indicates several elements of a situation; on the other, the languages like English in which a word indicates less than one element of a situation. Chinese provides an ideal fit between any situation and its restoration in language by representing one element with one word.

The definition of **word** is crucial to this, and other, typological classifications, in which *word* is used as a linguistic entity. For their usefulness will depend on an acceptable definition. Finck's definition is quite arbitrary, and would not be accepted today. Bloomfield's definition of *word* as "a minimum free form" is inadequate; yet an improved definition has not been provided by typologists in their classification. Since no adequate linguistic definition of *word* has been given, we cannot condemn Finck because his is inadequate; yet until one is provided, or another entity chosen as unit, use of a poorly defined *word* seriously reduces the value of typological classifications.

According to analysis, Finck arranged his eight typical languages in the order immediately following on the next page.

Eskimo (one word includes several elements of the situation)
Turkish
Georgian
Arabic
Chinese (one word corresponds to one element of the situation)
Greek
Samoan
Subiya (one word corresponds to less than one element of the situation)

As with his classification for synthesis, languages are not required to fit these selected types exactly. English, using more words than there are elements in a situation, would fall between Chinese and Subiya. Moreover, the eight types Finck proposed were not meant to be exhaustive, for others may still be discovered or may develop in the future.

According to synthesis these languages are arranged quite differently. Now at one pole stands Chinese, in which each word is isolated, uninflected, and equivalent to a root. At the other pole stands Eskimo, in which a word incorporates a variety of elements, though as in two other types they are not combined with the base. Between these fall the inflected languages.

Isolating	Chinese	root-isolating
	Samoan	stem-isolating
	Arabic	root-inflected
Inflected	Greek	stem-inflected
	Georgian	group-inflected
Elements Not Combined with Base	Subiya	juxtaposing
	Turkish	agglutinative
	Eskimo	polysynthetic or incorporating

Though Finck gave examples with commentaries of these eight types, he found only sporadic successors to apply his system more widely and thoroughly than he was able to do in a short book. Historical linguists continued to direct their chief energies at perfecting genealogical classification. When typological study was again undertaken, as by Sapir, purely formal analysis was preferred to that based on form and meaning.

3.3 Two approaches to typological classification have been made by structural linguists, without relation to each other. Independently of typologies based on grammar, phonologists, noting the configurations of entities and their constituents, have attempted to set up various types of sound systems. Typologists, dealing with grammar, especially morphology, have attempted to determine general grammatical features by which languages might be typed. Those proposed by Sapir were determined from characteristics observed in a wide variety of languages, not like Finck's from the application of semantics and psychology. Greenberg so modified Sapir's approach that typological classification may finally become widely applied. His modification permits classification of languages by selected structural features rather than by the entire language. Besides contributing to typological classification a flexibility necessary to deal with the diverse types of languages it also permits us to combine the previously separated phonological and morphological typologies.

In both phonological and grammatical classification for types any structural features may be utilized which are broadly represented in language. Only a beginning has been made to identify such features; those given here are intended as examples for further study.

3.4 In phonological classification much effort has been devoted to types by their arrangement of phonemes. Some languages have a triangular system of vowels, such as that of the short vowels of some Arabic dialects:

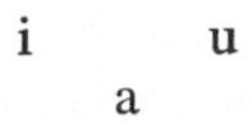

or the five-vowel system of Classical Latin:

i u
e o
a

or the seven-vowel system of contemporary Italian:

i						u
	e				o	
		ɛ		ɔ		
			a			

Other languages have rectangular systems, such as Tonkawa:

i	o
e	a

or the eight-vowel system of Turkish:

i	ü	ı	u
e	ö	a	o

or the nine-vowel system of some dialects of English:

i	ɨ	u
e	ə	o
æ	a	ɔ

Still other configurations could be cited. Yet it is cumbersome to compare configurations. One may more readily compare the use of distinctive features in phonological systems, by which configurations are determined. Such are position of articulation, manner of articulation, nasality, voicing, degree of opening, and so on.

Vowel systems may be classified for degrees of openness and closeness, with two in Arabic, Tonkawa, and Turkish, three in Classical Latin and English, four in Italian, and so on. Classifying these by number of distinctive positions from front to back would result in two for Tonkawa, three for English, and four for Turkish. The four of Turkish might however be reduced by assuming a system with three bases: high versus low, front versus back, rounded versus unrounded.

Consonant systems too may be classified for configuration of components. English has a relatively large number of fricatives, relatively few stops, a symmetrical arrangement of voiceless and voiced entities throughout the obstruent system and of stops and nasals, such as appear on the next page.

f	θ		s		š		
v	ð		z		ž		
					č		
					ǰ		
p		t				k	
b		d				g	
m		n				ŋ	
w	r	l		y			h

Sanskrit has a large number of stops, few fricatives and a symmetrical arrangement of aspirated and nonaspirated stops.

p		t		ṭ		c	k	
ph		th		ṭh		ch	kh	
b		d		ḍ		j	g	
bh		dh		ḍh		jh	gh	
m		n		[ṇ		ñ	ŋ]	
	v	l	r		y			
		s		ṣ		ś		h

Besides classification of phonological systems for their entities, ratios of entities might also be determined and compared from language to language, of obstruents to resonants, of stops to fricatives or to nasals, of other classes, of labials to dentals, velars, pharyngeals, and so on. The frequency of such classes in a running text might also be used for typing.

By classification for the distinctive features set up by Jakobson and his colleagues, vowels and consonants may be treated together (see page 62 for the terms used here). In this way the stop systems of Czech and French pattern like the vowel systems of Wichita and Arabic:

	Czech		French		Wichita		Arabic	
Compact	k	c	k		a	æ	a	
Diffuse	p	t	p	t	u	i	u	i
	Grave	Acute	Grave	Acute	Grave	Acute	Grave	Acute

The suprasegmental systems of languages may also be classified by the features on which they are constructed. English is characterized by a stress accent on words, with pitch used in marking intonations. Japanese is characterized by use of pitch for intonation, though pitch is also an inherent feature of words.

Other phonological features for use in typological classification are the role of quantity, that of juncture, the structure of syllables. The number of phonemes preceding and following the syllabic peak might be noted and compared. In Japanese the syllabic peak may not be followed by consonants, for example, *arimasu* 'is.' In English, it may be followed by relatively many consonants, as in *bursts*. In Russian a large number of consonants may precede the syllabic peak, as in /fsya/ 'all.'

Even more than genealogical classification, typological classification requires complete, accurate and consistent descriptions. If, for example, we follow a description of English which analyzes *tea* as /tíy/, *two* as /túw/, and so on, English may fall into a different phonological type from that resulting if we analyzed these items as /tí/ and /tú/. As more reliable descriptions become available, and as descriptive techniques are developed which will yield consistent descriptions, typological classification will occupy a more prominent and assured place than it has had in linguistic taxonomy.

3.5 Sapir's classification by morphological criteria resulted in four basic types of languages, *Language* 150–1. He also set up subclassifications and made a start towards quantitative indications of features; but his classifications, like those of Finck, are not precise, and are difficult to compare from language to language. Greenberg attempted to solve this problem by suggesting that classification of languages for their types be replaced by rankings for individual criteria.

Instead of labeling a language as synthetic or analytic, Greenberg proposed that a synthetic index, among others, be determined for any given language. Greenberg's synthetic index indicates the ratio of morphs per word in a given language. Sapir's sentence (1) *The* (2) *farm* (3) *er* (4) *kill* (5) *s* (6) *the* (7) *duck* (8) *ling* yields a synthetic index of 1.6, for it consists of eight morphs to five words. In selected examples, Greenberg found the synthetic index to be 1.68 for English, 3.72 for Eskimo, 1.06 for Annamese.

After such values have been determined, they may be used for comparison between languages, or languages may be given rank orders for any index.

Greenberg's second index is one of agglutination. When morphs are added to bases in a language like Turkish, many of them assume different shapes by automatic alternation. The genitive morpheme alternates in accordance with the form to which it is added; the genitive of *ev* 'house' is *evin,* of *göz* 'eye' *gözün,* of *at* 'horse' *atın,* of *yol* 'road' *yolun.* If all morphemes functioned in this way in Turkish, its index of agglutination would be 1.00. In English, the shape of morphs may or may not be predicted automatically; since *-ing* as in *farming* is invariant, it would be predictable in this way. Morphs of the past tense morpheme are not, for beside the regular alternation in verbs like *rounded, tripped* and *robbed,* we find past tense forms like *hit, went* and *rang.* Accordingly the index of agglutination in English is less than 1.00, though not as low as that of Eskimo.

A third index is that of morpheme classes per word, with subdivisions for root, derivational and inflectional morphemes. As in the sentence cited above, English has virtually one root per word; though some words, like *blackbird,* contain more than one root. It also has a relatively low index of derivational morphs per word, and a moderate index of inflectional morphs per word. Old English had higher indices of derivation and inflection, as does Sanskrit and Eskimo.

A fourth index is that of affixes per word. As in other Indo-European languages the index of prefixes is low in English, the index of suffixes relatively high.

Greenberg's fifth index deals with nexus, the indication of relationship by order (which Greenberg labels isolation), by pure inflection or by concord (agreement). Relationship in

English, as in Sapir's sentence, is largely indicated by order, to a much smaller degree by inflection, and to an even lesser degree by concord. We recognize that *duckling* is the object of *kills* by its order in following rather than preceding the word. In Old English, or Latin, on the other hand, an inflectional ending would have indicated the relationship, making the index of inflection much higher than it is in modern English.

The rank order determined by these five criteria seems to result in classification similar to that of Finck; of Greenberg's eight examples Eskimo has the highest ratio for synthesis, the lowest for agglutination. Annamese, similar in structure to Chinese which Finck used, has the highest ratio for isolation, the lowest for affixes per word. Under both systems of classification we might label Eskimo polysynthetic, Annamese isolating. Yet through use of form alone the criteria can be identified precisely so that other scholars can apply them with consistency. The indices also permit more precise comparison of languages. Yakuts Turkish as expected has a relatively high index of agglutination; yet its index of pure inflection is also high, higher than that of English. By determining separate index values for selected criteria, we are freed from the problem of labeling Turkish an agglutinative language in contrast to a supposedly inflectional language like English.

Criteria for ranking languages by syntax have also been tentatively proposed. One such is the ratio of particles to (full) words, proposed by Householder, *IJAL* 26, 195–7. Another ratio is based on the number of words before heads of constructions to words after them.

Of the three linguistic levels for which typological classification has been attempted, that for the morphological level is clearly the most successful. It may be advantageous therefore to produce phonological classifications in accordance with the techniques applied for morphology. If we do, phonological typing will be based on analysis of running texts rather than on analysis of phonological systems. That is, rather than classifying English by the number of fricatives in its phonological system, we would count the number of fricatives in a running text and determine the ratio of fricatives to stops, or consonants to vowels, and so on. Using this procedure we could determine criteria which would enable us to combine ratios for phonological features with those for morphological features. The most useful phonological criteria will have to be determined, like those for morphological features, by analysis of numerous languages.

Promising procedures for typological classification have at last been suggested. They are not the only possible procedures. Given adequate descriptions we could type languages for their phonological, morphological, syntactic and semantic structures, with no attention to the frequency of selected features in texts. At present, however, analysis of frequency of selected features is the most promising approach. It must be tested on a variety of languages and refined, as have been the procedures for genealogical classification.

3.6 Although the chief aim of typology is classification of languages, it promises new techniques for historical study. A small sampling indicates that the indices for selected Indo-European languages have changed in the course of time. The older Germanic languages, for example, have considerably higher synthetic indices than do those spoken today. Typological classification applied at selected stages of languages would enable us to mark their development on the basis of verifiable criteria. Such indices would not be based on a selected segment of the vocabulary, but would include borrowings, which hamper genealogical classification. Albanian and Armenian, and even English, with their many borrowings, would have indices which could be ranked with those of more conservative Indo-European languages like Lithuanian or Sanskrit. Until typological classification by indices has been carried out extensively for a great number of related languages, we cannot know what insights it will give us into language change, or language interrelationships. Its promise is such, however, that as much energy may be applied to it in the next decades as has been expended in the past on genealogical classification.

SELECTED FURTHER READINGS

The best introduction to typological classification is found in Edward Sapir's *Language* (New York, 1921), especially Chapter VI, Types of Linguistic Structures, although Chapters IV and V cannot be neglected.

F. N. Finck's *Die Haupttypen des Sprachbaus* (Berlin and Leipzig, 1909) gives a good example of the typological classification developed in the course of the nineteenth century. There are numerous statements of Marr's views; among the fullest is L. L. Thomas' *The Linguistic Theories of N. Ja. Marr* (Berkeley and Los Angeles, 1957).

For typology of phonological systems a fundamental work is N. S. Trubetzkoy's *Grundzüge der Phonologie* (Prague, 1939). A more recent discussion is available in Chapter 2 of C. F. Hockett's *A Manual of Phonology* (Baltimore, 1955).

The distinctive features which Roman Jakobson uses to classify both consonants and vowels, such as *compact* versus *diffuse, acute* versus *grave,* are discussed in *Fundamentals of Language,* pages 29–32, by Roman Jakobson and Morris Halle (The Hague, 1956). Compact is there defined as referring to "concentration of energy in a relatively narrow, central region of the spectrum," grave as "concentration of energy in the lower frequencies of the spectrum."

Use of distinctive features, such as *labial* versus *dental* articulation of consonants, or *front* versus *back* articulation of vowels, is sufficiently general for presentation without comment, or bibliographical reference.

Any future typological classification will have to start from Number 3, Volume 26 of *International Journal of American Linguistics* (July, 1960), in which was reprinted "A Quantitative Approach to the Morphological Typology of Language," by Joseph H. Greenberg, with three further articles including Householder's "First Thoughts of Syntactic Indices"; of these A. L. Kroeber's is most useful for an introduction to the possibilities for typological classification.

4 – The Use of Written Records

4.1 Materials of concern in historical linguistics are available only through written records, called **texts.** In order to interpret texts adequately a historical linguist must be equipped to deal with the writing system used to record them, even though he generally uses a standard transliteration. These however are often inadequate, occasionally even inaccurate; Greek *phi, theta, khi,* as here, are transliterated with two symbols and therefore in transliteration lack parallelism with other Greek consonants, such as *p b t d k g,* even though they are quite parallel with them in Greek writing and phonology. Similarly Sanskrit *bh dh gh* are the traditional transliterations for writing symbols quite parallel to those for Sanskrit *p t k* etc. The transliteration for Sanskrit aspirated stops has introduced into historical linguistics the further annoyance of complex symbols for phonemes in Proto-Indo-European. Though such transliterations are troublesome, they even become dangerous to anyone who does not know their background. We cannot expect revisions which remove such transliterational shortcomings, for the small number of historical linguists are expected to have enough resilience and energy to master oddities in transliteration. On the grounds that these would complicate the use of older handbooks, historical linguists have clearly had enough vigor to reject most attempts at modifications of transliterations. Accordingly one of the first tasks of a historical linguist is to master the writing systems of the languages with which he is concerned and their standard transliterations.

In addition historical linguists must understand the general development of writing systems. For new ones may be encountered, such as those discovered in Crete and now partially deciphered, or that discovered in Mohenjo-Daro and not yet deciphered. Moreover, in accordance with generally observable phenomena in their development, writing systems modify texts. That used for English, like those used today for all the other Indo-European languages developed from the Egyptian. By following its development we can observe the principles of development in writing, and some of the problems we face in dealing with texts.

4.2 The origin of writing is unclear. It may have resulted from attempts at artistic expression, like the animal figures found in various caves of Europe and Africa, or from attempts to depict figures for magical or religious purposes. Such figures may be compared with representations still used today, which have no direct relationship with language. Hunters in Africa may prop up a stick to indicate to another party the direction of their chase. Symbols reproduced on wampum belts by American Indians also represented a situation, with no attempt to depict its form in any selected language. Without understanding Indian languages the English-speaking William Penn was able to interpret the wampum belt recording his treaty. Such efforts to symbolize situations rather than speech we consider precursors of writing; we speak of writing systems only when symbols have been devised to represent elements of the language.

In the history of mankind only three writing systems have been devised which have gone through a long series of development and adaptation for various languages: those of Egypt, Sumer and China. They may actually be of one origin. Our data on their possible earlier relationship are inadequate. Only the Egyptian has been developed to an alphabet, a contribution of the Greeks. A history of the Egyptian, through its adaptation for West Semitic languages, for Greek, Latin, and from it to the languages of Europe, therefore incorporates the possible development of any writing system.

4.3 The earliest Egyptian texts we know, from the latter part of the fourth millennium B.C., already show the features of an advanced writing system. This consists of approximately five hundred symbols, known as **hieroglyphs.** Many of these are pictorial representations of the object represented by the word they stand for: a representation of a head stands for *tp* 'head'; a representation of a hand stands for *drt* 'hand'; a representation of a lotus stands for *sšn* 'lotus.' (Vowels were left undesignated by the Egyptians. Although Egyptologists have been able to determine the vowels of many words, the transcriptions of hieroglyphs generally do not indicate them.)

Other hieroglyphs are less directly related to the words they stand for. A representation of a seated man with his hand at his mouth stands for *wnm* 'eat'; a representation of a falcon may stand for *nsw* 'king.' Hieroglyphs as early as we know them may therefore represent words for actions or abstractions as well as for objects. For this reason the formerly used terms **pictograms** or **ideograms** are less appropriate than **logograms.** The symbols themselves we describe as **logographic.**

A further characteristic use of hieroglyphs supports this designation. Some homophones came to be indicated by the same hieroglyph. The word for 'ten thousand' *db'*, for example, was a homophone of the word for 'finger' and was represented by the symbol for 'finger.'

In a further development, some hieroglyphs came to be used for two consonants, because one of the consonants of a word was lost; other words may always have consisted of two consonants. For example, the word for 'swallow' was *wr;* this also came to be used for *wr* 'large,' and further as a partial representation of longer words, such as *wrd* 'be weary.' As a result of losses of further consonants, some hieroglyphs came to stand for words with only one consonant. The symbol for 'belt' represented *s,* that for 'water' *n,* and so on. Twenty-four such symbols in this way came to be used to represent syllables with one consonant. Their use illustrates the furthest development of the hieroglyphic system within Egypt. To the time of its progressive abandonment around the beginning of our era the Egyptian writing system maintained its full panoply of hieroglyphs, some of which represented syllables, others words.

Although not directly pertinent in the study of the development of our writing system, it is of interest to observe that a cursive script was developed early. When writing systems are used in everyday activities, writers find it difficult to maintain elegance and clarity of representation. With choice of writing materials, attempts at wide use of writing and rapidity of writing are responsible for many changes in the outward shapes of symbols.

Egyptians were no exception; the earliest cursive system is known as **hieratic.** It gave rise to another, more abbreviated system, known as **demotic.** The symbols of both hieratic and demotic are quite different from the handsome hieroglyphs which are usually depicted in handbooks and which a visitor can see in the tombs at Saqqara near Cairo and on other Egyptian monuments.

The decipherment of the hieroglyphic system, while also peripheral to historical linguistics, illustrates the dependence of historical linguistics on gifted philologists and cryptographers. It is generally known that possibly the most enduring of Napoleon's achievements in Egypt was the discovery in 1799 of the Rosetta stone by soldiers preparing fortifications. For some time, hieroglyphs had fascinated European intellectuals; there was accordingly tremendous interest in the Rosetta stone, for it was clearly a means to their decipherment since it contained a text in three writing systems, the Greek as well as demotic and hieroglyphic. From copies of the Rosetta stone a French scholar, François Champollion, in 1824 deciphered the hieroglyphic system; the demotic system was deciphered in 1848 by a German, Heinrich Brugsch. The Rosetta stone itself was taken to England in 1802 and is still in the British Museum.

4.4 It has long been suspected that our alphabet is an offshoot of the Egyptian writing system. At the end of the first century A.D., Tacitus stated this view in his *Annals,* 11.14: "The Egyptians first represented concepts by means of animal figures; these oldest monuments of human memory may still be seen engraved in stone. They claim to be the inventors of writing. From them the Phoenicians are said to have brought the script to Greece because they ruled the seas, and they received the credit for inventing what they only took over." Yet the link between the Western Semitic (Tacitus' Phoenician) and the hieroglyphic system was unknown. In 1904–1905 the archeologist, Flinders Petrie, found sixteen inscriptions in the copper and malachite mines of Sinai, which Sir Alan H. Gardiner later deciphered. These provided a link between the hieroglyphs and the Phoenician system; they also illustrate how the West Semitic twenty-two syllable system, like the twenty-four syllable system of the Egyptians, was based on hieroglyphs. To understand some of the modifications one must remember that the Semitic users of the symbols, and later the Greeks, were not consistent in their placing of the symbols. Some symbols were reversed, with ultimately a completely different appearance from those of the Egyptians.

Further modifications of shape were introduced when the Semitic system was borrowed by the Greeks, probably in the ninth century B.C. The Greeks wrote either from right to left, like the Semitic peoples, or from left to right, or both alternately **(boustrophedon).** Some characters then were reversed, for example, *B*. The ultimate shape of our alphabet was not fixed until the Latins took it over. Yet the essential modification of the Greeks was the conversion of the syllabic system of the Semites to an alphabetic system, and the introduction of symbols for vowels.

In naming the symbols the Semites and Greeks used the **acrophonic** principle. The second symbol was called *beta* by the Greeks, after its Semitic name, note Hebrew *beth*—house; the third *gamma,* see Hebrew *gimel*—camel; and so on. The first symbol was named for ', see Hebrew *'aleph*—ox; a consonant not found in Greek. When Greeks took over its name as *alpha,* it seemed to begin with *a* rather than with '. Accordingly they used it to represent a vowel rather than a consonant. The symbols for *e* and *o* developed similarly from consonantal symbols in which the initial consonant was lost. A further symbol, *i,* which to the Semitic users represented a vowel as well as a consonant, was used solely as a vowel by the Greeks, for the consonantal element had been lost in Greek. In this way the Greeks made the tremendous contribution of adding vowel symbols to the alphabet. This advance in writing systems has never been independently duplicated, nor have writing systems developed beyond it.

For a more complete representation of speech, symbols for accents and other suprasegmentals are essential. Accent symbols were also developed and used by the Greeks, in Alexandria. They did not, however, gain general currency in Classical times or subsequently. Only linguists in modern times have introduced them, to bring about the remaining essential of an accurate writing system.

Other modifications introduced by the Greeks are of interest, though not of fundamental importance to the structure of the alphabet. Among these are introduction of symbols for open *e* and *o* beside those for *epsilon* and *omikron* (close *e* and *o*). In Ionic Greek, *h* was not pronounced; the symbol for it, *H*, was taken over for *eta*, open *e*, comparing with the symbol *E* for close *e*. Apparently on this pattern an open Ω for *omega* was introduced beside *O*. These modifications illustrate the Greek readiness to modify the alphabet for practical purposes.

The Greeks introduced four additional characters to the Semitic alphabet, those for *upsilon, phi, khi* and *psi*. We do not know the sources for these. Pedersen, *Linguistic Science in the Nineteenth Century*, 208, suggests a relationship for *upsilon* and *khi* with symbols in the syllabary of Cyprus. Further, that the use of vowel syllables in Cyprus may have led to the introduction of vowel letters in the alphabet. The recent discovery that Linear B was used to write Greek from as early as 1450 B.C. and our consequently increasing knowledge of early Greek culture may help us to answer this problem and others in the Greek development of the alphabet.

4.5 Three other offshoots of the West Semitic syllabary, from Aramaic to Pehlevi, from Syrian to Mongol and Manchu and the Arabic writing system, developed vocalic writing only late, if at all. Another, the Indic **Brāhmī**, from which developed **devanāgarī** and many other south-Asian scripts, remained syllabic.

Based directly on Greek were, among others, the Gothic system, developed in the fourth century but soon extinct, and the two Slavic systems, the **Cyrillic** and **Glagolitic**, both of the ninth century. Cyrillic was based on majuscules, capitals; Glagolitic probably on minuscules, small letters. Cyrillic became established in Russia and has been adapted for a wide array of other Slavic and also non-Slavic languages.

The major continuant of the Greek alphabet was the Latin. It was transmitted to the Romans by Etruscans. In Etruscan the voiced : voiceless distinction between *g* : *k* was not made; accordingly the third letter came to stand for [k], as it still does in English before *a o u,* as in *cat cot cut*. Modifications of the alphabet by the Romans were slight; the most important is the introduction of a modified *C* for the *G* sound. Another modification is of interest in illustrating the dual function of the alphabet to represent numerals as well as sounds. When the Greek alphabet was imported for Latin some symbols were maintained for numerals: ᗐ or ⊥ for fifty (Greek *khi*); ⊙, ⋵ for hundred (Greek *theta*); ⊕ , ⋒ for thousand (Greek *phi*). The source of these eventually became unclear and they were modified to the more common letters *L C M,* which we use today when writing Roman numerals. A fourth of our Roman numerals, *D* for five hundred, was taken over from half of ⊕ . The three other symbols of the Roman numeral system *I V X* apparently had their origin in gesture-like signs.

Proper understanding of the dual use of the alphabet is essential in dealing with its history. When the Greek alphabet was taken over for Gothic, for example, a complete set of numerals was arranged, apparently as the first goal; then symbols were selected for sounds. The assumption that early makers of alphabets, like the Goth Wulfila, were incipient phonemicists is based on charming but inapplicable retentions from Romanticism.

Modifications which the alphabet underwent after its use for Latin are superficial. With the breaking up of the Roman Empire various "national hands" were developed in its political subdivisions. A ready example survives today for Irish.

Cursives were also introduced. Study of these is the subject of **paleography** and is not of direct concern to linguistics; paleography may however be essential to linguists dealing with medieval texts.

When scripts came to be too troublesome and unclear, reforms were introduced. The most important of these was the Carolingian, of about A.D. 800. Its importance results from the prestige which the Carolingian script enjoyed at the time printing was introduced in Europe. The favored form of letters was the Carolingian minuscule; our printed fonts continue this today. Other modifications, the selection of varying forms of *I* to stand for *I* and *J,* and of *U* to stand for *U* and *V,* the formation of *W* introduced no new principles; our alphabet today is not far different from the Latin.

Extensive modifications had been introduced in scripts for Germanic and Celtic languages, the bases of which are not wholly clear. The Germanic **runes,** clearly based in part on the alphabet, differ in order and purpose. The old runic alphabet contained twenty-four symbols, three series of eight, arranged probably according to a magical principle, later forgotten. The first six symbols of the first series are well known, through the name for the entire series, **futhark.** Runic symbols were used only for relatively short inscriptions, many of them at burials. The symbols we know from Latin were transparently adapted to simplify carving on wooden tablets, for example, ᚠ for *F,* or, because the runes were read in any position, ᚢ for *U.* Runic inscriptions are of interest to linguists as they provide our earliest Germanic texts, to philologists because they yield information about Germanic culture, covering especially the fifth to the tenth centuries, and to the general reader because of forgeries a number of which have attracted attention. The most notable of these is the Kensington Stone, which purported to prove that Vikings had penetrated to Minnesota in the Middle Ages. With other forgeries it is an illustration of a linguist's need to know the basis of his texts.

The **ogam** inscriptions, used for early Irish, are made by notching or lining the corners of posts. Series of one to five dots, or one to five lines extending to the right, to the left, or in both directions of an edge provided twenty symbols, five for vowels, fifteen for consonants. Though particularly subject to weathering, the ogam inscriptions when legible are valuable in giving us our earliest Irish and Welsh texts.

4.6 The writing systems we have surveyed may be classified into three groups, with transitional types:

1. **logographic**—symbols represent words, e.g., early Egyptian
   a. **logo-syllabic**—symbols represent words or syllables, e.g. later Egyptian
2. **syllabic**—symbols represent syllables, e.g., devanāgarī
   b. **syllabic-alphabetic,** e.g. West Semitic, in which symbols represent consonants with varying vowels
3. **alphabetic,** e.g. Greek

The systems in use at any time are rarely pure representations of one of these types. In contemporary English, numerals indicate words or morphemes such as 2, 4th, and are accordingly logographic, though the basic writing system is alphabetic.

Moreover, writing systems are rarely ideal. The alphabetic system used in English is uneconomical, for several entities may be used to indicate units otherwise represented by one entity: *ig* in *sign, i-e* in *sine, igh* in *sight, i* in *I.*

Worse still, English has a rare distinction of using the same symbols, *th,* to indicate two different phonemes besides separate entities, as in *porthole:* /ð/, as in *this,* and /θ/, as in *thin.* Possibly the restriction of /ð/ primarily to a small set of morphemes similar in use, and to initial position in these has permitted this rarity to persist.

When any graphemic material is analyzed, the type of writing system must be determined, and its degree of correspondence with the contemporary language. Often as in *sight,* see German *Sicht* [ziçt], writing systems reflect an earlier stage of the language. Obsolete spellings are helpful for historical study, though possibly difficult to interpret. It requires some study to determine when post-vocalic *gh* in English no longer represented a velar fricative. Our best evidence is derived from inverse spellings like Spenser's *whight* for *white.* This spelling would have been impossible when the velar fricative was still pronounced; from it therefore we receive information about the phonological development of English.

The most frequent imperfection in writing systems is failure to indicate some of the phonemes in a language. The writing system used for English is inadequate in failing to indicate suprasegmentals, pitch, stress and juncture; punctuation marks, unsystematically introduced from about the beginning of our era, and capital letters are only approximate indications for these. Another feature poorly indicated is quantity. No provision was made for indicating long vowels in Latin, and when the Latin alphabet was adapted for Germanic languages, long and short vowels were not distinguished.

When writing systems provide insufficient information, we attempt to supplement it in various ways, most commonly by the analysis of verse. Possibly our best means to determine Germanic quantities are based on the use of words in Germanic verse. The following lines from the *Beowulf* may illustrate how analysis of poetic texts adds information not provided by the Old English writing system.

710 Ða com of more under misthleoþum
Grendel gongan, Godes yrre bær;

Then came from the moor under cover of night
Grendel walking, God's anger he bore;

Since the manuscript does not use different symbols for short and long vowels, we cannot determine from it whether the *o*'s of *com, of, more, gongan, Godes* are short or long. But in Germanic poetry, certain requirements were placed on the poet: each verse was required to have two prominent syllables in which the vowels were long. Short vowels were permitted in the less prominent syllables, or in the prominent syllables if the lack of length was compensated for by a following consonant in the same syllable, as in *gongan,* or by an additional weakly stressed syllable, as in *Godes*. Since we know from the *m* alliteration of line 710 that *more* is metrically prominent, and since the *-re* of *more* is metrically significant, we must assume that its *o* is long; by converse reasoning we would assume the *o* of *of* to be short. Analysis of Old English verse therefore provides us with information about quantity and accentuation in Old English.

In this way, study of poetry may give us information beyond that provided by a writing system. Yet poetry manipulates phonemic patterns; it does not use them without modification. Therefore it must be interpreted with the same care as writing systems. Alliteration in Old English poetry assures us that the *g*'s of *Grendel, gongan* and *Godes* were similarly pronounced, and which other consonants were classed together by the Old English poets. But it tells us nothing about Old English vowels, for in Germanic verse all of the vowels alliterated with one another; further, when *g* became palatalized in Old English, as in *gieldan* 'yield' it continued to alliterate with velar *g*. Poetic conventions like writing conventions must be understood before they can be utilized to provide linguistic information.

Writing systems may also be inadequate because of conventions maintained from the area in which they were formerly used. The writing system taken over for Old English presents other problems than the lack of marking for quantity. Old English contained some vowels which could not be represented by the simple symbols used for Latin, such as the *eo* of *misthleoþum*. We have no contemporary description of the sounds it represented; accordingly its exact value is disputed. The compound symbol *eo* may reflect an Irish development. For in Old Irish manuscripts *e* is used before *o,* especially in weakly stressed syllables, to indicate the pronunciation of the preceding consonant. In Old English *menigeo* 'multitude,' we assume that *e* marked the preceding *g* as a palatal, with a pronunciation [menǐjo]. The Old English orthographic system is further complicated because it continues conventions of the Old Irish spelling system as well as the Latin.

Since writing systems are conventional and imperfect, we supplement in various ways the information we seek concerning the actual pronunciation. Misspellings help us to determine when conventional spellings do not reflect the spoken language. If humorists and bad spellers write *of* for *have* in modern English, we may infer that *have* is commonly pronounced /əv/. Scribal errors are similarly informative for older materials.

Moreover, languages are rarely isolated. Words adopted from other languages inform us of the sound systems of both languages, as do borrowings out of a language. The Biblical names found in the languages of Europe, from Old Church Slavic to Old English, give us information on them. If *Mary* is reproduced as *Marija* in Old Church Slavic, as *Maria* in Old English, we can infer the value of the symbols used from the spellings and from our knowledge of Latin and Greek pronunciation. Conversely we determine the pronunciation of names and words in Old Church Slavic, Old English and other languages from the manner in which they are represented when included in Latin and Greek materials.

We may also draw inferences from earlier or later forms of the language with which we are dealing. The Old English *o* in *of* is pronounced differently in Middle English and New English from that of *mod* 'mood.' We may also attempt to determine the pronunciation of Old English forms by comparing them with related forms in the other Germanic languages. But etymology may be misleading. Modern English *of* and *mood* have undergone various changes. We cannot insist that these reflect differences in Old English, although for these two words they do. If on the basis of their differing contemporary pronunciations we assumed different pronunciations for the vowels in the Old English forms of *good* and *mood,* our inference would be wrong. The vowels were alike in Old English; through subsequent changes they have become different. Because individual languages, and individual words, undergo various changes, etymological evidence must always be used cautiously in attempts to determine the pronunciation of related materials.

In recent attempts to interpret writing systems, increasing use has been made of structural evidence. Graphemic systems may be analyzed for the internal relationship of their elements and for their relationship with the phonemic system of the linguistic material they represent. Writers with no linguistic training are more aware of the phonemes than of the allophones of their language. If therefore we find beside Old English

i	u
e	o
æ	a

a *y,* as in *cyning* 'king' and an *oe* as in *oexen* 'oxen,' we may conclude that these symbols represent phonemes in some stage of Old English. From the composite form of *oe* we assume it represented a front rounded vowel. The symbol *y* fits best into the Old English system of symbols if we assume that it represented a somewhat higher front rounded vowel. In Old High German the first is spelled *kuning,* the second *ohson.* From these spellings we conclude that there was no phonemic difference between the *u* and *o* in these forms and those elsewhere. Though structural analysis may permit us to make inferences about the phonemic system represented by the orthography, in its interpretation we must be aware of possible complications, such as conventions imported from previous writing systems and those developed in the language. Interpretation of writing systems is best done by skillful use of all approaches.

Because of the shortcomings of methods of interpretation, we welcome contemporary descriptions of the language or its writing system. Greek and Latin grammarians provide some indication of the values of the alphabetic symbols they used. A grammarian in medieval Iceland has given us similar information about Old Icelandic. Less explicit but equally valuable help comes from the rare writer, who like Orme, modified traditional system in an attempt better to indicate his pronunciation. Various ingenious methods have been developed in attempts to determine the pronunciation and phonological systems underlying texts. We may illustrate some of these by noting further systems of writing.

4.7 The **cuneiform** or wedge-shaped script was developed by Sumerians in the fourth millennium B.C., taken over by Akkadians in the middle of the third millennium, and from them by various neighbors: by the Hittites and other groups in Asia Minor, who produced texts in the second millennium B.C., by the Elamites, with texts in the two last millennia B.C., and by various less well-known groups: the Cosseans, Mitanni (1400 B.C.) and the people of Lake Van, ninth to seventh centuries B.C. It passed out of use in the fourth century A.D., and subsequently became completely unknown, until cuneiform texts were deciphered in the nineteenth century.

A long inscription at Behistan, Iran was the avenue to relearning cuneiform. This inscription of the Persian king Darius (521–486 B.C.) was copied in part by travelers in the eighteenth century, by H. C. Rawlinson, 1836–1847, and recently by G. G. Cameron, 1948. Early scholars noted that inscriptions from the Old Persian area were composed in three languages: Old Persian, Elamite and Akkadian. By assuming that the Behistan inscription was to be attributed to the Persian kings, they substituted their names, compared readings of nonproper names with Avestan and Sanskrit words, and eventually mastered the Old Persian texts and through them the cuneiform system of writing.

The Old Persian texts furnished a relatively ready access to decipherment of cuneiform because for Old Persian only thirty-six syllabic characters, with five additional signs, had been maintained. Mastery of them led to the reading of Akkadian, the third language of the Behistan inscriptions, for the proper names provided ready comparison. Other Akkadian texts were then read; among them were lists and grammars indicating the values of symbols in Akkadian. Still other texts were avenues to Sumerian. The reading of cuneiform in this way gave access to the history of the Middle East from the fourth millennium B.C. Many cuneiform texts remain to be uncovered and interpreted.

The earliest Sumerian texts indicate that the cuneiform system developed from pictures. An early form of the symbol for 'star, god, heaven' is ✳, for 'vegetation' ⚘, for 'enclosure' □. As these symbols were inscribed with a stylus on clay tablets, they came to be stylized in wedge-shaped forms (and shifted by ninety degrees to keep the scribe from smudging his copy). Ultimately ✳ was written with three strokes 𒀭. Complex symbols also were developed; that for 'garden' was ⚘□. Moreover, characters could be used merely for their phonetic value; 𒀭 was read as the syllable *AN* as well as the word 'god.'

When cuneiform symbols were taken over by Akkadians, another complexity was introduced: symbols could be read either by their Sumerian or their Akkadian values. Since 'god' in Akkadian is *ILU* and 'heaven' *ŠAMU*, 𒀭 in Akkadian texts may have these readings among others, such as the Sumerian *AN*. When taken over by the Hittites the cuneiform system could be read with Sumerian, Akkadian or Hittite values, compounding the complexity further. Without parallel texts and dictionaries, interpretations of the Hittite texts would have been fantastically difficult.

The reading of cuneiform texts is aided somewhat by the presence of **determinatives,** symbols used with nouns to indicate morphological and semantic classes, such as plurals, gods, men, rivers, wooden articles, and so on. Determinatives, used also by the Egyptians, are markers which themselves have no phonetic value, somewhat like capital letters for proper nouns and adjectives in English or for nouns in German. The symbols used for them may also be read as word symbols.

The cuneiform system therefore is a combination of a logographic and a syllabic system. In Old Persian it was virtually modified to an alphabetic system.

4.8 A third system of writing, the Chinese, has remained logographic. In Japan, however, it has been modified to a syllabic system, which is generally used in conjunction with logographs. Like the Egyptian hieroglyphs and the Sumerian cuneiform symbols, Chinese characters developed from pictures. In early inscriptions the symbol for *mu*^{4} 'tree' was 米, for *jih*^{4} 'sun' ⊙, for *men*^{2} 'gate' 門. As Chinese characters were inscribed on wood rather than on bone, the lines of characters were straightened, and the characters became stylized. Today *mu*^{4} is written 木, *jih*^{4} 日, *men*^{2} 門.

A small number resulted from combinations of simple characters. That for 'east' is 'the sun rising through a tree' 東. Another small group are symbolic pictures: *yen*^{2} 'speak' is a mouth producing speech 言, earlier [illegible]. The largest group was made up of components, one of which represents the meaning, the other the pronunciation (often called phonetic). A homonym of *men* 'gate' indicates plurality. The character developed for this consists of a form of 'man' 亻 and the character for 'gate' 門; the composite character is 們. A similar process gave rise to 悶 *men*^{4} 'mournful' (*men* plus 'heart') and 捫 *men*^{1} 'feel' (*men* plus hand).

The large number of characters of this last type provided the means for the most common arrangement of Chinese dictionaries. Characters are arranged by a characteristic element, called *radical*, and the number of additional strokes. Although in writing rapidly, Chinese produce characters in cursive form, the stroke order and the number of strokes in conventional writing are still keys to their identification. 們, for example, is listed under 亻, radical nine, and further classified by its eight additional strokes.

Until very recent times, the system of characters was the

sole method of writing Chinese. Since Chinese morphs are monosyllabic and uninflected, the writing system was efficient, except for the need to memorize thousands of characters. In this century various attempts have been made to develop a simpler system of writing Chinese. None has succeeded in replacing the character system.

Various systems of transliteration have also been developed. That of Wade and Giles is used most commonly for transliterating Chinese in Latin letters. Transliteration has given rise to pronunciations of Chinese place-names which are sometimes far from the original, such as *Peking* for something like [bey ǰiŋ], which may serve as an illustration of one of the problems caused by transliteration.

When the Chinese system of characters was carried to Japan, means were devised to indicate inflectional syllables and particles. Certain characters were selected to indicate syllabic values, as for the particle *ka*. In the early period a great many such characters were so used, but in the course of time they came to be restricted in number and stylized. The character 加 'add to' was the one selected to indicate the syllable *ka*. Forty-eight such characters make up the Japanese **kana** syllabary. Of this there are two forms: the **hiragana,** used normally; the **katakana,** which compares in use to our italics. Hiragana symbols developed from rapidly written forms of characters; the hiragana for *ka* is か, in which 口 has become a simple stroke. The katakana symbols developed from abbreviated forms; the katakana for *ka* is カ, in which the 口 has been entirely omitted.

Japanese is still written in a combination of characters with kana. In the word for 'walk,' for example, the Chinese character 歩 must be supplemented by the kana symbol for *ku* く to indicate the positive *aruku;* the negative *arukanai* is written 歩かない. This character has a totally different value when used in the compound for 'infantry' 歩兵 *hohei.* As a result of these different uses the Japanese writing system is possibly the most complicated today.

4.9 Both the cuneiform system and the Chinese system follow the development that we traced in the Egyptian–Greek system, though neither carried it as far. The farthest developments of them, in Old Persian and Japanese, were to syllabic systems.

The three writing systems we have dealt with started with pictures, as did other writing systems which we will not discuss: the Aztec, Mayan, Proto-Indic, Proto-Elamite, Cretan, and Hieroglyphic Hittite. Of these, only Hieroglyphic Hittite has been securely deciphered, although Mayan seems to be in process of decipherment. Each of the three was conventionalized and modified by the writing materials.

As a further stage, syllabic systems developed. This stage, clear in the twenty-four Egyptian syllables, the Sinitic and West Semitic scripts, in the Hittite and Elamite cuneiform, and in the Japanese kana, also has representatives in the Cyprian syllabary, in Linear A and B, and an interesting modern creation, Sequoia's invented syllabary for Cherokee.

Syllabic symbols developed toward consonantal symbols in the West Semitic area.

The last stage of development, in Greek, led to the creation of a pure alphabet, in which symbols are used for vowels as well as consonants. The Greek alphabetic system was widely adopted and imitated. New writing systems devised today are alphabetic. In a complete writing system symbols would also be used to indicate suprasegmentals. Although the Greeks introduced symbols for pitch accent, they did not become a standard part of their writing system nor of those based on it. Only linguists of recent times have introduced symbols for all the phonemic entities in a language.

SELECTED FURTHER READINGS

D. Diringer's *The Alphabet,* 2nd ed. (New York, 1948), furnishes a general introduction, with numerous illustrations. One of the most thorough, detailed and well-illustrated treatments of writing is H. Jensen's *Die Schrift in Vergangenheit und Gegenwart,* 2nd ed. (Berlin, 1958). Both Diringer and Jensen should be consulted primarily for their data and their illustrations.

For a structural analysis of writing systems, see I. J. Gelb's *A Study of Writing: the Foundations of Grammatology* (Chicago, 1952). Gelb presents a typology in accordance with which writing systems developed. When it differs from that of Diringer and Jensen, his identification of the characteristic structure of writing systems should be accepted.

Brief statements on writing systems may also be found in the standard handbooks, such as Bloomfield's *Language,* Chapter 17.

Although discussions of writing systems generally deal with their interpretation for linguistic purposes and their decipherment, none is as readable as are the pertinent sections in Holger Pedersen's *Linguistic Science in the Nineteenth Century.* An excellent earlier discussion of various steps in the development of the alphabet and theories concerning it is Kurt Sethe's *Der Ursprung des Alphabets* (Berlin, 1916).

5 – The Comparative Method

5.1 Analysis of texts available in writing and of modifications in writing systems provides us with one method of determining linguistic change. When in sixteenth-century texts we find *delight* spelled with *gh,* we assume that *gh* no longer indicates a consonant, but that the former consonant has been lost with an effect on the vowel. For *delight* earlier was spelled like *rite* rather than *right.* After the consonant indicated by *gh* had been lost, words like *delite* < ME *deliten* < OFr *deliter* < Latin *dēlectāre,* were misspelled on the pattern of words like *light* < OE *lēoht,* compare Germ. *Licht,* in which the *gh* was etymologically justified. Since spelling systems are conservative, this method of determining change is cumbersome. Moreover, it can be applied only when we have a continuous series of texts. Especially for prehistoric languages, a surer method of defining change and determining earlier forms has been developed which is known as the **comparative method.**

In using the comparative method we contrast forms of two

or more related languages to determine their precise relationship. We indicate this relationship most simply by reconstructing the forms from which they developed.

If for example we wish to determine the third singular present of the verb 'be' in Proto-Indo-European, our first step is to compare forms such as Skt. *ásti,* Lith. *ẽsti,* Gk. *ésti,* Goth. *ist,* and others. In these four forms our chief problem is the Sanskrit *a;* we infer from other forms that all PIE *e* > Skt. *a.* We then reconstruct the Proto-Indo-European form *ésti.* For our comparisons we use phonemic, not phonetic, analyses; our reconstructions are accordingly phonemic.

After we reconstruct forms, we attempt to verify them, using various means. One is to locate a contemporary form. For Proto-Indo-European this is manifestly impossible; for Proto-Romance on the other hand it may be quite possible. By another means we compare additional forms, either from the same root or of the same category.

Examining first singular and plural forms of the root 'be':

1 sg.	Skt. *ásmi*	Lith. *ẽsmi*	Gk. *eimí*	Goth. *im*
1 pl.	Skt. *smás*	Lith. *ẽsme*	Gk. *esmén*	Goth. *sijum*

we reconstruct the two further forms PIE *ésmi* and *smés.* (Detailed analysis of the developments in the various forms cited would require lengthy discussion.) These and still further forms of the verb 'be' lend credence to our reconstruction *ésti,* as would reconstructed forms of other verbs.

We note from the first that the reconstructed forms are limited in validity by the amount of information on which they are based. The comparative method has the serious limitation that it offers no means of reconstructing elements which are completely lost in subsequent stages of the language. Today we reconstruct the Proto-Indo-European third singular *ˀésti,* but with the help of another method. From the comparative method we could not determine that the Proto-Indo-European form began with a glottal stop, since this is not attested in forms that have come down to us.

Besides comparing the set of forms from one root, we compare sets of phonemes: the set of vowels in two or more languages, of stops, and so on. If we wished to support our reconstructed *s* and *t* in the Proto-Indo-European third singular of 'be,' we would attempt to determine the entire Proto-Indo-European obstruent system.

5.2 We may illustrate the application of the comparative method to sets of phonological entities with forms containing Greek and Latin obstruents (the forms are cited in transliteration):

		1	2	3	4
1	Gk.	patḗr 'father'	beltī́ōn 'better'	phrā́tēr 'brother'	
	Lat.	pater	dē-bilis 'weak'	frāter 'brother'	
2		treîs '3'	déka '10'	thúrā 'door'	heptá '7'
		trēs	decem	foris	septem
3		he-katón '100'	génos 'kin'	khamaí '(on the) earth'	
		centum	genus	humus	
4		poû 'where'	baínō 'come'	phónos 'murder'	
		tís 'who'		theínō 'strike'	
		quod 'what'	veniō	dē-fendō 'ward off'	
		quis 'who'			

For the first three rows of the first two columns—the voiceless and voiced orders of the labial, dental, and velar series—the results of our comparison would permit little dispute for the entities with which we are concerned. In both Greek and Latin we find oppositions between voiceless and voiced stops, between labials, dentals and velars, and we assume the same phonemes for Proto-Indo-European. We would posit accordingly for the system from which the obstruent systems of Greek and Latin developed:

Greek		Latin		Proto-Indo-European	
p	b	p	b	p	b
t	d	t	d	t	d
k	g	k	g	k	g

For the last two columns and the last row, however, we would be unable to posit earlier forms on the basis of the material provided here. We can suggest earlier forms only if we add material from other Indo-European languages.

The comparative method was sharpened largely by its application to the obstruent system of Germanic. In Germanic the obstruents had undergone various changes which baffled scholars before the studies of Rask and Grimm. By careful comparison these two founders of historical linguistics demonstrated the changes which had taken place in Germanic, and the usefulness of the comparative method. Their work and that of their successors also indicated the need for precise comparison between languages. Adding to our Greek and Latin examples cognate words from Germanic and Indic illustrates how they enable us to fill out our reconstruction of the Proto-Indo-European obstruents. (Unless otherwise labeled the Germanic examples are from Gothic. Examples in a wide variety of dialects to support the reconstruction of PIE *b* do not exist. We therefore must cite a cognate from Baltic, and admit that these post-date Proto-Indo-European, as do the examples for *b* in the chart on page 85.)

		1		2	3	4
1	Gmc.	fadar	Eng.	pool	broþar	
	Skt.	pitā́	Lith.	balà 'swamp'	bhrā́tā	
2		þrija		taihun	daur	sibun
		tráyas		dáśa		saptá

3	hunda	kuni 'race'	guma 'man'
	śatám	jánas	kṣā́s 'earth'
4	OIcel. hvat 'what'	OHG queman	OE gūþ 'battle'
	kás 'who'	gámanti 'they go'	ghnánti 'they strike'

The examples cited here support the inferences drawn from comparison of Greek and Latin, and supplement them, especially for column four. If we posit an obstruent system based on these four dialects, we reconstruct it as follows:

Proto-Indo-European

p	b	bh	
t	d	dh	s
k	g	gh	
k^w	g^w	g^wh	

Without a great deal of additional material and involved analysis the forms of the fourth row and the third column are poorly supported. For the fourth row we may find comfort in the Germanic and the Latin evidence; for the third column in the Sanskrit forms. We will not offer further evidence here in favor of these conventional reconstructions. Additional discussion would be pertinent for the study of Indo-European historical grammar rather than the comparative method. Greater understanding of the comparative method may be better achieved by more thorough examination of the Germanic obstruents. Reviewing the nineteenth-century study of the Germanic phenomena contributes to understanding the development of both the comparative method and that of historical linguistics.

5.3 Rask pointed out in 1818 the relationships between the Germanic obstruents and those of the other Indo-European dialects. In 1822 Grimm made the important contribution of indicating the system underlying the relationships. Proto-Indo-European voiceless stops of all four series are represented by voiceless fricatives in Germanic, Proto-Indo-European voiced stops by Germanic voiceless stops, Proto-Indo-European voiced aspirates by Germanic voiced fricatives. Grimm's achievement in systematically relating the Germanic obstruent system to those of the other Indo-European dialects securely established the comparative method. The consistency of correspondences in other positions, such as medially in the examples below, clearly indicates its value in historical linguistics; cf. Table 2, page 89.

By means of these and other examples we may verify the obstruents just posited for Proto-Indo-European. We can most simply state the development of the Proto-Indo-European obstruents into Germanic by using the following formulae. We read > 'became' or 'developed to.'

PIE p t k k^w > PGmc. f θ χ χ^w
PIE b d g g^w > PGmc. p t k k^w
PIE bh dh gh g^wh > PGmc. ʋ đ ǥ ($ǥ^w$)
PIE s > PGmc. s

We could state similarly with appropriate formulae the development of the Proto-Indo-European obstruents in the other Indo-European dialects.

If we wish to indicate the relationship of the obstruents from dialect to dialect we use the sign = in our formulae, reading it "correspond(s) to," for example:

Skt. p b bh = PGmc. f p ʋ
Gk. t d th = OCS t d d

We could also state our previous formulae in reverse order, for example:

PGmc. ʋ đ ǥ ($ǥ^w$) < PIE bh dh gh g^wh

reading < 'developed from.'

5.4 In a study of the relationships between two languages, we should make comparisons for all environments, not merely as

TABLE 2

Gk.	anepsiós (?)		nephélē 'fog'	
Lat.	nepōs	Lith. trobà 'building'	nebula	
Skt.	nápāt	OWelsh treb 'house'	nábhas	
Gmc.	OE nefa 'nephew'	Go. þaurp 'village'	Germ. Nebel	
Gk.	phrā́tēr	édomai	eruthrós	hestía 'hearth'
Lat.	frāter	edō	ruber	Vesta
Skt.	bhrā́tā	ád-mi	rudhirás 'bloody'	vásati 'lives'
Gmc.	OE brōðor 'brother'	OE etan 'eat'	OE rēad 'red'	wisan 'be'
OCS	bratŭ	jadętŭ 'they eat'	rŭdrŭ	
Gk.	déka	agrós	lékhetai 'sleeps'	
Lat.	decem	ager	lectus 'bed'	
Skt.	dáśa	ájras 'plain'		
Gmc.	taihun '10'	OE æcer	ligan 'lie'	
Gk.	lúkos 'wolf'	érebos 'underworld'	nípha 'snow'	
Lat.	lupus		nix, nivis	
Skt.	vr̥kas		Av. snāežaiti 'it snows'	
Gmc.	OIcel. ylgr 'she-wolf'	riqis 'darkness'	OE snāw	

we have done here for the initial and the intervocalic after accented vowels.

In such comparisons we find a variety of interrelationships.

1. The entities concerned may have been maintained in both languages. Latin *p* in *pater* and Greek *p* in *patḗr* are examples.

2. The entities concerned may have been maintained in one language and may have undergone change in the other. Latin *p* in *pater* and Gmc. *f*, as in Goth. *fadar*, are examples.

When only two languages are attested, it may be difficult to determine which maintains the original form. One may look for unchanged entities in certain environments in either language as guides. The occurrence of *p* after *s* provides the conclusive evidence in reconstructing PIE *p* from Latin and Germanic, for after *s* Germanic has preserved *p*, as in Goth. *speiwan*, see Lat. *spuō* 'spit.' We may therefore assume that in other environments as well, Latin *p* more closely represents the Proto-Indo-European entity than does the Germanic *f*.

3. The entities concerned may have undergone change in both languages, as in Lat. *nebula* and Germ. *Nebel*. Reconstructing the etymon of such forms may be very difficult. After a century and a half of attention the etymon of Greek *ph*, Latin *f/h*, Sanskrit *bh*, Germanic ᴜ has not been determined to everyone's satisfaction. If unchanged items cannot be found in certain environments, as in Goth. *speiwan*, one must rely on knowledge of the various kinds of sound changes.

Here too we may have a variety of developments.

a. The entities concerned may merge completely, as in OCS *jadętŭ* 'they eat' and *rŭdrŭ* 'red.' Such complete mergers cause great difficulties for reconstruction. We cannot determine whether a voiced stop in the Slavic languages developed from a Proto-Indo-European voiced stop or a voiced aspirate.

b. The entities may merge in part, as in Lat. *ruber* 'red' and *nebula* 'fog.' By comparing parallel entities in other series of the language with such coincidences, for example, the Latin dentals *edō* : *ruber* and the velars *ager* : *lectus*, one may place less credence in forms with mergers, such as the Latin dental series, than on those in related languages. The lack of parallelism in the Latin reflexes of PIE *bh dh gh* leads us to suspect marked changes in this order between Proto-Indo-European and Latin.

Moreover, the merger may be highly complex, as in Greek *poîos* "of what kind" (where Gk. *p* = Lat. *qu*) : *patḗr* (where Gk. *p* = Lat. *p*) and *tís* 'who' (where Gk. *t* = Lat. *qu*) : *treîs* (where Gk. *t* = Lat. *t*). Again, one must sort out the situation in the language concerned. Further analysis of Greek indicates that the reflexes of Proto-Indo-European k^w and the other labiovelars show up as labials before *a o* and as dentals before *e i*. Accordingly the complex merger is the result of an inner Greek development. To the extent we can judge from our Linear B materials, labiovelars were still maintained in Greek until approximately 1300 B.C.

Sound change is dealt with in Chapter 10; the changes sketched here are designed to indicate complexities in the application of the comparative method.

5.5 The comparative method has been highly successful in disclosing relationships between languages, and in permitting us to reconstruct earlier forms than those attested. Although the evidence for the labiovelar order is not clear in the widely known dialects of Indo-European, they were generally reconstructed for Proto-Indo-European; when Hittite texts were discovered, even from the troublesome Hittite writing system there is evidence for velar and labial articulation, which supports the reconstruction of Proto-Indo-European labiovelars. The Hittite form corresponding to Gk. *tís* is written *ku-iš*.

Another reconstruction by the comparative method which was later verified is Bloomfield's Proto-Algonquian cluster *çk,* which he proposed on the basis of Fox and Ojibwa *šk,* Cree and Menomini *hk,* and related clusters. Later in Swampy, Cree, he found a distinct reflex of this cluster, *htk* and other evidence

to support his reconstruction; *Language* 5.99–100 (1928).
Since use of the comparative method has in this way been demonstrated to be successful, careful application of it is highly trustworthy.

The comparative method, however, has various shortcomings. We use it to determine earlier entities from allophones, not from phones. Accordingly we can make reconstructions only at the phonemic, not the phonetic, level. On the basis of Greek *ph,* Germanic *ʋ*, Slavic *b,* Latin *b,* Sanskrit *bh* and Armenian *bh* we may posit PIE *bh,* but we cannot determine precisely its pronunciation. Similarly the Proto-Indo-European labiovelars; we do not know whether they were articulated as velars followed by labial rounding, as velars with simultaneous labial closure, or still other sounds. When we use the comparative method, our reconstructions are less precise phonetically than the information on which they are based.

We lose information also in the complexity of the language we reconstruct. In normal use of the comparative method we proceed backwards by triangulation, and eventually posit for each subgroup a dialect-free phoneme. In reconstructing the Proto-Indo-European voiceless velar stop, for example, we proceed from comparison of Greek *k* with Italic *k,* to comparison with Germanic *g,* with Indo-Iranian *ś* and so on. It is likely, however, that some of the dialects of Indo-European were not uniform; further, that they reflect a nonuniform situation in the parent language. Some forms, for example, which are expected to have a sibilant in Baltic and Slavic, have a velar, e.g.

Lith. *akmuõ* OCS *kamy* versus Skt. *aśmā*, Av. *asman-* 'stone'
Gk. *ákmōn* 'anvil'

Although we should reconstruct a dialect-free Proto-Indo-European, such irregularities suggest that the parent language already was composed of various dialects. With care we may apply the comparative method in all rigor and from forms like those for 'stone' assume dialects within the parent language.

Yet the method itself is not designed to yield anything other than a dialect-free corpus.

5.6 Throughout the nineteenth century the comparative method was being refined. We may illustrate its development by observing the increasing precision applied to the description of the obstruent system of Germanic in its relation to that of Proto-Indo-European and those of the other dialects.

In 1822, J. Grimm published general statements on the relations between Germanic obstruents and those in the other languages. Labeling *p t k* **Tenues,** *bh dh gh* (and *f* θ χ etc.) **Aspiratae** and *b d g* **Mediae,** he stated that Indo-European **T** > Germanic **A,** Indo-European **A** > Germanic **M,** Indo-European **M** > Germanic **T,** producing a circular scheme which has often been reprinted:

On the basis of subsequent changes in the High German area, where *t* later became *ts,* as in German *zu* versus English *to,* he assumed that this change repeated itself in the Germanic languages and therefore considered it a law. Subsequently the formulation has been called **Grimm's law.** Though many of his successors have gained a somewhat restricted renown through the discovery of a "law," which describes a minute change in some language, there has been considerable objection to use of the label "law" for a statement of correspondences. Today we may retain the label for established laws, like Grimm's, but prefer to be more modest if we make discoveries of correspondences in any language.

Grimm's contemporaries soon discovered "exceptions" to his law. Accounting for these contributed greatly to the development of historical method in the nineteenth century.

The first exception concerned the maintenance of Proto-Indo-European voiceless stops after Germanic fricatives. Note the example that follows on the next page.

Goth.	*hafts** 'married'	=	Lat.	*captus* 'captured'
	speiwan	=		*spuō* 'spit'
	ist	=		*est* 'is'
	skadus 'shadow'	=	Gk.	*skótos* 'darkness'
	nahts	=	Lat.	*nox, noctis* 'night'

In these and other examples the stop after fricative had not undergone change. The lack of change was ascribed to the environment. Within decades after Grimm had published his law scholars accounted for the first exception by stating that voiceless stops remained unchanged when they followed Germanic voiceless fricatives.

This solution indicated the importance in historical linguistics of examining immediate environments and observing phonetic characteristics. Though Grimm himself showed little interest in phonetics, his successors studied the production of sounds thoroughly. As a result articulatory phonetics was greatly developed in the nineteenth century, reaching a high level in the works of Sievers and Jespersen.

Explanation of the second group of exceptions gave rise to a further methodological advance. Involved here were Germanic voiced fricatives and stops which seemed to correspond irregularly to Indo-European voiced stops rather than to voiced aspirated stops, as in

Goth.	*-biudan* 'offer'	=	Skt.	*bodhāmi* 'notice'
	dauhtar	=		*duhitá̄* 'daughter'
	gagg 'street'	=		*jan̄ghā* 'leg'

If the correspondences had been in accordance with Grimm's law, the cognates in Sanskrit should have had initial aspirates.

Hermann Grassmann accounted for the lack of correspondence by pointing out that all such forms contained Proto-Indo-European aspirates in two successive syllables. Further, that in Indo-Iranian and Greek one of the two successive aspirates had been dissimilated to a stop. Accordingly the irregularity was not to be ascribed to Germanic, but rather to the supposedly more archaic Sanskrit and Greek.

We will examine the Sanskrit and Greek dissimilation of aspirates at greater length in the next chapter. Here we are chiefly concerned in a further refinement of the comparative method based on Grassmann's findings. Observing that his explanation was based on examination of the elements in successive syllables, linguists now learned that they could not deal only with entities and their immediate environments, for sounds might be affected by noncontiguous sounds. Grassmann's discovery led them to examine entire syllables and words, as well as individual sounds.

Accounting for the third set of exceptions led to a further refinement. These exceptions comprise forms in which a Proto-Indo-European voiceless stop had become a voiced fricative in Germanic rather than a voiceless fricative. Examples are:

> Goth. *sibun* OE *seofon* OS *sivun* OHG *sibun;*
> Skt. *saptá* Gk. *heptá* '7'
> Goth. *fadar* OIcel. *faðer* OE *fæder* OHG *fater;*
> Skt. *pitā́* Gk. *patḗr* 'father'
> OE *sweger* OHG *swigur;* Skt. *śvaśrū́ṣ* Gk. *hekurā́*
> 'mother-in-law'

A Danish linguist, Carl Verner, noted that the accent in Sanskrit and Greek never preceded the consonants which corresponded in Germanic to voiced rather than voiceless fricatives. Including Gmc. *z* < PIE *s* (*r* in all Germanic dialects but Gothic), for it behaved similarly, as in

> OIcel. *snør* OE *snoru* OHG *snura;* Skt. *snuṣā́*
> Gk. *nuós* < **snusos* 'daughter-in-law'

Verner formulated the following "law":

Germanic voiceless fricatives became voiced fricatives in voiced surroundings if the chief accent did not stand on the immediately preceding vowel in Proto-Indo-European.

Verner's article, written 1875, published 1876 in the *Zeitschrift für vergleichende Sprachforschung* 23, pages 97–130 under the title "Eine Ausnahme der ersten Lautverschiebung," probably had a greater effect on linguistics than has any other single publication.

As one result, linguists noted that they could no longer limit their attention to consonants and vowels, but that they had to consider accent as well. The suprasegmentals began to receive attention. In the late decades of the nineteenth century one observes in linguistic journals a tremendous attention to the suprasegmental patterns manipulated in verse. Many articles attempted to explain sound changes by recourse to suprasegmentals. Though some of these were overly enthusiastic, after 1876 linguists regarded the pitch and stress patterns of language, as fourteen years earlier they had learned to regard entire words, and several decades earlier they had learned to regard immediate environments. Accordingly, after Verner linguists dealt with all the phonological markers of an utterance.

5.7 Verner's explanation of the last large group of exceptions of Grimm's law had the further effect of giving linguists complete confidence in their laws or formulations. Observing that greater attention to the matter of language permitted them to account for residues and for diverse developments, a group of linguists after 1876 proclaimed that "sound laws operate without exceptions." These linguists, referred to as **neogrammarians** by somewhat scornful elders, proclaimed that if one assembled all the facts, analyzed them accurately and thoroughly, one could state exceptionless principles or laws for the development of language.

The new movement centered around Leipzig. Its leading young scholars, Brugmann, Osthoff, Leskien, and others adopted the label neogrammarian for themselves, and encouraged by their new scientific method proceeded to deal with a tremendous number of problems. They also attracted to Leipzig brilliant young students, such as Leonard Bloomfield. Through their students as well as their publications, the neogrammarian school exerted a great effect on linguistic theory. The principle that sound laws operate without exceptions encouraged linguists to uncover all the facts involved in language change, for it assured them that thorough study would yield results. It also led occasionally to undue pedantry and explanations based more on method than on matter. In spite of occasional excesses, the neogrammarians applied the comparative method with great skill to various problems in language. They also produced handbooks which have not been superseded to this day, such as K. Brugmann's *Grundriss der Vergleichenden Grammatik der indogermanischen Sprachen,* 2nd ed. (Strassburg, 1897–1916). They may further be credited with final development of the comparative method.

SELECTED FURTHER READINGS

A. Meillet's *La méthode comparative en linguistique historique,* Instituttet for sammenlignende kulturforskning Serie-A II (Oslo, 1925) is still the best introduction to the comparative method.

Good accounts are given in any of the competent handbooks. Among these are Bloomfield's *Language,* Chapter 18, E. H. Sturtevant's *An Introduction to Linguistic Science,* Chapter XV.

The most recent comprehensive treatment is Chapter XII of H. Hoenigswald's *Language Change and Linguistic Reconstruction* (Chicago, 1960). Here the comparative method is presented so comprehensively and rigorously that students should first read several briefer accounts, like those noted above.

6 – The Method of Internal Reconstruction

6.1 In explaining the second group of exceptions to Grimm's law, Grassmann made use of the comparative method. His decisive evidence, however, was furnished by observation of patterns within Sanskrit and Greek. For application of the comparative method to Germanic, Sanskrit and Greek data would not indicate which language better reflects the situation in the parent language. Irregularities within Sanskrit and Greek clearly show however that in some environments these languages had made the departure from the Indo-European distinction between aspirates and stops.

Some of the best evidence for the departure is found in reduplicated verb forms of Sanskrit and Greek. The perfect in Sanskrit and Greek is generally marked by reduplication of the first consonant (or consonants) of the root, followed by a vowel, for example:

Skt. *da-dau,* Gk. *dé-dō-ka,* cf. Lat. *de-dī* of the present *dō* 'give'

When however in Sanskrit and Greek, roots with an aspirate

are reduplicated, the reduplicating consonant does not maintain aspiration, for instance:

Skt. *ba-bhū-va* 'he has become.' Gk. *pé-phū-ka* of *phū́ō* 'develop'

Since the *p* of Greek is an unaspirated voiceless stop while the *b* of Sanskrit is an unaspirated voiced stop, we assume that the loss of aspiration took place separately in Sanskrit and Greek. In accordance with the patterns of reduplication we expect to reconstruct on the basis of information derived from within each of these languages:

Skt. **bha-bhū-va*	Gk. **phé-phū-ka*	on the pattern of
da-dau	*dé-dō-ka*	

Such a procedure, taking no outside language into account for reconstruction, we call the **method of internal reconstruction.**

We do not find the starred forms **bha-bhū-va* and **phé-phū-ka* for Sanskrit and Greek because in each language one of two aspirates of successive syllables was dissimilated. The changes may be described in Grassmann's formulation: the first of two aspirates beginning successive syllables or a syllable which also ended with an aspirate lost its aspiration.

The examples cited from the Sanskrit and Greek perfect indicate one type of complexity resulting from the loss of aspiration. Another is found in inflected forms, when aspirates are modified by contiguous elements. The nominative of 'hair' in Greek, for example, is *thríks,* the genitive *trikhós*. This paradigm seems to select willfully from the two possible aspirates. Yet each form is readily explained. In the nominative the aspiration was lost when the nominative marker *s* was appended after *kh* as in *ónuks, ónukhos* 'claw'; accordingly there was no aspirate with which the initial *th* might be dissimilated. In the genitive on the other hand the medial *kh* was maintained, requiring dissimilation of the initial consonant. Again comparing similar inflections like *kêruks,* gen. *kḗrūkos* 'herald,' in which the consonants remain unchanged, we could reconstruct internally from Greek alone pre-Greek *_thrikh-_ $<$ PIE _dhrigh-_.

6.2 The method of internal reconstruction is based on the occurrence of sound change without regard to morphological classes. As illustrated in Chapter 5, sound changes take place by allophones, regardless of their morphological role. A sound may undergo change in a number of morphs of a morpheme in which it occurs in specific phonological surroundings; in others it may remain unchanged. For example, we may analyze perfect reduplication in Sanskrit as a morpheme, with the structure (simplified): C_1a–C_1 . . . In those morphs with initial aspirate the dissimilation took place, yielding allomorphs of a characteristically different structure. When we find such varying allomorphs in a later stage of a language, we can hypothecate the prior form, as we do for perfect reduplication in Sanskrit. In dealing with morphophonemic variations, our use of internal reconstruction is dependent on a knowledge of the various patterns of sound change.

As with the dissimilated aspirates of Sanskrit, the new phones generally merge with those of other phonemes. Sanskrit _b_ resulting from the dissimilation of _bh_ in _ba-bhū-va_ merged with the existing /b/. When we apply internal reconstruction we may be able to determine such merged phones by their characteristic phonological environment. In Sanskrit, for example, we suspect any /b/ which is initial in its syllable and precedes an aspirate of being a reflex of earlier /bh/.

6.3 If morphological patterns are adequately structured, phonemes which have disappeared may be reconstructed by internal evidence. Most Indo-European roots have a structure CeC-, e.g. _bher-_ 'bear,' _g_^{w}_em-_ 'come,' _sed-_ 'sit.' (Note that root is a term which has become established for Proto-Indo-European base morphemes, as opposed to derivational and inflectional morphemes.) A small number of widely attested roots, however, differ by having only one consonant, e.g. _ag-_ 'lead,' (_s_)_tā-_

'stand,' *dhē-* 'place,' *es-* 'be.' Saussure suggested in 1879 that at an earlier stage of Indo-European these were parallel with roots of the structure CeC-; he posited for that stage consonants which subsequently disappeared. Saussure's suggestion was not widely accepted. When Kurylowicz dealt with Hittite, however, he found reflexes for some of Saussure's vanished consonants, which subsequently had been called laryngeals. Today therefore we reconstruct these roots with two consonants, *heg-* instead of *ag-*, (*s*)*teh-* instead of (*s*)*tā-*, *dheʔ-* instead of *dhē-*, *ʔes-* instead of *es-* (see 5.1). The validation of Saussure's brilliant suggestion through Hittite has added considerably to our confidence in the method of internal reconstruction.

6.4 When phonemes are restricted in occurrence to specific allomorphs of a morpheme, we may apply the method of internal reconstruction to determine the basis of the restriction, and the earlier situation. We find such restrictions for PGmc. *s* : *z*. For the Proto-Germanic forms of 'choose' we posit:

	Inf.	Pret. 3 sg.	Pret. 3 pl.	Pret. ptc.
	kiusan	kaus	kuzun	kuzan-
cf. 'freeze'	friusan	fraus	fruzun	fruzan-

From these forms, occurrences of /z/ may seem characteristically intervocalic, after *u*. Yet from other forms we know that the distribution is related, not to specific vowels, but to the former position of the accent, as may be verified by comparing related Sanskrit forms (page 95, Verner's law), for example:

PGmc. nesan 'be saved' : nazjan 'save'

Examining all the occurrences of PGmc. *z* versus *s* would verify this conclusion.

By the time of the individual Germanic dialects the original distribution was even more obscured, for in Old Icelandic, Old English, Old Saxon, Old High German and less well-attested dialects the reflexes of PGmc. /z/ had fallen together with those of PGmc. /r/. Of 'choose' we find the following forms in these dialects:

OIcel.	kiōsa	kaus	køron	kørenn
OE	cēosan	cēas	curon	coren
OS	keosan	kōs	kuran	gikoran
OHG	kiosan	kōs	kurun	gikoran

Since both /r/ and /s/ are widely distributed in the Germanic dialects, only detailed study of their interrelationships will lead to internal reconstruction of the Proto-Germanic situation, and from this of the Proto-Indo-European.

Study of the distribution of similar phonemes is useful. For parallel with the PGmc. *s* : *z* contrast we find that of þ : ð, *h* : *g*, and their reflexes, as in:

OE	sēoþan	sēaþ	sudon	soden	'boil'
OHG	siodan	sōd	sutun	gisotan	
OE	tēon	tēah	tugon	togan	'pull'
OHG	ziohan	zōh	zugun	gizogan	

As illustrated in the Old English infinitive for 'pull,' later changes may completely obscure the original pattern. If we had only Modern English and no Old English materials, the only verb paradigm showing the original Proto-Germanic distribution of voiceless versus voiced fricatives would be *was* : *were*. The distribution to be sure is maintained also outside of inflectional paradigms, as in *frost* : *frozen,* in the increasingly rare *seethe* : *sodden,* which is now used only as an adjective. After languages have undergone further changes, the original patterns may be very difficult to reconstruct from internal evidence.

6.5 The verb paradigms given here illustrate that internal reconstruction may be applied with greatest assurance in morphological paradigms. Excellent examples are the irregular, or strong, verbs of the Germanic languages. We list forms in

Gothic and Old English, though Gothic alone would be adequate for our reconstructions:

1	Go.	beitan	bait	bitun	bitans	'bite'
	OE	bītan	bāt	biton	biten	
2	Go.	kiusan	kaus	kusun	kusans	'choose'
	OE	cēosan	cēas	curon	coren	
3	Go.	-bindan	-band	-bundun	-bundans	'bind'
	OE	bindan	band	bundon	bunden	

Although sound changes have obscured some of the relationships, we have enough early Germanic material to assume that these apparently different verb classes were originally one. If we label *b t k s d* Consonants and *i, un* and *u* of stressed syllables Resonants, we can state the original class with its variation:

PGmc **CeRC-** **CaRC-** **CRC-** **CRC-**

From analysis of the Gothic materials, we can readily posit the Proto-Germanic variation. From the later Old English materials, internal reconstruction would be somewhat more difficult.

Examining further Germanic verbs we find the same variation in the first two forms of classes 4 and 5, which have a Proto-Germanic structure **CeC-** (the preterite plural and preterite participle are different in pattern and will not be accounted for here).

4	Go.	stilan	stal	stelun	stulans	'steal'
	OE	stelan	stæl	stǣlon	stolen	
5	Go.	wisan	was	wesun	wisans*	'be'
	OE	wesan	wæs	wǣron	wesen	

A highly structured set of forms, like those of the strong verb in Germanic, assists us greatly in reconstruction of prior stages of a language from internal evidence alone. We are also fortunate in having cognate forms in Indo-Iranian, Greek, and other dialects which support our reconstruction of these Germanic verb classes into one original class. Substituting PIE *o* for PGmc *a* we posit PIE:

Ce(R)C- **Co(R)C-** **C(R)C-** **C(R)C-**

6.6 Since these Proto-Indo-European formulae represent morphs restricted in distribution, we may make the further assumption that in an earlier stage the three different vocalisms are to be reconstructed as one. We posit the original form as **Ce(R)C-**, assuming that with accentual variation this became **C(R)C-**, as in Skt. *dr̥ṣṭás* 'seen' beside Gk. *dérkomai* 'I see.' **Co(R)C-**, as in Gk. *dédorka* 'I have seen,' we also derive from **Ce(R)C-**, with less assurance about the element conditioning the change of *e* to *o*. These vowel variations in the Indo-European languages, as in NE *bite, bit, bitten* : *choose, chose, chosen* : *bind, bound, bound* : *steal, stole, stolen* : *was, were,* are known by the term **ablaut** or **apophony.** They have been accounted for through principles of internal reconstruction developed in the study of historically observable sound changes. The effort that has been devoted to arrive at an understanding of ablaut, and the obscurities still remaining, may indicate the complexities involved in the reconstruction of poorly attested languages, as well as the hope of some success, if an adequate number of forms with morphological variation are maintained through subsequent periods of sound changes.

6.7 If the sound changes which take place yield a complete merger, the method of internal reconstruction can be used only in situations like the Proto-Indo-European root, where we have clearly definable morphemes. By examining their varying structures, we can suggest earlier forms. When, however, we find complete merger in morphemes of varying shapes, we cannot apply the method. In Iranian, for example, *bh* and the other aspirates fell together with unaspirated stops, and we have no evidence for Grassmann's law.

If on the other hand sound changes result only in a partial merger, as the dissimilated Sanskrit aspirated voiced stops with unaspirated voiced stops, we can apply the method of internal reconstruction, unless the resulting morphophonemic variation has been obscured by subsequent sound changes, or by analogical changes (see Chapters 10 and 11).

Generally, isolated forms like *frost* or *sodden* preserve longest the evidence which we can use in internal reconstruction. Yet from isolated forms it is very difficult to apply a technique using morphophonemic variations. Alternating morphemes from the most frequent layers of the vocabulary, such as *was* : *were,* are also likely to preserve means for applying the method of internal reconstruction; because they retain the original grammatical variation, as well as the phonological, they are more useful than are isolated forms.

The constant changes and losses in language eventually obscure entirely the morphophonemic variation resulting from earlier sound change. Ultimately they eliminate the morphophonemic contrasts which may be used in internal reconstruction.

SELECTED FURTHER READINGS

Chapters 7 and 10 of Henry Hoenigswald's ***Language Change and Linguistic Reconstruction*** deal generally with the method. In "Internal Reconstruction of Phonemic Split," *Language,* 32.245–53 (1956), J. W. Marchand treats it in one pattern of change.

Additional control over the method can best be secured by study of its use in dealing with specific problems. It may be of interest to survey in greater detail than is presented here the application of the method to problems in Proto-Indo-European. An introduction may be found in my *Proto-Indo-European Phonology,* especially Chapters 2, 3, 15; additional readings are cited there. Another application, with discussion of the theory involved, may be found in Wallace L. Chafe's "Internal Reconstruction in Seneca," *Language,* 35.477–95 (1959).

7 – Study of Loss in Language; Lexicostatistics

7.1 The techniques known as the comparative method and the method of internal reconstruction are both applied to selected speech material with the aim of determining linguistic relationships and reconstructing earlier stages of a language. Both methods are based on our knowledge that languages change. Besides changing, languages also undergo loss. The phenomenon of loss in language has not been widely explored, but we know from general reading that losses of vocabulary may occur with changes in culture. Today, for example, we find the technical terms used in astrology difficult; few of us could distinguish between horary and judicial astrology, let alone the nomenclature employed in each. The terms went out of use with the practice. Only recently has there been much attention to loss of vocabulary items. The concern arose out of attempts to use rate of vocabulary loss, or percentage of retention to determine chronological linguistic relationship, a procedure referred to as **glottochronology.** The broader term **lexicostatistics** may be used for statistical study of vocabulary for historical purposes.

7.2 Several basic assumptions underlie glottochronology. The first is that some items of the vocabulary are better maintained than others: the lower numerals, pronouns, items referring to parts of the body, to natural objects—animals, plants, heavenly bodies, and so on. These items are referred to as the **basic core vocabulary.**

Another underlying assumption is that the rate of retention of items in the basic core is constant. Conversely, that their rate of loss is approximately the same from language to language. If then the percentage of cognates in the basic core is determined for two related languages, the length of time that they have been separated can be stated.

In applying glottochronology to two related languages one compiles the vocabulary items referring to a selected number of elements, determines which are related, and uses the percentages to posit the length of separation. One might, for example, use a list of five items: those for "animal, four, head, I, sun" and compile one's percentages. In standard German, one would elicit for the above-listed items: "Tier, vier, Kopf, ich, Sonne." These show 60 percent agreement with English, for *animal* and *Tier, head* and *Kopf* are not related. If there were a standard scale to determine the time of separation expected from 60 percent agreement in basic-core vocabulary, we could apply it and propose the time when English and German separated.

A scale for determining the length of separation for two languages was devised by Lees, *Language,* 29.113–27. By this formula the time of separation, or **time depth,** is equal to the logarithm of the percentage of cognates, **c,** divided by twice the logarithm of the percentage of cognates retained after a millennium of separation, **r:**

$$t = \frac{\log c}{2 \log r}$$

Using our five items from English and German we determine t as follows (assuming a rate of retention of 85 percent):

$$t = \frac{\log 60\%}{2 \log 85\%} = \frac{-.511}{2 \times -.163} = 1561$$

By this formula, English and German separated approximately 1561 years ago, around the year A.D. 400.

7.3 In such a short list, the range of error may be great. To reduce it, one would prefer a long, carefully designed list. Swadesh has devised several. In most investigations either of his two lists, one of one hundred, another of two hundred words, has been used. (The lists are reproduced at the end of the chapter.) Even with such lists, the range of error must be computed; see Lees, *Language,* 29.124, or Gudschinsky, *Word,* 12.204–5. Typical conclusions are given in length of separation plus or minus a number of years, determined from the range of possible error. Gudschinsky for example concludes that "Ixcatec and Mazatec were a single homogeneous language, 2,200 ± 200 years ago." (*Word,* 12.205)

Even proponents of glottochronology urge caution in the acceptance of absolute times of separation. They suggest instead determining the "degree of lexical relationship" **(dips).** Dips are determined by the formula

$$d = .014 \frac{\log c}{2 \log r}$$

For our example this would be 21.854, again with possibility of error. Since variations have been found from language to language, a relative set of figures may be less misleading than an attempt to indicate precisely the time of separation.

7.4 The work which has been done in glottochronology has indicated various problems in its use. No common basic core has been found from culture to culture. G. and A. Sjoberg, for example, have shown, *American Anthropologist,* 59.296–

300, that in the cultures of South Asia some items referring to natural objects like the sun cannot be included among the basic core; for they belong to the widely borrowed religious vocabulary.

Moreover, considerable duplication has been found within languages for elements which have been posited in the basic core as different. In applying Swadesh's lists to Athapaskan languages Hoijer noted that over half of the items fail to meet Swadesh's criteria, *Language,* 32.53ff. In Navaho, for example, "this, that" corresponds to five items, no one of which can be clearly matched to the items on the English list; similarly, nouns like "tree, seed, grease" and verbs like "eat, kill, know." Gudschinsky has proposed methods which may deal with such problems; they need further study.

It has also been doubted whether the rate of retention is constant from language to language. Meillet long ago pointed to a gypsy dialect of Armenian which contained few Armenian lexical items, while showing the central structure of the language. Clearly, the rate of loss in English, Lithuanian, Greek is much lower than that for this Armenian dialect. If different rates of retention must be proposed from language to language, the generality of glottochronology is eliminated, and its usefulness greatly diminished.

Glottochronology accordingly needs considerable further exploration before conclusions based on it can be accepted. There is even question whether it is a useful procedure. For languages may be unique in their semantic structure as well as in their grammatical structure. If they are, no universal list can be devised. Moreover, no one rate of retention may be applicable for all languages. Conclusions of such variety have resulted from applications of glottochronology that some linguists dismiss it entirely; others are attempting to apply it soberly and determine how it can be used reliably.

If on the other hand the aims of glottochronology are reduced, if it is used within a language group and a culture area for the more modest goals of determining relative dates of separation, or for establishing subgroups of languages, the problems discussed above may be avoided in part. Glottochronology may then give us useful information about languages attested only from recent times which are related and which are spoken in areas of similar culture.

As one of its contributions, glottochronology has focused attention on the problem of loss in language. Though it may be unworkable in study of time depth because of the diversity of its results, the wider study, lexicostatistics, may be useful in investigating general principles underlying change and loss in language, especially when data-processing techniques are applied to large amounts of material. Numerous instances are attested of languages going out of use: Cornish in the eighteenth century, Dalmatian in the nineteenth, and today many indigenous languages throughout the world. Thorough documentation of the stages leading to their extinction would be of great interest to historical linguistics. For many languages of which we know are now extinct; the steps to their extinction may be understood more clearly if we have thorough descriptions of languages now on the way to extinction.

SELECTED FURTHER READINGS

Possibly the best statement describing the use of glottochronology is Sarah C. Gudschinsky's "The ABC's of lexicostatistics (glottochronology)," *Word,* 12.175–210 (1956). It contains a bibliography of the work to 1956, including the numerous articles of M. Swadesh, who is to be credited with the recent interest in the subject. His article "Diffusional Cumulation and Archaic Residue as Historic Explanation," *Southwestern Journal of Anthropology,* 7.1–21 (1951), relates glottochronology to general linguistic and anthropological theory.

Numerous additional articles could be cited. The following may be among the most useful in providing an introduction to the applications made and varying views on the subject: Harry Hoijer,

"Lexicostatistics: A critique," *Language,* 32.49–60 (1956); John A. Rea, "Concerning the validity of lexicostatistics," *IJAL,* 24.145–50 (1958); D. H. Hymes, "Lexicostatistics so far," *Current Anthropology,* 1.3–44 (1960), with thorough discussion and extensive bibliography.

The following list of two hundred words is taken from Gudschinsky's article; the list of one hundred used by Rea is set in italic, with additional words appended. In view of the uncertain results of glottochronology, and on the other hand its relative ease of application, students should carry out their own investigations to the extent practicable.

1. *all*
2. and
3. animal
4. *ashes*
5. at
6. back
7. bad
8. *bark*
9. because
10. *belly*
11. *big*
12. *bird*
13. *bite*
14. *black*
15. *blood*
16. blow
17. *bone*
18. breathe
19. *burn*
20. child
21. *cloud*
22. *cold*
23. *come*
24. count
25. cut
26. day
27. *die*
28. dig
29. dirty
30. *dog*
31. *drink*
32. *dry*
33. dull
34. dust
35. *ear*
36. *earth*
37. *eat*
38. *egg*
39. *eye*
40. fall
41. far
42. *fat*–grease
43. father
44. fear
45. *feather*
46. few
47. fight
48. *fire*
49. *fish*
50. five
51. float
52. flow
53. flower
54. *fly*
55. fog
56. *foot*
57. four
58. freeze
59. fruit
60. *give*
61. *good*
62. grass
63. *green*
64. guts
65. *hair*
66. *hand*
67. he
68. *head*
69. *hear*
70. *heart*
71. heavy
72. here
73. hit
74. hold–take
75. how
76. hunt
77. husband
78. *I*
79. ice
80. if
81. in
82. *kill*
83. *know*
84. lake
85. laugh
86. *leaf*
87. leftside
88. leg
89. *lie*
90. live
91. *liver*
92. *long*
93. *louse*
94. *man–male*
95. *many*
96. *meat–flesh*
97. mother
98. *mountain*
99. *mouth*
100. *name*
101. narrow
102. near
103. *neck*
104. *new*
105. *night*
106. *nose*
107. *not*
108. old
109. *one*
110. other
111. *person*
112. play
113. pull
114. push
115. *rain*
116. *red*
117. right–correct
118. rightside
119. river
120. *road*

121. *root*
122. rope
123. rotten
124. rub
125. salt
126. *sand*
127. *say*
128. scratch
129. sea
130. *see*
131. *seed*
132. sew
133. sharp
134. short
135. sing
136. *sit*
137. *skin*
138. sky
139. *sleep*
140. *small*
141. smell
142. *smoke*
143. smooth
144. snake
145. snow
146. some
147. spit
148. split
149. squeeze
150. stab–pierce
151. *stand*
152. *star*
153. stick
154. *stone*
155. straight
156. suck
157. *sun*
158. swell
159. *swim*
160. *tail*
161. *that*
162. there
163. they
164. thick
165. thin
166. think
167. *this*
168. *thou*
169. three
170. throw
171. tie
172. *tongue*
173. *tooth*
174. *tree*
175. turn
176. *two*
177. vomit
178. *walk*
179. *warm*
180. wash
181. *water*
182. *we*
183. wet
184. *what*
185. when
186. where
187. *white*
188. *who*
189. wide
190. wife
191. wind
192. wing
193. wipe
194. with
195. *woman*
196. woods
197. worm
198. ye
199. year
200. *yellow*

94. *breast* 95. *claw* 96. *full* 97. *horn* 98. *knee* 99. *moon* 100. *round*

Note that in eliciting one must not search for cognates. Exact cognates exist for the words used in 7.2, e.g., *Haupt* for *head* and *cup* for *Kopf,* yet the normal response of a German speaker asked to give the equivalent of head is *Kopf*. Equivalents in usage rather than etymological cognates must be used as basis for glottochronology.

8 – Broadening of Language Materials; Dialect Geography

8.1 The growing convictions about the regularity of sound change after 1870 led to great interest in the study of various strata of speech, especially geographical dialects. In spite of the clarifications produced by Grassmann and Verner for the first Germanic consonant shift, and by other linguists for such problems elsewhere, some elements in the standard languages under investigation still showed irregularities. It was then tentatively assumed by some linguists that standard languages contained irregularities because they were mixed. To find pure languages one would have to collect the speech of the everyday people, commonly known as dialect. Interest in dialects prompted by a search for regular language development was supported by interest aroused by the Romantic movement.

Following Rousseau, scholars and literary figures came to concern themselves with folkways from the end of the eighteenth century. Using more than the occasional phrases of "rustic dialect" found in Wordsworth, writers like Burns and Hebel preferred their native speech to the more general literary languages. In an attempt to show that dialects as well as literary languages had respectable pedigrees, some linguists devoted their attention to dialects, for example J. A. Schmeller, who in 1821 published the first grammar of a dialect, Bavarian. Although Schmeller was followed in his aim by other scholars, dialect study before 1875 was more concerned with social and historical than linguistic problems. Scholars attempted to relate contemporary dialects with ancient tribal groups. In nomenclature and popular conceptions they have had a lasting effect. Old English is still often referred to as Anglo-Saxon. With this label the suggestion is made that Angles carried to Britain the Anglian dialect, Saxons the Saxon dialect, where they subsequently merged to form English. Similarly in Germany, the labels for dialects continue old tribal names which are still used as area names: Bavarian, Franconian. In subsequent dialect study less colorful, and also less misleading, labels are used, such as Northern, Midland, and Southern in the United States. Remains of nineteenth-century views are also maintained in popular conceptions, such as that pure Elizabethan English is still spoken in the Kentucky uplands. One can indeed find resemblances to present-day unfamiliar dialect forms in older material, such as the Shakespearian plays, but must not base unfounded conclusions on these; the speech of Kentucky mountaineers has undergone considerable modification since the seventeenth century, as have more widely spoken strata of English. By a similar unfounded statement the dual is supposed to survive in the Bavarian dialect form *enk* 'you.' This reflex of a Germanic dual form has come to be used in the plural, with no reflection at all of the old dual category, which is totally lost in German as well as in English. Although they may contain such inaccurate views, the first efforts to record popular speech are useful for their collections of data.

Under superficial examination, the early dialect study seemed to support the view that "sound changes take place without exception." In standard English, for example, initial *v* and *f* both represent Old English *f,* apparently without pattern, as in *vat, vixen* versus *father, folk.* Yet in the Somerset dialect spoken by Sophie Western's father in *Tom Jones* every Old English *f-* is a *v-*. Squire Western says *vather* and *volk* as well as *vat* and *vixen.* Though Wenker set out to collect similar material in German dialects, to find similar consistency there, his work led virtually to the converse of his original aim, and contributed greatly to our understanding of complexity in language.

Wenker's dialect work has the further importance that with his counterpart in France, J. Gilliéron, it furnishes almost classical contrasts in dialect investigation. Subsequent studies and conclusions have been largely based on the activities of these two men.

8.2 After restricted investigation in the Rhineland, Wenker began to collect material from every section of Germany. His procedure was to prepare forty sentences and send them out to schoolteachers in 40,736 localities, later expanded to 49,363. The sentences dealt with everyday matters, and were chosen carefully to give data on dialect differences. Sentence one reads: *Im Winter fliegen die trocknen Blätter durch die Luft herum.* "In winter the dry leaves fly around through the air." (See Mitzka, *Handbuch,* pages 13–14 for the entire set.) Teachers were asked to transcribe the sentences in accordance with the characteristic speech in their districts. Sets were then returned to Marburg for analysis. Each of the sources for material was eventually to be put on a map, and the characteristic features of dialects plotted by the location of their occurrences. Publication of the maps did not get under way until 1927 and is not yet complete. The plotting of dialect distribution on maps, however, led to the terminology used in detailed study of the varying strata of language.

The study of the varying forms of speech in one language

is known as **dialect geography** or **dialectology.** In plotting their findings on maps, dialect geographers compiled **dialect atlases** containing maps of the features investigated. Terminology and views on dialect spread are fashioned after those used in map-making. On the pattern of isobar and isotherm, **isogloss** is a term used for a line drawn from location to location along the outer limits of characteristic features. The interpretation and linguistic significance of varying patterns of isoglosses was developed as the German and French dialect materials were analyzed and described. Moreover, procedures of collecting dialect materials were improved as subsequent dialect geographers profited by the experience of their predecessors.

The great advantage of the German collection is its broad coverage. For a relatively small area like that of Germany, close to fifty thousand recordings provide tremendous breadth of information. Yet Wenker's dialect project also had numerous shortcomings; one of the greatest is that it has not been completely published. To this day scholars who wish to use the German materials must go to the archives in Marburg. Further, transcriptions were made by untrained observers. Everyone has individual differences in recording; with a great number of untrained workers there can be no attempt to correct these, or even to note them. These shortcomings are especially serious in phonological study, for which the German project was best suited. For the forty sentences provide little material on morphological variation, less on lexical differences. Since these shortcomings became apparent, various efforts were made to repair them.

To provide material collected by trained observers, young scholars undertook the collection and description of speech in various localities. Numerous monographs were published, supplementing the inadequate materials of the atlas. A. Bach, *Deutsche Mundartforschung,* gives a densely printed selection of them, pages 214–26. To provide the deficient lexical material, Mitzka in 1938 sent out a second set of materials, questions designed to secure names of everyday items, such as plants and animals. His results are being published in a German word-atlas, and in monographs dealing with individual words. To provide contemporary records of pronunciation, E. Zwirner undertook in the nineteen-fifties to collect tape recordings of German dialects from more than 1200 localities. Although brief, his recordings preserve speech for subsequent interpretation. Tape recordings have the further advantage that copies may be provided to other investigators. With these supplements ample materials are available for German dialect study, and provision has been made to remedy the shortcomings of Wenker's initial undertaking.

Jules Gilliéron, editor of the French atlas, planned from the start to avoid the shortcomings of his German predecessor. He selected and trained one worker, Edmond Edmont, to collect all material for the French atlas. Equipped with a good ear, Edmont provided accurate, reliable and consistent records. Moreover, cycling from point to point, where he established himself in congenial surroundings, he collected material by direct questions, rather than through a highly restricted set of sentences. In the years of collecting, 1896–1900, Edmont gathered material from 639 locations, providing less coverage than had the German project. Under its superb organization, however, the French atlas had the further distinction of completed publication by 1910. Gilliéron must therefore be credited with providing the pattern according to which the German materials and those of many subsequent projects were published.

8.3 The advantages which later dialect studies derived from the German and French undertakings may be illustrated by the American project. Sponsored by the American Council of Learned Societies, this was planned to avoid mistakes made in previous collections. (See the report of Hans Kurath in the *Handbook of the Linguistic Geography of New England.*) Its planning, which resulted in great part from earlier dialect studies, also reflects the realization of the complexity of language.

Under the direction of its carefully chosen editor, Hans Kurath, great attention was given to:

1. Selection and training of field workers.
2. Selection of informants and locations to investigate.
3. Preparation of a questionnaire.

Already highly trained linguists, the field workers were given further training in the summer of 1931 under two of the eminent dialect geographers, Jud and Scheuermeier. For an area as large as New England, a number of field workers is essential in spite of the resultant diversity of recordings. Yet this diversity was not unduly great. Moreover, it provided a check on the characteristics of individual workers which was missing in the excellent work of Edmont.

Just as the selection and training of field workers illustrates the increase in precision of dialect geography since 1876, the care in selection of informants indicates the increasing awareness of the complexity of language. Informants were chosen from each age group. Since this was the first large-scale dialect study in the United States, particular care was taken to include speakers more than seventy years old. Moreover, speakers from three arbitrarily selected social groups were included: those with little formal education and restricted social contacts; those with some formal education; those with advanced education. All information about informants and other pertinent data about speech communities were carefully noted, and are available to analysts.

For the preparation of worksheets comprising the questionnaire, samplings were made to determine points of variation among speakers, accordingly, items to investigate. Worksheets were thereupon designed to elicit specific forms, but also for flexibility. Moreover, field workers were to note if an informant indicated that a form was rarely used, old-fashioned, amusing, or whether it elicited from him still other attitudes or responses. Adequate information was collected and made available so that linguistic facts could be understood not only by linguists, but also by historians, geographers, sociologists, and others interested in the social and cultural history of New England (Kurath, *Handbook,* ix). Apart from simultaneous tape recordings now possible, with which other linguists might check transcriptions, techniques were developed adequate to collect material of any breadth and precision that scholarly resources, finances, and time would permit. The American project covered New England, with subsequent publication of an atlas, 1939–43. Further collecting in America has been carried out. A concise statement of the status of collecting and availability of materials has been provided by R. I. McDavid, Jr. in Chapter IX, "The Dialects of American English," of W. N. Francis', *The Structure of American English* (New York, 1958). The work involved in covering a territory the size of the United States is so huge that numerous smaller projects have now been undertaken. Elsewhere as well the arranging of dialect collections in multiple projects now forms the general pattern rather than preparation of national atlases. For unless a language area is small and homogeneous, the results of dialect collection are so tremendous and diverse that they are not readily accessible. In France, too, numerous studies covering only a section of the country have been undertaken in attempts to provide fuller information than that in Gilliéron's atlas.

Changes in language and costs of publication make it likely that future results will be available in archives rather than atlases after the French pattern. However the collections are made available, linguists now have access to a broad array of linguistic data. The extent of collections may be determined from Sever Pop's survey of 1400 pages, *La Dialectologie* (Louvain, 1950). These must now be interpreted for their contributions to our understanding of linguistic development. (See map 1.)

8.4 The contributions by dialect geographers to our understanding of language were not long in coming. Very early in investigations it became quite apparent that the boundaries between languages and those between dialects could not be neatly defined. Isoglosses differ from item to item. Since the division between High German and Low German was among the most highly investigated among language interrelationships, many of the procedures of dialect geography were worked out in solving problems concerning it.

The chief items differentiating High German from Low German are the reflexes of Proto-Germanic *p t k*. These remained in Low German, as in English, but have become fricatives and affricates in High German.

A summary of the changes in initial, medial and final positions may be given as follows:

1. late Proto-Germanic *p- t- k- -pp- -tt- -kk-* > Old High German *pf ts k*(*x*) (we may use the unchanged English items to indicate the original, Proto-Germanic sounds).

E. pool: G. Pfuhl	E. shape: G. schöpfen
E. tongue: G. Zunge	E. sit: G. sitzen
E. cow: G. Kuh, but Swiss kxū	E. wake: G. wecken, but Swiss wekxen

2. late Proto-Germanic *-p- -t- -k- -p -t -k* > Old High German -*f*(*f*) -*s*(*s*) -*x*(*x*).

E. hope: G. hoffen	E. up: G. auf
E. water: G. Wasser	E. it: G. es
E. cake: G. Kuchen	E. book: G. Buch

Map 1. The pronunciation of *yeast* in the Atlantic States. Note the precision which is used in providing the information, and the insert map giving the distribution of pronunciation in southern England, by which the sources of American dialect forms can be explored. Taken from *Pronunciation of English in the Atlantic States* by Hans Kurath and Raven I. McDavid. Ann Arbor: The University of Michigan Press, 1961. Included with the permission of Hans Kurath.

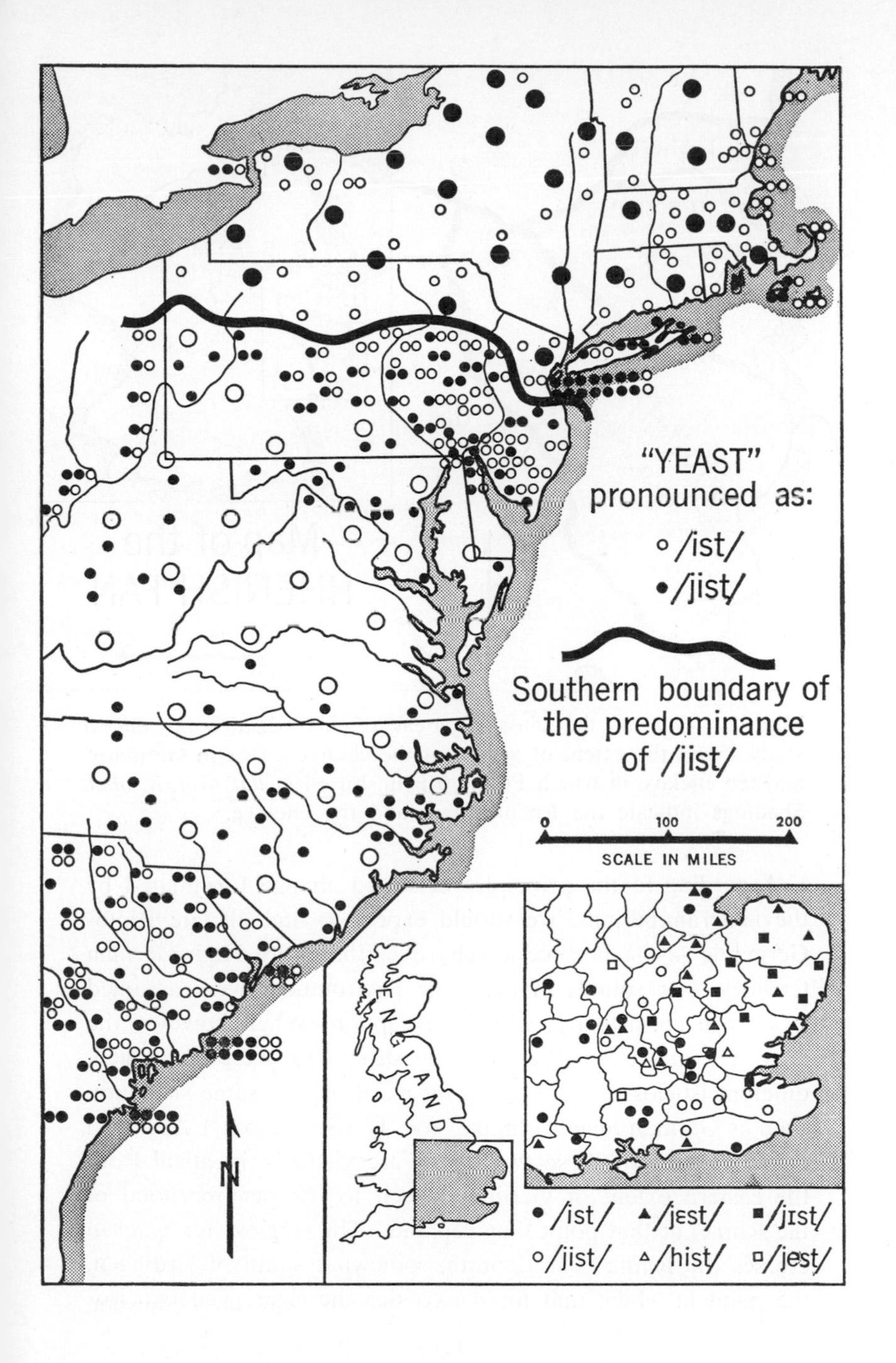
"YEAST"
pronounced as:
○ /ist/
● /jist/
Southern boundary of
the predominance
of /jist/
0
100
200
SCALE IN MILES
ENGLAND
● /ist/
▲ /jɛst/
■ /jɪst/
○ /jist/
△ /hist/
□ /jest/

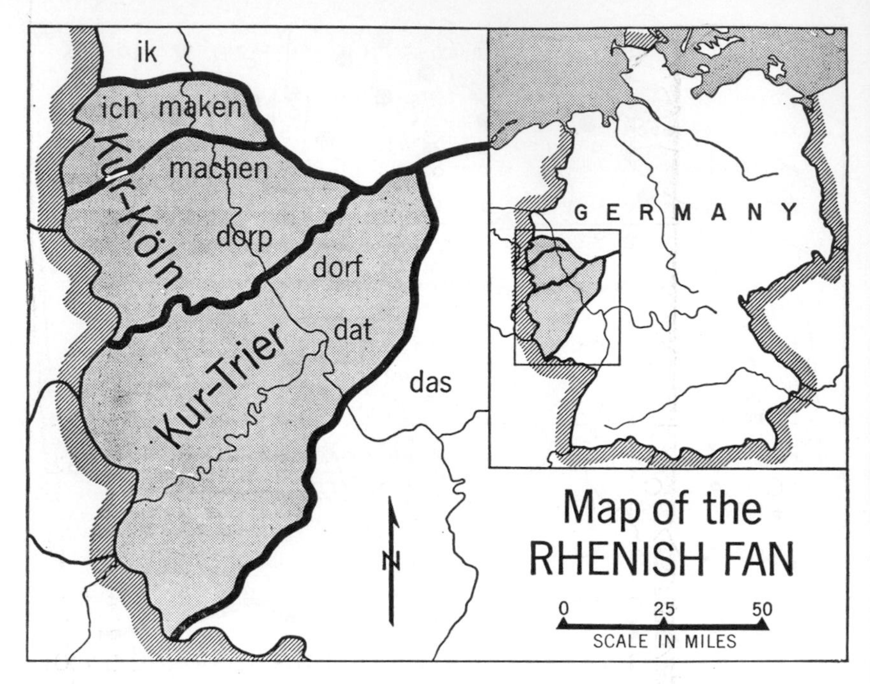

Map 2. One of the classical areas of investigation in dialect study shows the extent of spread of the change $k > x$ in Germany, and the enclave in which PGmc. *t* is unshifted in *dat, wat, it, allet*. Shadings indicate the Rhenish fan, and the enclave.

According to the principles of sound change formulated by the neogrammarians, we should expect to find all late Proto-Germanic *-k- -k* become *x* (ch) over the entire High German territory. For sounds in the same environment were assumed to change consistently, without exception. When however the data assembled by Wenker's questionnaire were examined, different isoglosses were found for words of the same structure, such as German *machen* 'make,' *ich* 'I.' (See map 2.) Although the isoglosses for these two words are virtually identical from the eastern extent of German speech to the neighborhood of the Rhine, at that point they separate. The isogloss for *machen* crosses the Rhine near Benrath, somewhat south of Ürdingen, the point at which that for *ich* crosses the river. The two isoglosses are labeled after the villages the *Benrath line* and the *Ürdingen line*. Their divergence near the Rhine plus that of other isoglosses which fan out at this point led to the label, the *Rhenish fan,* and require an explanation.

This can be furnished from cultural history. The Benrath line corresponds to the extent of Cologne's influence from the thirteenth century; the Ürdingen line to its influence from the fourteenth to the sixteenth centuries. (See Bach, *Deutsche Mundartforschung,* 133–34.) The forms for 'make' were fixed at the early time; those for 'I' later. One can account for the different isoglosses by assuming that a sound change, $k > x$, had taken place in southern Germany, and that its effects were gradually extended northward. The extent of spread of innovation in any word is determined by the cultural prestige of speakers who use it. Findings like those for German *machen* and *ich,* repeated many times over in various dialect studies, led to a more accurate understanding of language change and to greater concern with cultural patterns of communities in which a given language is spoken.

Another kind of problem was raised by the unshifted *t* in *dat it wat,* the German forms for *that it what* in the Mosel Franconian area. Here *-t* shows up as *-s* in words like *great,* G. *gross,* but not in the words cited or the *-et* ending of the adjective, for example, *allet* rather than standard German *alles,* nom. sg. nt. 'all.' Though scholars are not unanimous in their explanations for these unshifted forms, they may be ascribed to difference in syntactic environment. We may assume that the unshifted *dat it wat allet* were spread to all environments from weakly stressed sentence positions, in which the change $t > s$ was not carried through. Again, information concerning the use of forms required broadening, to include their precise environments within sentences, not only within words.

8.5 Such problems encountered in dialect geography studies led to a questioning of former views concerning (1) the regularity of sound change and (2) the usefulness of setting up dialects. Extremes in the rebellion against the tidy view of language ascribed to the neogrammarians may be illustrated by the slogan: *every word has its own history* and by Gaston Paris' statement on the virtually imperceptible gradations from dialect to dialect in French, even into Italian.

No one can deny that every word, like every social convention or every artifact, has its own history. But the statement is as misleading as is the slogan: sound changes take place without exception. A word is a composite of morphemes and phonemes. Since the allophones of the phonemes vary with their environment, every word will have undergone changes different from all other words. To conclude that one should describe every word separately, indicates a poor understanding of the social functioning of language. Even worse are the linguistic studies which deal with the history of individual sounds, from proto-languages to the present. Studies based on such methods resemble lists rather than descriptions; for the essentials of languages are phonemes not sounds, morphemes not words. Neither phonemes nor morphemes are independent entities in language; rather, they pattern with other sets and subsets of phonemes and morphemes. Fortunately, dialect geographers, like historical linguists who learned much from the neogrammarians, have come to understand the disadvantage of basing methodology on slogans.

The usefulness of positing dialects was graphically questioned by Gaston Paris in his story of the traveler who proceeds slowly from Paris to Italy. Traveling a few miles at a stretch, and adapting his speech constantly to each local dialect, such a traveler would scarcely notice differences in speech in the French area; he might not even notice when he crossed the supposedly greater boundary from France to Italy. For even here he would not find an abrupt speech cleavage such as he might encounter if he crossed into Germanic territory.

In spite of the absence of sharp dialect, or language, boundaries, dialect geographers have not abandoned subclassification of languages. For dialect classification they have progressed from a reliance on isoglosses for important linguistic features, such as the *machen* isogloss, through **bundles of isoglosses** to correlation methods. Contemporary investigators seek to learn whether a list of features is present at given points. They then correlate their results and connect points with similar correlation coefficients with lines known as **isopleths** or **isogrades.** These may not only represent various isoglosses, but also folk customs, such as tales, superstitions, agricultural practices. Further, they may reflect earlier political boundaries which in turn were probably determined by geographical features (Weinreich, *Word,* 10.397–98). Isopleths accordingly circumscribe areas of culture which have exerted a uniform effect on language. These for linguistic purposes are called language or dialect areas.

8.6 Although given a common label, the speech of language areas is not uniform. Language areas generally center about a point which is touched by relatively few isoglosses. Such points, areas of prestige, are known as **focal areas.** Innovations transmitted from them are accepted by surrounding areas as far as the prestige of the focal area extends. As an example we may cite the distribution of *tonic* (soda water) in New England. Its general use around Boston indicates the extent of influence exerted by the speakers in the Boston area. Outside the area, *tonic* has not succeeded in replacing older forms.

At the limits of well-defined speech areas we find **transition areas.** These may show characteristics of two neighboring focal areas, as do western New Hampshire, central Massachusetts and Rhode Island in their terms for soda water.

Further characteristic types of area, known as **relic areas,** lie beyond the extent of expanding isoglosses. Relic areas are generally found in locations which are difficult of access for cultural, political, or geographic reasons. They may be discontinuous, as are the relic areas on map 3 in which final *r* is preserved.

The status of preconsonantal and final *r* in New England, as in *hard, far,* may illustrate the various types of area. Around Boston there is little evidence for this *r;* isoglosses would be remote from the city. We conclude, as from the word "tonic," that Boston is a focal area. In western Massachusetts, and elsewhere along the Connecticut River, usage is divided, with some speakers pronouncing, others dropping, *r*. This is a transition area between the *r*-speech of the Hudson Valley and the *r*-less speech of Boston. In addition we find the *r* of this environment maintained on Martha's Vineyard, Marblehead, and Cape Ann, which are relic areas.

Since the time of the German and French dialect projects, which established much of the methodology of dialect geography, many studies have been made of speech communities and their subdivisions. In an approach referred to as neolinguistics,

Map 3. Shows the distribution of preconsonantal and final *r,* illustrating the influence of the focal area Boston, transitions to other dialect areas, and relic areas.

An *r* preceding a vowel, as in *road, borrow, far out,* is pronounced in all parts of New England. But before consonants and finally, as in *hard, how far?,* usage is regional: in western New England and in New Brunswick the *r* is regularly pronounced, in most of eastern New England it is dropped, while the Connecticut Valley is mixed and unstable in practice.

Martha's Vineyard, Marblehead, and Cape Ann, all secluded communities, appear as "*r* islands" in eastern New England, where this *r* is still losing ground. On the other hand, the *r* is gaining ground in the Connecticut Valley.

The largest circles indicate regular use of this *r,* the smallest ones sporadic use, and the remainder rather evenly divided usage.

Taken from *Handbook of the Linguistic Geography of New England* by Hans Kurath in collaboration with Marcus L. Hansen, Julia Bloch, and Bernard Bloch. Providence, R. I.: Brown University, 1939. Copyright, 1939, by The American Council of Learned Societies. Included with the permission of Hans Kurath.

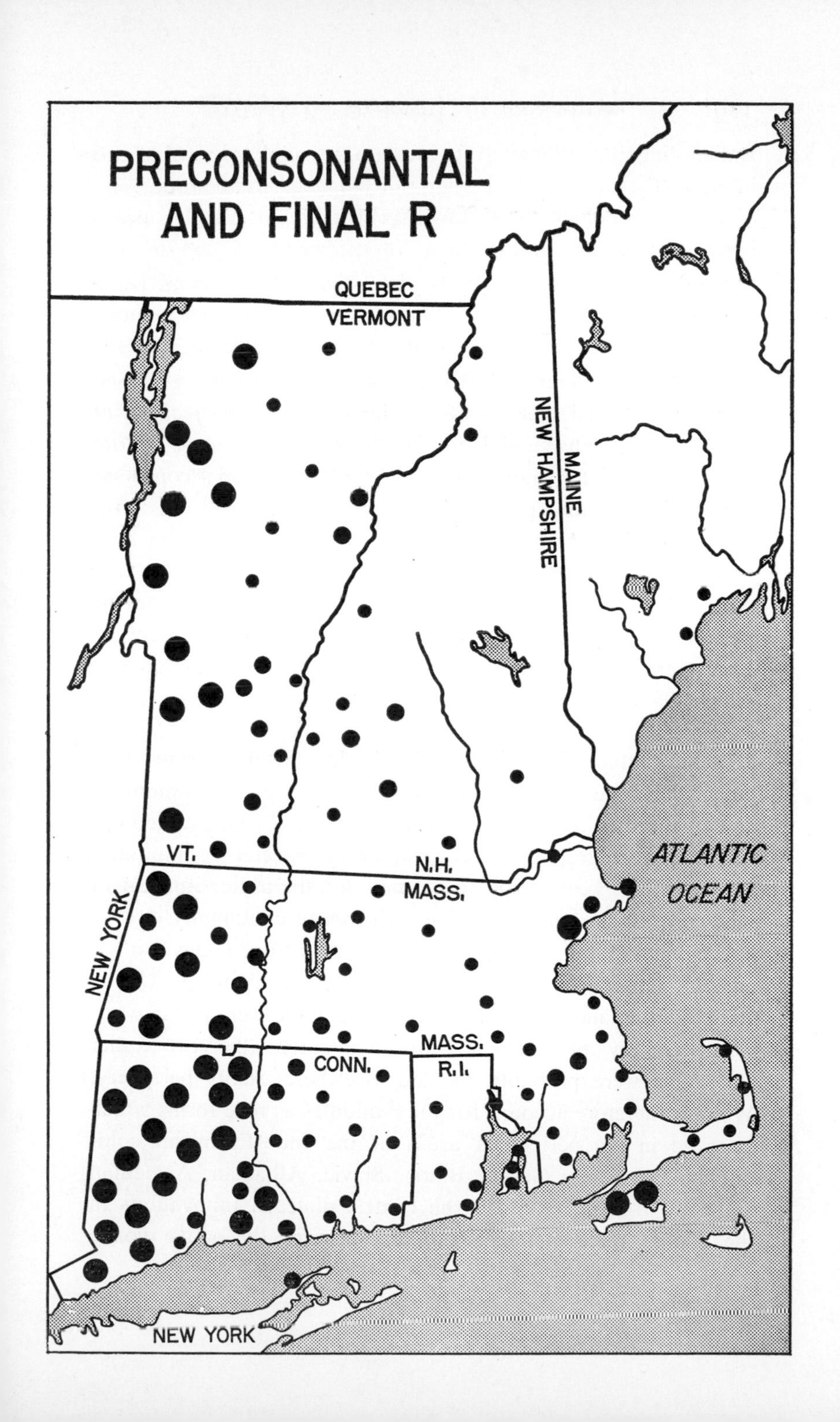
PRECONSONANTAL
AND FINAL R
QUEBEC
VERMONT
MAINE
NEW HAMPSHIRE
VT.
N.H.
MASS.
NEW YORK
ATLANTIC
OCEAN
MASS.
CONN.
R.I.
NEW YORK

Italian linguists attempted to set up principles by which to interpret the complex phenomena of language. Without devising a new methodology, other linguists interpreted complex problems, such as the varying forms of the words for 'house' and 'mouse' in the Netherlands, by investigating the social background of linguistic entities. In attempting an interpretation one may observe how words similar in structure, e.g., MLG *hūs, mūs,* have different histories partly because they are used in different social dialects of the language, partly because of different geographical dialects. In the word for 'house,' more likely than that for 'mouse' to be included in formal conversation, an innovating pronunciation of a focal area has also been disseminated more widely. Successive innovations for both words, however, spread from the cities of Antwerp and later Amsterdam which were focal areas, leaving relic areas on the periphery of the country. Moreover, on the borders between Low German and Dutch speech we find a transition area in which the spread of innovations was checked.

8.7 Such studies of dialect distribution within various languages have led to better understanding of speech communities and of the distribution of linguistic features. From the findings of dialect geography in contemporary speech communities attempts have been made to explain the linguistic situation of past periods, as in the Proto-Indo-European community.

Among the Indo-European languages verb endings with a characteristic *r* to mark the middle voice are limited to Celtic, Italic, Hittite, and Tocharian. Celtic and Italic were at the western periphery of the Indo-European area; the two other subgroups were probably located elsewhere on its periphery. We may therefore account for the *r*-middles as relic forms which survived in the peripheral areas of the Indo-European community. Germanic, Greek, Baltic, Slavic, Albanian, Armenian and Indo-Iranian make up the central dialects. Innovations in the middle voice, patterned on endings for the active voice, were spread through this central area, but did not eliminate the *r*-endings on the periphery.

Another innovation which spread through a part of the central area is the change of some *k* to sibilants, as in the word for 'hundred' (see page 27). The languages with the innovation are Indo-Iranian, Armenian, Albanian and imperfectly Slavic and Baltic. Applying the findings of contemporary dialect geography in this way to ancient speech areas has given us a much more flexible, and realistic, view of their interrelationships.

Linguistic study may also lead to an understanding of earlier cultural relationships. For example, if we had only linguistic information about prior settlement patterns in Louisiana and Texas, we could still determine from the distribution of words for a 'small bonus' the predominant influence of French and of Spanish settlers (see map 4). After millennia have elapsed such distribution may become clouded, and its interpretation require intricate analysis. Nevertheless, interpretations of this sort have been attempted for areas of present-day Romance languages, with the aim of determining prior language groups. But, since no data survives from these, the conclusions must be viewed with reserve.

8.8 The history of individual words has also been clarified by dialect geographers, especially by Gilliéron. He was greatly interested in the relationships of homophones to each other, assuming that in the course of time one of them would be eliminated. In the French collections he found good material in support of his thesis. The word *viande,* from Lat. *vīvenda* nt. pl. of the quasi gerundive of *vīvere* 'live,' replaced *char* < *carne* in the focal area of Paris, where *char* came to be homophonous with *chère* 'dear' < Lat. *cara.* In this way he provided one explanation for some losses in language, although his successors suggest that he exaggerated the extent of "loss by collision." Yet the examples they provide are from different subsystems of the language, such as the noun *bear* and the verb *bear,* or *two,*

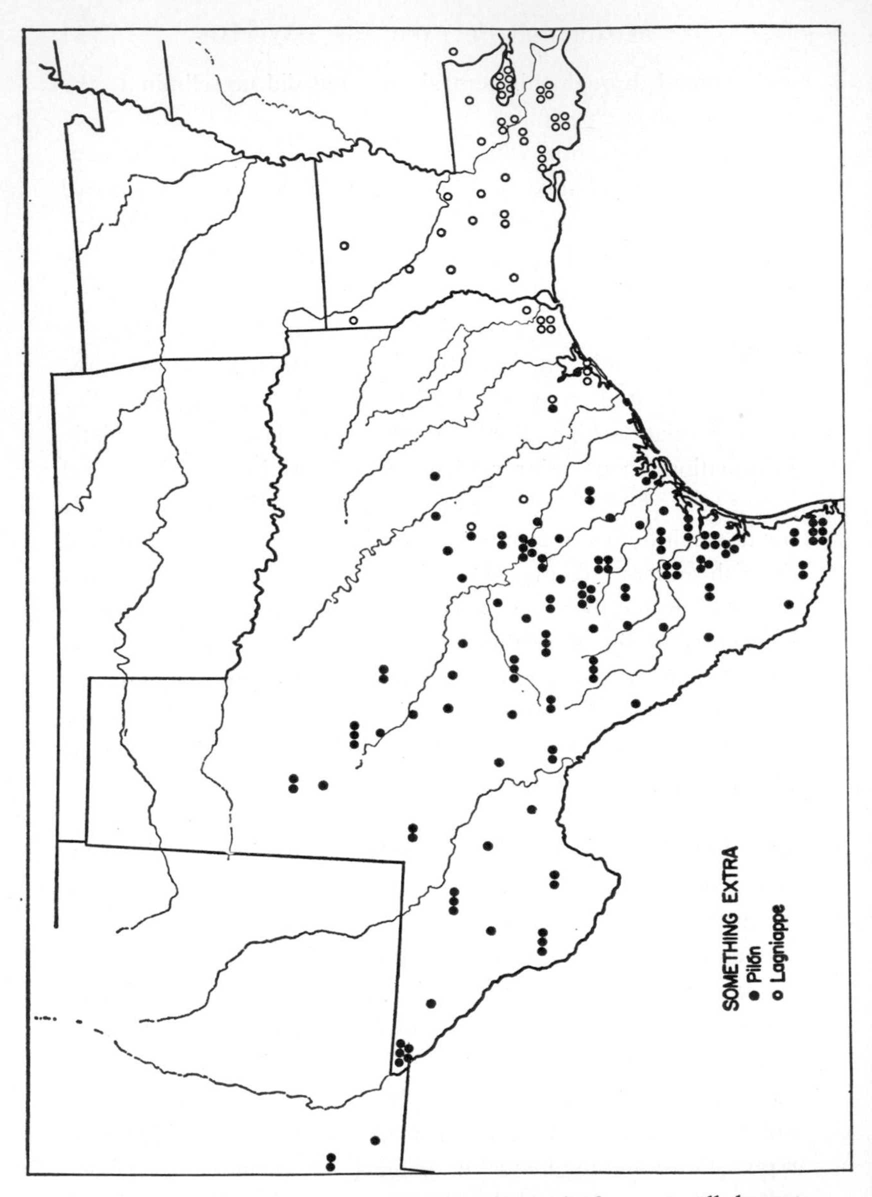

Map 4. Indicates the distribution of words for a small bonus, *lagniappe* and *pilon,* in the Texas area. The extent of French influence is clearly demarcated from that of Spanish. Taken by permission from *The Regional Vocabulary of Texas* by E. Bagby Atwood. Austin: The University of Texas Press, 1962.

too and *to*. When sound changes lead to homonymity for items used in similar environments such as *char,* or *gat,* for 'cat' and 'rooster' in southwestern France, the likelihood of substitutes for one of the homonyms is great. In one of his classical studies Gilliéron demonstrated how the words for 'pheasant' and 'vicar' were substituted for the old word for 'rooster' in precisely the area where it coincided with the word for 'cat.'

Another phenomenon accounted for by dialect geography studies is the occurrence of **blends.** These occur in various formations. In western Germany two words for 'potato,' *Erdapfel* and *Grundbirne,* gave rise to *Erdbirne.* In the western Taunus area, two words for 'brake,' the native *Hemme* and *Meckenick* from Fr. *mécanique,* have given rise to *Hemmenick* (see Bach, *Deutsche Mundartforschung,* 158ff. for these and others). Such blends are found particularly in transition areas.

8.9 Because dialect studies have been especially successful in explaining individual forms, dialect geographers have concerned themselves primarily with single items rather than with structures or substructures of language. This concern may have been further magnified by the necessity of constructing isoglosses for individual items, rather than for segments of a substructure. Besides treating linguistic facts individually, dialect geographers have even raised the question whether their study can be structural (e.g. U. Weinreich, "Is a Structural Dialectology Possible?" *Word,* 10.388–400, 1954).

The question was already answered by Bloomfield, when in *Language,* page 323, he demanded of a dialect dictionary that it "give a phonemic scheme for each local type of speech . . . ." Yet dialect geographers other than a few like Weinreich have disregarded this demand, possibly because of the complexity of their subject. Any dialect geographer with a sizable questionnaire collects enough material from one informant to produce a skeletal grammar. Pressed for time, however, he proceeds to a further speaker without actually producing such a grammar. Instead, he deposits the materials in an archive for further study. Subsequent scholars using the archive generally are interested primarily in noting common linguistic features. They can determine these from unprocessed questionnaires, and accordingly structural statements rarely result. A possible solution lies in the application of data-processing techniques.

One of the contributions of dialect geography to the present lies in making us aware of the tremendous variety of language. Through the diversity and wealth of forms which it has disclosed, dialect geography has broadened greatly our views of language. Historical grammars no longer treat languages as single strata, but rather as complexes composed of numerous strata. A given speaker masters some of these. But the complete language is discernible only as one collects material from a variety of speakers.

The linguists at the beginning of the nineteenth century concerned themselves essentially with the standard language. Early dialect geographers went on to explore the geographically varying strata. Subsequent study aroused concern for strata determined also by social, by functional, and by occupational differences. In this way a view of language more complex than that of Grimm and Rask, even more complex than that of the neogrammarians, has been contributed to historical linguistics by the study of dialect geography.

SELECTED FURTHER READINGS

There has probably been more study and publication in dialect geography this century than in any other field of linguistics. To master its principles, one may best find from Sever Pop's *La Dialectologie,* and after 1950 from the *Linguistic Bibliography,* the primary publications in one's special field of interest—Italian, Swiss, Finnish, and so on—and deal with the data themselves.

Besides the publications providing such data there are handbooks which are standard for each area. For English, one should consult H. Kurath, *Handbook of the Linguistic Geography of New Eng-*

land, for general principles as well as a statement on the work carried out in New England. The recent summary by R. I. McDavid in W. N. Francis' *The Structure of American English,* brings this up to date for American English. U. Weinreich's article in *Word,* 10.388–400 (1954) supplements it theoretically. Work in England has unfortunately not proceeded to the point where a general handbook has been produced.

For German, one can consult A. Bach, *Deutsche Mundartforschung;* for French, A. Dauzat, *La géographie linguistique.*

Individual studies which illustrate the application of the principles of dialect geography to restricted fields are E. B. Atwood's *A Survey of Verb Forms in the Eastern United States* and H. Kurath and R. I. McDavid, *The Pronunciation of English in the Atlantic States.*

ABC

9–Models of Language

9.1 In summarizing views on phenomena as complex as language groups, it is useful to state them by proposing a model. For models provide a convenient and graphic means of concisely indicating general conclusions. To the extent they are accurate, they assist in clarifying views, in posing and solving problems. To the extent they reflect superseded views, however, they may hinder advances. In the century and a half of historical linguistic study various models have been proposed. Only by recognizing what these are, what their advantages and their shortcomings are can we understand the use of many contemporary terms and scholarly disputes of the present and the past.

The first useful model widely used in historical linguistics was the family. After Sir William Jones called attention to the connections between Sanskrit, Greek, Latin, Germanic, linguists set out to determine and represent the relationships between these languages. They did so by likening various languages to various members of a family, and in this way created terminology which we may deplore in its literal sense but in great part maintain.

We speak of the Indo-European group and other such groups as a **language family.** Greek and Latin, and other Indo-European languages, may be called **sister languages.** Other relationship terms such as uncle, aunt, we now find naive and reject. However, we may still speak of the **parent language,** Proto-Indo-European, or refer to it as the **mother language.** If we wish to avoid the cruder overtones of the family metaphor, we use Latin terms, such as **cognate** instead of **related.** We also say that French is **descended** from Latin (or Proto-Romance). In the course of time terminology like related or cognate has become so technical and colorless, that it gives rise to few misconceptions.

The family model was useful in working out the alignment of languages. The Germanic languages had obviously undergone changes different from those of Greek or Latin; how better to indicate the subsequent independence than by labeling them sisters, since 'language' is a feminine noun in German. Shortcomings of the family model however are obvious after some thought, for modern Germanic languages like English and German are related to modern Greek, but not as sisters, rather as distant cousins. When viewed over a great expanse of time, a language family behaves differently from a natural family, for its members may grow old without dying, and may develop new interrelationships which are hard to label with relationship terms that are not cumbersome. Shortly after the middle of the nineteenth century a new model was proposed which solved some of these problems, continued others, and raised still others—the **family tree.**

9.2 The suggestion that the relationship between subgroups of a language is similar to that between branches of a tree was vigorously propounded by a linguist trained in biology, August

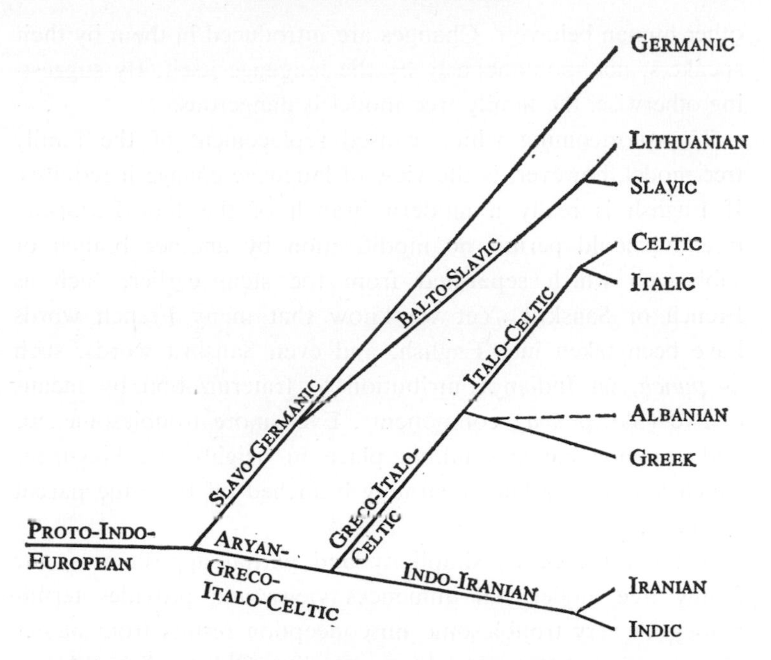

Schleicher's Indo-European family tree, *Compendium* 9.

Schleicher, who was strongly influenced by Darwin's views on evolution. His model is more sophisticated than that of the family, permitting a clear view of languages and also their various further developments—from original branches through smaller and smaller subbranches which show relationships in both time and space.

As with the family model, we use terminology today which is based on the view of a language group as a tree. We say that English **branched off** from Germanic, which in turn is a branch of Indo-European, and so on. But very early, dangers in this model became apparent.

One shortcoming it shares with the family model is its depiction of a language as a biological organism. Languages do not have an independent existence, like an animal or a tree. They are sets of conventions, like conventions of fashion, games, and other human behavior. Changes are introduced in them by their speakers, not spontaneously by the language itself. By suggesting otherwise, the family tree model is dangerous.

The shortcoming which caused replacement of the family tree model, however, is the view of language change it requires. If English is really a modern branch of the Indo-European tree, it should permit no modification by another branch or subbranch which separated from the stem earlier, such as French or Sanskrit. Yet we know that many French words have been taken into English, and even Sanskrit words, such as *punch,* an Indian contribution to fraternization by means of five (Skt. *pañca*) components. Even more troublesome, we find common changes taking place in neighboring languages which long before had separately branched off from the parent language.

Yet because of its simplicity and partial appositeness, the family tree model still influences views and provides terminology. A very troublesome misconception results from names of successive stages of a language, like Old English, Middle English, New English. These terms suggest that we view New English as a direct descendant of Old English. We know however that modern standard English developed from the London dialect, a Midland form of speech, while our chief Old English materials have come down to us in a West Saxon form. To try to trace modern standard English directly to the language of the *Beowulf,* or of Alfred's works, causes difficulties. Similarly New High German and Middle High German. New High German is essentially a central German dialect, while Middle High German was an upland dialect. In using the family tree model these important facts of linguistic history are concealed.

9.3 Primarily because of its inadequacy in accounting for linguistic change, the family tree model was soon replaced by a model designed for this purpose, and accordingly referred to as a theory, the **wave theory.** By this model languages are spoken side by side over a given area and influenced by changes introduced at one point; these then spread like the waves on a pond which are caused by an object hitting the surface of the water. With this theory, proposed in 1872 by Schmidt, the Indo-European languages may be depicted as follows:

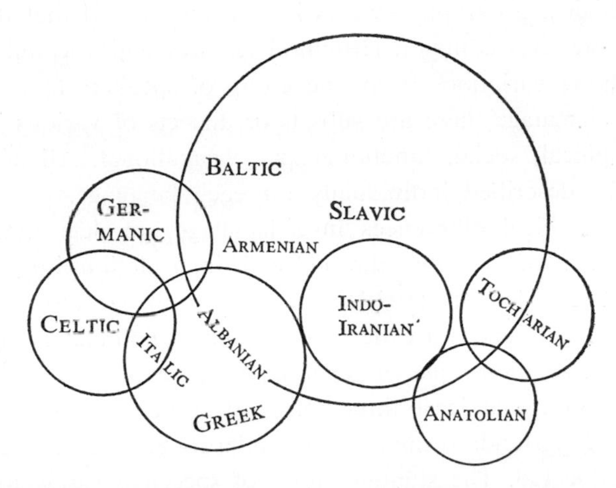

A reformulation of Schmidt's representation of the distribution of the Indo-European languages.

In permitting us to show flexibly interrelationships between languages, and changes affecting them, the wave theory is preferable to the family-tree theory. Both however share the defect of depicting language as a set composed of a single layer rather than multilayered phenomena.

9.4 Either theory was adaptable to the neogrammarian approach, with its simple view of language. For "sound changes could take place without exception" either along the branches of a tree, or over an expanse in which languages existed side by side. When however study of dialect geographers showed that a language is subdivided in area into dialects—and by different social and occupational groupings—any bidimensional model, even when supplemented by the third dimension of time, becomes insufficient. We now view language as a set of social conventions so complex that a simple biological or geometrical model is totally inadequate. Rather than force one on language, we attempt to understand it in its complexity.

9.5 Dialect geography studies have demonstrated that though a language has common structural features and vocabulary, it also shows variations from one group of speakers to another. In any language there are subsets or dialects of various types: geographical, social, functional and occupational. All of these must be described individually for each language.

Geographical differences in a language are determined by the extent of its use, the cultural interrelationships of its speakers, the length of settlement of its speakers, and so on.

Social differences are determined almost completely by cultural interrelationships. In general we may expect even in nonliterate groups at least three forms of speech: a cultivated, a common or standard, and a nonstandard—in modern societies, an uneducated. The standard form of speech is rarely used as such in literary, religious, prophetic, or even political utterances. Nonstandard forms may be found among antisocial groups, such as criminals, or a rebellious younger generation, or among rustics.

Functional differences again reflect cultural interrelationships. Although their variety differs from language to language, we may speak of at least two styles, formal versus informal, in many languages more. In Japanese, there is besides a formal and an informal, an epistolary style, for use in formal letters; further, a style used only to and by dignitaries. Only the Japanese emperor may use *chin* 'I.' A reflection of this style was applied with humorous effect in the *Mikado,* a term meaning 'honorable gate' used for the emperor formerly in somewhat the same way as the 'Sublime Porte' was used for the former Turkish government.

All such subsets are imposed on each other. There may be, for example, formal and informal varieties of nonstandard, standard, and cultivated speech. Somewhat different are occupational subsets. Specialists of various kinds: engineers, jockeys, biochemists, linguists, have developed their own jargons, which consist largely of special vocabularies. These may be applied in any of the subsets mentioned above.

All of these subsets in a language provide the possibility of additions, changes, losses. As technological features are introduced, modified, or retired, language referring to them will probably change. In this way variety in language virtually provides built-in mechanism for change. The complexity of language also is difficult to symbolize in a model simple enough to clarify its structure and development.

9.6 We have been discussing language only as a complex set of conventions used by a group of speakers. Subsets are also found within an **idiolect,** the language of a single speaker. A speaker may change his place of living, his social status, his relations to his associates, his occupation, and by these changes virtually be forced to introduce changes in his language. If we constructed a model for a language, we would have to include in it such multistrata units for each idiolect. Idiolects are rarely used for nonsocial purposes, however, and accordingly our chief concern is with dialects, or **dia-systems.** These in their variety effect various changes as they are used in conjunction with each other.

In sketching the complexity of language to this point we have been viewing language used by a generation of speakers. As new speakers acquire a language, further possibilities are provided for the introduction of change. Since change in language is the prime concern of historical linguistics, we must view the modifications of the various subsets of language in the additional dimension of time. We may arbitrarily select any two points of time for such study. Our results are more useful, however, if we compare the varying language of two or more periods which have been differentiated by marked changes in structure (see pages 18–19).

9.7 Such changes may be introduced in the interplay of geographical subsets, dialects. They may also be introduced from without, from other languages. Upon introduction, they may be imposed from speaker to speaker, along lines of communication. If so we may find wedge-shaped isoglosses along basic routes of travel, such as the Rhine. Changes may on the other hand be transmitted from center to center. Kurath points out that all the chief colonial centers in America except Philadelphia lost preconsonantal *r;* apparently Philadelphia—the second largest city of the British Empire in the eighteenth century—alone withstood spread of this change from across the Atlantic.

Changes in social subsets may be introduced similarly. Some beat locutions are extended from patron to patron of an espresso joint. Others may be transmitted from San Francisco to New York, without affecting Omaha or Peoria. Similarly occupational jargons. Atomic physicists may transport new usages from Berkeley to Brookhaven, with little effect on intervening areas. With increase in complexity of communication, the origins and spread of language change have also become increasingly complex.

9.8 If we choose to produce a model of language then, we should depict it as a complex of various strata, in each of which individuals employ composites of the extant possibilities. The variety of these allow many possibilities of interaction, and change. On the other hand the pressures towards ease and accuracy of understanding, which are highly exacting in complex societies, work against the introduction of change.

9.9 When changes have occurred, historical linguists determine them, and earlier forms of language, by use of the comparative method and the method of internal reconstruction.

They determine variation in language by the methods developed in dialect geography. Through detailed field work, it has become clear that no idiolect or language is perfectly symmetrical; we find variation, inadequacy and imbalance in all languages, especially in areas of cultural change. In such positions, innovations and changes are likely. If a new cultural fashion, such as interest in highly rhythmic music, becomes popular, jive talk, technical language associated with it, may fill out areas inadequate in the previous language for its discussion. Similarly, new technological developments, such as electricity, medicine, machines. Space exploration disclosed an inadequacy in technical terminology in various languages. The Russian term *sputnik* has filled one of the gaps.

Imbalance in the structure of a language is much more difficult to deal with than is that of vocabulary, as we may illustrate by means of oral and nasal stops in English.

The English voiceless and voiced stops, and nasals, provide a symmetrical scheme:

p	t	k
b	d	g
m	n	ŋ

In outline, this subset is balanced. In distribution, however, the balance is incomplete; /ŋ/ is not used initially. When we proceed to the fricatives, we do not find the symmetry continued: /f/ is labiodental, not bilabial; /θ/ is interdental, not alveolar, /s š/ do not balance /k/. If we examine clusters of these phonemes preceded by /s/, we find a further imbalance: /sp st sk sf sm sn/ occur, but no others. Change often is introduced in such unbalanced patterns of the phonological (and morphological) systems, as in unbalanced locutions in the vocabulary, but there has been inadequate study to make convincing statements about it. The next chapters will deal with the phenomena, mechanism, and to some extent effects of such changes.

SELECTED FURTHER READINGS

For application of the family tree and wave models to the Indo-European languages, see H. Pedersen, *Linguistic Science in the Nineteenth Century,* 311–18, and L. Bloomfield, *Language,* 311–18.

A. Martinet, *Éléments de linguistique générale* (Paris, 1960), deals with linguistic diversity in Chapter 5.

10—Change in Phonological Systems

10.1 When languages are compared at various periods, we find correspondences between their entities. In comparing Middle English with Modern English, for example, we observe obvious correspondences between ME *set,* NE *set,* somewhat less obvious between ME *wīf,* NE *wife,* ME *hūs,* NE *house.* We conclude that NE *set, wife, house* are the contemporary forms of ME *set, wīf, hūs,* and we label these Modern English forms **replacements** for the Middle English. The investigation of such replacements between successive stages of a language is one of the chief concerns of historical linguistics. In this chapter we will deal with the patterns of replacement in sound systems and with phonological correspondences between entities at two or more stages of a language.

10.2 Between the English of Chaucer (†1400) and that spoken today probably all entities in the phonological system have changed. Some of the changes were very minor; Chaucer's pronunciation of ME *set* would probably be understood by us today, though in details it might seem odd. Other pronunciations of his we might not understand at all, such as his ME *see* /sē:/ versus our NE *see* /síy/, ME *tōth* /to:θ/versus our NE *tooth* /túwθ/. Historical grammars concern themselves largely with such striking changes. Yet to understand the process of change in language we must also deal with replacements which do not modify the system, and which therefore seem minor or not worth notice in general surveys dealing with the history of a language.

One feature of Chaucer's pronunciation of *set* which may seem odd to us is his articulation of /t/; it would probably remind us of the *t* used by a Spanish speaker. For at one time English /t d n/ were dentals. Over the past centuries their articulation has been progressively retracted, so that they are now alveolars. As this retraction took place, it caused no changes in the morphological system of the language. Nor was the system of phonemic contrasts affected. NE /t/ contrasts with NE /p k/ etc. just as did ME /t/ with ME /p k/ etc.

While such modifications are apparently going on constantly in language, we have little information about them. For only when phonological systems are altered, do speakers, including scribes, take account of changes. Since we have very few detailed descriptions of past languages, we will be able fully to understand sound changes only after linguists have compiled numerous statements on gradual modifications as well as phonemic changes in language. Such information has been assembled only recently, as for the voicing of American intervocalic /t/, as in *bottle, latter*. It must be gathered from all languages in which changes are observable.

10.3 For languages of the past we hypothecate modifications in pronunciation chiefly on the basis of subsequent changes in the system. In Middle English we do not posit a phoneme /ŋ/. We assume that /n/ had an [ŋ] allophone before velars. For when final /g/ was lost in forms like early NE *sing, sing* did not fall together with *sin.* Moreover, in his partial rimes, Layamon paired *stronge* and *londe* (see H. Pilch, *Layamons "Brut"* [Heidelberg, 1960], page 150). We assume therefore that ME /n/ before /k g/ was pronounced [ŋ], as in NE *stronger, finger.* In some stage of the language before Middle English, possibly very much earlier, [n] before /k g/ had undergone a subphonemic change to [ŋ].

The constant changes taking place in language may in this way lead to modifications in sound. These modifications have no effect on the system until some further disruption occurs; by one such the conditioning element for a specific allophone may be lost, as in early NE *sing.* The appearance of new phonemes on such occasions informs us of previous allophonic changes in the language.

As a further example we may note pre-OE [y]. With [u] this must have been an allophone of pre-OE /u/; [y] occurred before /i i: j/, [u] elsewhere. Since the interchange was automatic, no new allophones of /u/ would have been apparent to the speakers. Only when in late pre-Old English the conditioning elements were modified was [y] distinguished from [u]. At that time [y] became a separate phoneme, as in OE *fyllan* 'fill' < **fulljan* versus OE *full.*

Scribes generally indicate contrasts which distinguish meaning, or betray them by inconsistencies or errors of spelling. With a long series of texts, we therefore are usually aware of any changes in the phonological system which have taken place over periods of a language.

10.4 In dealing with changes affecting a phonemic system we now require grammars to note not only individual changes but also that they present them within the systems of the two stages. In comparing Middle English and Modern English, for example, we expect that the Middle English and Modern English consonants as well as the vowel systems be provided us. Since grammars of the past dealt largely with individual phonological entities, they have rarely provided phonological systems of the languages under discussion. With our present awareness of the importance of structures and substructures in language, we find such historical grammars inadequate and look forward to improved presentations.

Comparing the Middle and Modern English consonant systems, we find little difference between them in number of phonemes.

Middle English	Modern English
p t č k	p t č k
b d ǰ g	b d ǰ g
f θ s š x h	f θ s š h
v ð z	v ð z ž
m n	m n ŋ
w l r y	w l r y

One Middle English consonant phoneme /x/ has been lost, as in *thought*. Two new consonant phonemes have been added: /ŋ/ as noted above, and /ž/, which developed from clusters of /z/ and /y/, as in *vision,* and in French loanwords, such as *rouge*. In structure, and number of members, the consonant systems of the two successive stages are markedly alike.

10.5 The vowel systems, however, are strikingly different. We give first the Middle English system, using a notation similar to Middle English orthography.

Short vowels	Long vowels	Diphthongs
i u	i: u:	
e o	e: o:	ei eu oi ou
a	æ: a:	ai au

Apart from rearrangements, vowels of the Middle English short-vowel system underwent few modifications, as we may illustrate:

ME ship NE ship ME busch NE bush
ME set NE set ME lock : NE (Brit.) lock
ME bak (OE bæk) NE back

In the environments given here, the allophones of the Middle English short vowels agree with those of Modern English, though ME /a/ was probably articulated farther back than is NE /æ/. Simply listing these correspondences, however, gives a completely inadequate view of the relationships between the two systems. For between Middle English and Modern English, additional vowel phonemes were added to the system, and the characterization of vowels by quantity was abandoned. Further, ME [ə], an allophone of ME /e/, has become a Modern English phoneme, with many additions from ME /u/, which in general became NE /ə/ except after labials, where it may have been restored, as in *put, bush, full, wolf*. The number of Modern English vowels was expanded by reduced long vowels which lost their quantity before two or more consonants. Before reviewing examples, we may compare correspondences between the Middle English long vowels and their Modern English counterparts.

Between Middle English and the present, the long vowels have changed markedly, undergoing a series of changes known as the Great English Vowel Shift. This shift is remarkable, for all the Middle English long vowels are modified similarly, by raising; /i: u:/, however, were already high vowels and could be raised no further. Their counterparts in Modern English are diphthongs, with first element at the lowest position of simple vowels, resulting in /ay/ and /aw/. ME /e:/ and /æ:/ have fallen together to NE /iy/; ME /a:/ was fronted and raised to the approximate position of the vowel in ME *seen;* ME /o:/ was raised to NE /uw/. Examples are:

ME	NE	ME	NE
wīf /wi:f/	wife /wáyf/	hous /hu:s/	house /háws/
seen /se:n/	seen /síyn/	spon /spo:n/	spoon /spúwn/
see /sæ:/	sea /síy/	name /na:me/	name /néym/

These remarkable changes alone would have resulted in a totally different vowel system, but the Middle English symmetrical system of diphthongs (the three low short vowels followed by the two high) was also markedly changed, especially those ending in *u*.

Middle English /ei ai/, which had probably fallen together by the time of Chaucer, coalesced with ME /a:/, e.g., ME *vein,* NE *vein* /véyn/, ME *day, dai* /dai/ > NE *day* /déy/.

ME /oi/ remained unchanged, e.g., ME *boi, boy* /boi/ > NE *boy* /bɔy/.

ME /eu/ coalesced with /uw/ from ME /o:/, e.g., ME *fruit* /freut/, NE *fruit* /frúwt/ (also /yuw/, e.g., *pure*).

ME /ou/ remained unchanged, e.g., ME *boue* /boue/ > NE *bow* /bów/.

ME /au/ became a low, back vowel, e.g., ME *cause* /kauze/ > NE *cause* /kɔz/.

It is clear from these examples that the Middle English vowel system was modified so markedly that it is difficult to plot the Modern English system beside it, as we have done for the consonants. Following the diphthongal analysis, proposed by Sweet, Wyld, Bloomfield, Bloch, Trager and others, we may present the Modern English vowel system of one idiolect as follows:

i ship		u bush	iy see			uw spoon
e set	ə some		ey say			ow bow
æ back	a lock	ɔ cause	ay wife		aw house	
				ɔy boy		

Some sources, by no means all, for the fourteen entities listed here have been given above to furnish patterns of replacement. Further Middle English sources will be listed below, though for a complete account one must consult an English historical grammar.

10.6 From the changes between the Middle English and the Modern English phonological systems we may illustrate the essentials necessary for general understanding of sound change. Since sound changes of the types we have observed take place with modifications of sounds to sounds with similar articulation (for example, ME [e:] became NE [i:] rather than the totally different [u:] or [s]), thorough knowledge of articulatory phonetics is essential for understanding the mechanism of changes or shifts. By **shifts** we mean any modifications in sounds, whether or not they lead to changes in the phonological system. When they do lead to changes in the phonological system, for example when PGmc -[ʋ]′- from PIE /p/ merged with PGmc [ʋ] from PIE /bh/, or when ME /n/ split into NE /n/ and /ŋ/, the rearrangements follow certain patterns, mergers, and splits. To understand sound change we must accordingly observe both the mechanism and the patterns which may be involved.

10.7 Understanding the mechanism of sound change involves a knowledge of the types of modification that sounds have undergone, as well as an understanding of articulations themselves. In setting up correspondences between Middle and Modern English we have provided only the simplest, and proceeded as if all Middle English phonemes had merely one **reflex** in Modern English, for example, as if all ME /u/ had become NE /u/. Such a highly simple treatment is unrealistic. For sound changes of the type we have been considering take place by allophones. ME /u/, for instance, is reflected as NE /u/ only after labials (see page 151); elsewhere it became /ə/. The differing developments correlate with differing allophones in Middle English. The changes we have been discussing we therefore label **change by allophones.**

Allophones of phonemes are generally restricted to certain environments; here they are conditioned by their surroundings. When such allophones undergo a change, we speak of a **conditioned** or a **combinatory change.** Examples are: ME /u/ to NE /u/ after labials; PGmc /f θ s χ/ to /ʋ đ z g/ when not preceded by the chief stress; some American English intervocalic /t/ to /d/, through [t̬]. Much more rarely all phones of a phoneme change, and we speak of an **unconditioned change.** Examples are: PIE /o/ to PGmc /a/, as in Goth. *asts* 'branch' < PIE /ósdos/, with loss in Germanic of the second vowel; PGmc /z/ to OE /r/.

Whether conditioned or unconditioned changes take place, when a shift occurs it generally involves modification of a distinctive feature of articulation. NE /t/, for example, is a stop, produced by alveolar closure while the velum is raised and the glottis is open. Some of its allophones may be further modified by aspiration. Its allophone before stressed vowel is aspirated, as in *top;* that after /s/ as in *stop* is unaspirated. Similarly /t/ in American English (*butter, bottom* etc.) was unaspirated and very short; articulated in this way it became voiced between voiced sounds, with some restrictions. In accounts of shifts we accordingly identify the distinctive features of allophones, for through their modification sound changes take place.

10.8 A shift may take place because of a change in **place of articulation:** labials may become labiodentals, dentals may become alveolars, velars may become palatals, and so on. A shift of labial to labiodental occurred when PIE /p/ became PGmc /f/; cf. Gk. *patḗr* = Goth. *fadar*. A shift from dental to alveolar, when PGmc /t/ became OHG /s/; cf. Eng. *hate* = Germ. *hassen*. A shift of velar to palatal, when early PIE /k/ under certain conditions became [š]; cf. Lat. *centum* = Skt. *śatam*.

A shift may take place in **manner of articulation;** stops may become fricatives or affricates, aspirates may become unaspirated or vice versa, and so on. A shift from stop to fricative occurred when PIE /p/ became /PGmc /f/; cf. Lat. *pater* = Goth. *fadar*. A shift from stop to affricate, when PGmc /p/ became OHG /pf/; cf. Eng. *pool* = Germ. *Pfuhl*. A shift from aspirate to lack of aspirate, when PIE /bh/ became PGmc /ʋ/; cf. Skt. *bharati* 'he bears' = Goth. *bairiþ*.

A shift may take place in the **position of the velum;** nasal sounds may become denasalized, non-nasals may become nasals. OIcel. *ellefo* 'eleven' corresponds to Goth. *ainlif;* OIcel. *annar* 'other' on the other hand corresponds to Goth. *anþar*. Nasal consonants were lost in Old English, with lengthening of the preceding vowel, when they occurred before voiceless fricatives; cf. Eng. *five* = Germ. *fünf*, Eng. *goose* = Germ. *Gans*. Nasal articulation may not be lost completely, but may affect neighboring vowels, as in Fr. *vin* [vẽ] < Lat. *vinum* 'wine.'

A shift may take place in the **position of the glottis;** voiced sounds may be devoiced, voiceless sounds voiced. An example of voiced sounds becoming devoiced is PIE /b d g/ becoming PGmc /p t k/; cf. Lat. *duo* = Eng. *two*. An example of voiceless sounds becoming voiced, PGmc /f θ s χ/ without chief stress on the preceding syllable becoming /PGmc /ʋ đ z ǥ/. As a remainder of this shift we may cite Eng. *r* < PGmc /z/ varying morphophonemically with *s* in *frore* versus *frost*.

In discussing shifts we may deal separately with those affecting vowels, though the modifications may be similar to those for consonants.

Shifts may take place in the degree of vowel opening. Open vowels may become more closed, closed vowels more open. In Middle English, /æ:/ as in *sea,* became more closed, so that we now rime its vowel with that of *see*. The closed vowels /i:/ and /u:/ of *wife* and *house* on the other hand came to be more open.

Shifts may take place in the degree of fronting. Back vowels may become front vowels, and vice versa. When the umlaut was carried through in pre-Old English, when for example /u:/ became /y:/ as in /my:s/ the plural of /mu:s/ 'mouse,' a back vowel was fronted.

Shifts may take place in labial articulation. The /y:/ of /my:s/ which was fronted in pre-Old English times later lost its lip rounding and coalesced with /i:/, so that in Middle English the vowel of *mice* fell together with that of *wife*.

A knowledge of articulatory phonetics is accordingly essential for the understanding and the interpretation of shifts. For the allophones of phonemes are determined by their phonetic environment; when sound changes take place, the direction may be a result of the earlier phonetic surroundings of the sounds concerned. Since phonemes are used to mark meaning in a language, however, they and their allophones generally are maintained without change. For if they, or allophones of the phonemes which comprise their environment, change, distinctions in the language are lost. When the allophones of English *t d n* became alveolar rather than dental, the number of distinctions in the language remained unchanged. When on the other hand /y y:/ became unrounded and merged with /i i:/, the possible distinctions for English were reduced. When the allophones of PGmc /f/ after vowels which did not have the chief accent split from the phoneme and fell together with allophones of PGmc /ʋ/ < PIE /bh/, there were in this environment only voiced fricatives; accordingly the number of contrasts was reduced. Allophonic shifts may in this way lead to rearrangements in the morphological and semantic structure of a language; for when contrasts are eliminated, the number of potential morphological and semantic markers is reduced. Such rearrangements follow general patterns. Besides a knowledge of articulation, which permits us to understand the mechanism of sound changes, we must therefore know the patterns according to which phonological structures are rearranged.

10.9 There are two such patterns, mergers and splits. By **mergers** we refer to coalescences of phonemes. ME /e:/ and /æ:/ coalesced in NE /iy/; ME /a:/, /ai/ and /ei/ coalesced in NE /ey/.

By **splits** we refer to bifurcation of phonemes. ME /n/ developed to NE /ŋ/ and /n/; ME /u/ to NE /ə/ as in *run* and to NE /u/ as in *put*.

Merger is the more important of these patterns; for often when a sound change results from a split, the rearrangement has taken place in such a way that one of the split allophones has merged with allophones from another source. The [ʋ] which split off from PGmc /f/, for example, merged with [ʋ] which resulted from PIE /bh/. Moreover, allophones may become phonemes when their conditioning entities merge with others; pre-OE [y] and other rounded allophones became phonemes when following *i j* merged with reflexes of other weakly stressed vowels or were lost. Merger may therefore be considered the central process in sound change.

Merger may be conditioned or unconditioned. Unconditioned merger, when a phoneme merges completely with another phoneme, is relatively infrequent. An example is PGmc /z/, which merged in pre-Old English and other Germanic dialects with PGmc /r/. When such mergers take place, we cannot determine the earlier forms solely from one language. Using English alone we cannot distinguish the source of the *r* in *were* (PIE *s*) from that of the *r* in *four* (PIE *r*). Examples of other unconditioned mergers are: that of PIE /o/ with PIE /a/ to PGmc /a/; those of PIE /bh dh gh/ with /b d g/ in Iranian, Baltic, Slavic, Celtic.

Much more frequent is conditioned merger, with primary split. PGmc [ʋ], an allophone of PGmc /f/ after weakly stressed vowels, merged with /ʋ/ from PIE /bh/, leaving [f] as the sole allophone of the /f/ phoneme. Numerous instances of such merger can be cited: NE /u/ from /u:/ in closed syllables merged with earlier ME /u/, both becoming NE /ə/ except after labials (see page 151), as in *blood,* cf. Germ. *Blut,* and *nut,* cf. Germ. *Nuss;* NE /ž/ from [zy] merged with /ž/ in borrowings from French, like *rouge.* Often after such mergers we find alternations which reflect the earlier situation such as the /ž/ in *vision* which alternates with the /z/ in *visible.* As noted in Chapter 6, these are useful in applying the method of internal reconstruction.

Besides merger, the examples in the preceding paragraph illustrate primary split. When **primary split** occurs, some allophones continue the original phoneme, others merge with a different phoneme. PGmc /f/, ME /u:/ and NE /z/ were all maintained after the allophones discussed above had been regrouped. Primary split generally leads to an expansion of the members of one phoneme, with reduction in the members of another, but not to a new phoneme in the system.

New phonemes may be introduced by a split if the conditioning features for one set of allophones are modified or lost. Such a phenomenon we refer to as **secondary split.** The pre-Old English front rounded allophones of /o o:/ and /u u:/ became phonemes when the conditioning /i i: j/ were modified. Pre-OE /o o: u u:/ were continued, but from some of their allophones four new phonemes /ø ø: y y:/ were added to the system. On the other hand, no new phonemes were produced when at the same time the fronted allophones of /a a:/ fell together with /e e:/ by secondary split. The essential difference between primary split and secondary split, therefore, is not the result but rather the process by which the sound change takes place.

Many sound changes involve **loss.** OE /h/ before /l n r/ was lost, as in *loud* < OE /hlu:d/, *nut* < OE /hnut/, *ring* < OE /hring/; ME [g] was lost after [ŋ], as in *long.* It may simplify presentation of such sound changes to consider loss a merger with zero. Moreover, as in ME *rime* 'hoar-frost' < OE *hrīm* and *rime* 'rhyme' < OE *rīm,* the loss of sound may result in a homophone with a word in which there was no sound, so that a loss literally results in merger with zero. We may then account for the origin of NE /ŋ/ in secondary split, for the previous conditioning element -*g* was modified by merger with zero.

10.10 In the paragraphs above we have dealt with sound changes that arise from the rearrangements of allophones. Some allophones of one phoneme in the course of time come to resemble allophones of another phoneme and may merge completely or in part with them. In sound changes of this type all allophones which are similar in articulation undergo the change. Moreover, when the change has taken place, the new alignment is maintained, until another shift occurs. NE /ŋ/, for example, has remained distinct from /n/ since the loss of a following /g/. Besides such change we find in language **sporadic changes** which affect sounds only in some of their occurrences, and may not be permanent. Since these changes involve a direct change from one phoneme to another, with no gradual modification of allophones, we refer to them as **changes by phonemes.**

As an example we may cite the pronunciation of NE *seven* [sévm̩]. There has been no long gradual development of a final alveolar nasal to a labiodental or bilabial nasal. Speakers use either one of the two phonemes. We find such changes especially in rapid, informal speech, although their results may often be maintained in a language. They are especially common in everyday words. Though a similar change is often to be observed for NE *eleven* [əlévm̩], it would be rare, or nonexistent, in *leaven,* which has the same phonetic environment for *n,* but a different environment in the social strata of the language.

Speakers are often conscious of changes by phonemes, though they are unaware of the changes by allophones, as in the gradual voicing of NE *water, bottle,* and so on. Except for self-conscious speakers, who in this period of general advanced education flourish more widely than at any previous time, changes by allophone are carried through in all morphs in which the allophone occurs; the *t* in Modern English forms like *better, bottom,* for example, is consistently modified. The different attitude of speakers to change by phonemes on the other hand probably results from an awareness that such phenomena are associated with movement from one social dialect to another.

Changes by phoneme like changes by allophone, are governed by articulatory possibilities and can best be understood by observing the underlying changes in articulation.

10.11 The most frequent such changes are assimilatory. **Assimilation** is a change in the articulation of a sound to one more like that of neighboring sounds. To illustrate we may note changes of the consonant of Latin *ad* 'to' when it was prefixed to morphs beginning with consonants. (For the sake of simplicity, examples are given from contemporary English, even though the assimilatory changes took place in Latin and their results were borrowed into English. The varying forms of the English morpheme *ad,* as in *adjourn,* illustrate morphophonemic interchanges; I rely here on morphophonemic variation to provide a compact series of examples because it is difficult to illustrate sound changes without citing a huge amount of material.) *Apparatus,* from *ad* + *pārāre* 'make ready,' illustrates assimilation in **place of articulation;** the dental *d* was changed to a labial. *Assimilation,* from *ad* + *similāre* 'resemble,' illustrates assimilation in **manner of articulation;** the stop *d* was changed to a fricative. *Annex,* from *ad* + *nectere* 'bind,' illustrates assimilation in **position of the velum;** the oral *d* was changed to a nasal. *Attempt,* from *ad* + *temptāre* 'try,' illustrates assimilation in **position of the glottis;** the voiced *d* has become unvoiced.

As in these four examples, the preceding element is most commonly assimilated, and the articulation of the second element is anticipated. This type of assimilation is referred to as **regressive.**

The articulation of the prior element may also be maintained, as in [sévm̩]; in this pronunciation the labial articulation is maintained for the nasal from the preceding fricative. This type of articulation is referred to as **progressive.**

The articulation of both elements may be modified, by **reciprocal assimilation,** as in [sébm̩]; in this pronunciation the closure of the second element is anticipated in the *b,* and the position of the *b* is maintained for the nasal.

The assimilated sound may not always be contiguous with the sound to which it is changed. An example is Eng. *orangutang,* which was taken over from Malay *orang* 'man' + *ūtan* 'forest; wild.' The nasal of *ūtan* was modified to the velar position of the nasal in *utang* by **assimilation at a distance.**

Assimilation may be complete, as in *annex,* or partial as in [sévm̩]. Partial assimilation is common in inflection, as in the German weak verb. The past of *lieben* [lí:bən] 'love' is *liebte* [lí:ptə], of *sagen* [zá:gən], 'say' *sagte* [zá:ktə], of *reisen* [ráyzən] 'travel' *reiste* [ráystə], in all of which the final consonant of the stem was once voiced. The past of Eng. *live* is [livd] but that of *lick* [likt].

Word boundaries often fall before junctures, and accordingly the final sounds of words may be assimilated, especially to voicelessness. In German, for example, voiced stops become voiceless when final: *lieb* [lí:p] 'dear' but *liebe* [lí:bə], *Hund* [húnt] 'dog' but *Hunde* [húndə], *trag* [trá:k] 'carry' but *trage* [trá:gə].

10.12 Assimilation in word-ending position may lead to development of an additional consonant, as in the pronunciation [sinst] for *since.* In this pronunciation the tongue makes a closure against the alveolar ridge before articulation of the word is completed. The closure is heard as a stop. Such additional consonants are referred to as **excrescent.** Further examples may be taken from English, e.g. *varmint* < *vermin,* or from German; compare Germ. *Axt,* Eng. *ax;* Germ. *Sekt* 'champagne,' Eng. *sack* 'dry sherry'; Germ. *Habicht,* Eng. *hawk.*

We may also view **apocope,** the loss of final vowels, as assimilation to post-word juncture. In Old English, the first singular present ended in *-e,* for example, *helpe.* Such final vowels were lost in the late Middle English period. Apocope and **syncope,** the loss of medial vowels, are prominent in languages with a strong stress accent on initial syllables. In the Germanic languages there has been continuous loss of vowels, until in present-day English many of the native words have become monosyllabic. The Old English first singular preterite of *temman* 'tame' was *temede;* both weakly stressed vowels have been lost, to yield NE *tamed* [teymd].

Final assimilatory changes we associate with delimitation of words by some type of juncture. We may find other indications of junctures in erroneous word division. NE *newt* is from *an ewt/eft,* wrongly divided; since the forms *a/an,* like *my/mine,* etc., were interchanged in accordance with the following sound, speakers not completely conversant with a word might not know where to make the division. *Newt* has remained in English beside *eft*. The reverse type of erroneous division was made in *adder,* cf. Germ. *Natter,* and *apron,* cf. OFr. *naperon*. Such forms, plus assimilation of final elements, enable us to draw inferences about juncture phenomena in the past.

10.13 We have been viewing assimilation as a sporadic sound change, involving change by phonemes. Yet we can also understand as assimilatory many changes by allophone that have taken place. We cannot therefore associate assimilation solely with sporadic changes, but must expect it in any articulatory changes. In the history of English we may observe many instances of assimilation of dentals and alveolars, some of which are sporadic; others are allophonic changes leading to modifications of the system. The following assimilatory changes occur sporadically in Modern English:

won't you	did you	miss you	raise you
[wównčə]	[díǰə]	[míšə]	[réyžə]

These forms may be used in rapid speech, are considered informal by some speakers, substandard by others, and have by no means replaced the more careful [wównt yùw] and so on.

Similar changes took place in early Modern English, and many of the changed forms have remained in the language. From the eighteenth century [ty] is attested with the pronunciation [š], as in *nation;* similarly [sy] as in *issue,* and especially before [yu:] as in *sugar, sure, assure*. (This change also took place in such words as *assume, consume, suet*, but subsequently [s] was reintroduced in these words as a **spelling pronunciation.)** Similarly [zy] became [ž] as in *measure, pleasure, treasure;* [dy] became [ǰ], as in *soldier, grandeur, Indian, educate,* *hideous;* here too all words but *soldier* and *grandeur* were remodeled by spelling pronunciation. *Injun* has survived only as a pejorative term; many *educators* consider the regular pronunciation of this word undignified and insist on the spelling pronunciation.

In pronunciations like [dídʒə díǰə] of *did you,* which has not universally replaced the nonassimilated form, and [sówlǰər] of *soldier,* which has, we observe the same articulatory phenomenon: the neighboring sounds have been assimilated to one another. In [dídʒə díǰə], the [ʒ] is closer in articulation to [d] than is [y]. Generally in speech, allophones result which accord with neighboring sounds.

10.14 Native speakers are not aware of allophonic modification. Foreign speakers, however, hear languages other than their own with their native allophonic and phonemic system, and they distinguish between allophones in a foreign language if these are similar to phonemes in their own language. As example we may note the Japanese form of English *cap.* In English a front variant of /k/ is used before front vowels, as in

keep cape cap

a back variant before back vowels, as in

coop cope cop

The five vowels of Japanese /i e a o u/ are equated by native speakers to the vowels in these words, with /a/ corresponding to the vowels of both *cap* and *cop*. Yet when *cap* was taken into Japanese, speakers observed the front [k] and reproduced it as *ky,* to yield *kyappu* [kyap:ɯ].

We may use the Japanese development to speculate on possible future changes of English /k/. As long as the present articulation of English /k/ with that of following vowels is maintained, there will be no sound change. If however [k] before [æ], as in *cap,* should become sufficiently like the allophones of /š/ to be interchangeable with them, a primary split would occur, and all /k/ before /æ/ would merge with the /š/ phoneme. If on the other hand the conditioning vowels should merge, e.g. /æ/ and /a/, a secondary split would occur; all /k/ before former /æ/ might then merge with the /š/ phoneme, or they might become a separate phoneme.

10.15 Changes of this type, in which consonants have been assimilated to a neighboring [j] or to front vowels, have taken place at various times in the history of English, and even more widely in Baltic, Slavic and other Indo-European languages. Such assimilation of consonants to front vowels and [j] is referred to as **palatalization.**

In early Old English, allophones of /k/ and /g/ were palatalized in the neighborhood of front vowels, so that modifications arose as follows:

cīdan 'chide'	cū 'cow'	geard 'yard'	gold 'gold'
[k'i:dan]	[ku:]	[g'εard]	[gold]
pic 'pitch'	bōc 'book'	dæg 'day'	longum 'long' d. pl.
[pik']	[bo:k]	[dæg']	[loŋgum]

Gradually the palatalized allophones, as in *chide, pitch, yard, day,* came to be further differentiated from the velar allophones, as in *cow, book, gold, longer.* Eventually by primary split the palatalized allophones of /k/ fell together with reflexes of [tj] as in *feccan* [fetjan] 'fetch' and the new phoneme /č/ arose; the palatalized allophone of /g/ fell together with the earlier phoneme /j/ as in OE *gear* 'year' and split from the /g/ phoneme. For some time after this split and this merger /k g/ occurred only before consonants and back vowels in English.

Palatalization has been much more prominent in the Slavic languages, where it has occurred repeatedly. Some phonemes of Slavic can be ascribed to the palatalization which took place in the Indo-European speech community and gave rise to the isogloss which separated the *satem* languages from the remainder of the Indo-European family. Note the following.

OCS pĭsati 'write'	cf. Gk. poikílos 'variegated'
OCS zrĭno 'corn'	Goth. kaurn 'corn'
OCS zemlja 'earth'	Gk. khamaí 'on the earth'

At a later time, velars were again palatalized in Slavic, for example:

OCS četyre 'four'	cf. Lat. quattuor 'four'
OCS žena 'woman'	Gk. gunḗ 'woman'
OCS žęti 'strike'	Hitt. kuenzi 'strikes'

Later still in Russian, all consonants were palatalized before front vowels, so that today consonants are found in two series: palatalized and nonpalatalized.

10.16 Assimilation may also take place in the articulation of vowels. When clusters of vowels or vowels plus certain consonants, such as [j], occur in a language, neighboring vowels may become more alike in articulation. PIE /e/ before [j] became raised in Germanic, so that PIE /ey/ > PGmc. /i:/, as in OE *stīgan,* OHG *stīgan* 'climb,' compare Gk. *steíkhō* 'come.' Modern English cognates are *sty* and *stile.*

PGmc. /e/ was also assimilated to an *i* in the following syllable, as in Goth. *midjis,* OE *midd* 'mid' = Lat. *medius.*

The most far-reaching of these assimilations in the Germanic languages took place in the early period of the individual dialects, and is generally known by the term **umlaut** or **mutation.** Pre-OE short and long *a o u* standing before *j* or short or long *i* of the following syllable became fronted; *a > e, o > ø,* later *e, u > y,* later *i.*

Germanic umlaut provides excellent examples of split. By secondary split the fronted allophones of *o u* became phonemes when the conditioning *j* was lost or the conditioning vowels merged to a central vowel. By primary split the fronted allophones of *a* merged with the earlier *e.* Compare the Proto-Germanic or Gothic and the Old English cognates:

PGmc. mūsiz > OE mȳs 'mice'
PGmc. dōmjan 'judge' > OE døman > dēman > NE deem
Goth. satjan = OE settan 'set'

Since umlaut is an instance of split, we expect to find morphophonemic variants in the later language. These exist abundantly in English and in German, as in *mouse* : *mice, louse* : *lice, goose* : *geese, doom* : *deem, man* : *men.*

Umlaut is an example of regressive assimilation at a distance.

Vowels may also be modified by progressive assimilation, as in the **vowel harmony** of various languages. Examples below illustrate how the vowel of Turkish *-dir* 'is, are, am' varies from *i* to *ü* to *ı* to *u*, depending on the vowel of the final syllable of the base; since the *d* is also assimilated to *t* when following a voiceless consonant, *-dir* may occur in eight forms, of which four are given here.

iyidir 'it is good'	süttür 'it is milk'
kızdır 'it's a girl'	kuştur 'it's a bird'

As illustrated here, vowels may be assimilated to back as well as front articulation.

10.17 Back assimilation is relatively prominent in Old Norse. Pre-ON *a* before *u* became *ǫ* [ɔ], e.g. *lǫnd* 'lands' from **landu*. Before *w* pre-ON *a* > ɔ, *e* > *ø* and *i* > *y*, as in *søkkua* 'sink' < **sekkwa, lyng* 'heather' < **lingwa.* Since the vowels are also rounded, the assimilation in these Old Norse forms involves **labialization,** a type of change less frequent than is palatalization.

Other types of assimilation occur from language to language. One such is **pharyngealization,** which is prominent in the Semitic languages; in Semitic grammar it is generally referred to by a translated term, **emphasis.** In forms made from roots with emphasis, both consonants and vowels are pharyngealized. In Egyptian Arabic ʔab 'father' is pharyngealized, ʔ*um* 'mother' is not. When the dual and plural suffixes are added, they are pharyngealized after ʔab but not after ʔ*um,* cf.

dual	ʔabbe:n	ʔumme:n
plural	ʔabbaha:t	ʔummaha:t

10.18 Assimilation may also lead to weakening in articulation, and even to loss. Intervocalic NE *t,* for example, has been voiced, like neighboring sounds, as in *bottle, butter, bottom.* That this is assimilation may be demonstrated by absence of voicing before *n,* as in *button;* here the articulation of the following alveolar has apparently served to check the assimilatory voicing of *t.*

Assimilation of *w* to following back vowels in early Modern English, evident in NE *sword,* has led to its complete loss in some environments.

10.19 Losses may be complete, with an effect on a neighboring element, often lengthening it. When for example [χ] was lost in *night, height, fight* and so on in early Modern English, the preceding vowel was lengthened. This phenomenon is known as **compensatory** lengthening. Other examples are OE *gōs* < pre-OE **gans,* cf. Germ. *Gans* 'goose,' OE *ūs* < pre-OE **uns,* cf. Germ. *uns* 'us,' in which nasals were lost before voiceless fricatives, with compensatory lengthening of the preceding vowel. The same change occurred earlier in OE *brōhte* < PGmc. /branχta/ 'brought,' OE *þōhte* 'thought.'

Weakening of articulation may also lead to the introduction of vowels or consonants, so-called **epenthesis.** We find epenthetic vowels for example in OE *æcer,* cf. OIcel. *akr* 'acre,' OE *ofen,* cf. OIcel. *ofn* 'oven,' and in many other words before *r l m n;* we find epenthetic consonants in OE *bræmbel* beside *brēmel* 'bramble,' OE *gandra* beside *ganra* 'gander,' and so on. Prothetic vowels were introduced in French and Spanish before *s* plus consonant, as in Fr. *école* < OFr. *escole,* Span. *escuela,* Port. *escola* from Lat. *schola, scola* 'school.'

10.20 A much more subtle change occurred in Middle English, when syllables were balanced. At this time short vowels in open syllables came to be lengthened, as in ME *māken* 'make,' cf. OE *macian,* ME *stēlan* 'steal,' cf. OE *stelan,* ME *wēvel* 'weevil,' cf. OE *wifel,* ME *hōpe* 'hope,' cf. OE *hopa,* ME *wōde* 'wood,' cf. OE *wudu*. Conversely long vowels in closed syllables—before long consonants or some consonant clusters—came to be shortened, as in ME *ledde* 'led,' cf. OE *lǣdde,* ME *kepte* 'kept,' cf. OE *cēpte,* ME *wimman* 'woman,' cf. OE *wīfman,* ME *softe* 'soft,' cf. OE *sōfte,* ME *huswif* 'hussy (housewife),' cf. OE *hūswīf*. Similar balancing of syllables took place in German, and other languages. In Modern English, Modern German, and other such languages there is then no phonological differentiation between light and heavy syllables, as there was in Old English, Greek, or Latin. In spite of attempts to the contrary, poets accordingly cannot reproduce the rhythm of Old English, Greek or Latin verse in Modern English. For the regularization of syllabic quantity has brought about a completely different rhythm.

Balancing, like assimilatory changes can be viewed as resulting from a tendency of languages to develop towards ease in articulation. For when two sounds are produced more like each other, the effort involved in their production is obviously lessened. Accordingly assimilation seems to function in keeping with the "principle of least effort"; since we can find instances of assimilation in virtually any language, the conclusion may seem justified that languages are evolving towards simpler forms. Not enough evidence has been assembled to argue with assurance for or against this conclusion.

One may point to facets of a language which seem comparable to those in another language, yet the two languages are going different ways rather than moving in parallel fashion to forms which require least effort. The weakening and voicing of intervocalic *t,* for example, is occurring only in American English, not in British, Australian or other English dialects. The velar fricative [χ] was lost before consonants in English, see *light,* but not in German, note *Licht*. Languages are so complex in structure—they contain so many substructures that are themselves in some kind of balance and at the same time in balance with other substructures—that we cannot select a random change as evidence of development towards simplicity. Moreover, simplicity in the muscular activity involved in the articulation of speech may differ from simplicity in the neural activity underlying that articulation.

10.21 It is apparently to a tendency towards simplification of neural activity that we can ascribe **dissimilation,** the production of sounds so that they will be more unlike one another. For we find dissimilation particularly among the more complex sounds, such as *l* and *r,* as in NE *turtle* < Lat. *turtur,* NE *pilgrim* < Lat. *peregrinus,* NE *marble* < Lat. *marmor.* It is less commonly attested for stops, as in Germ. *Kartoffel* 'potato,' in which the initial *k* was dissimilated from *t* in the seventeenth century; the earlier term was *Tartuffeln,* which was borrowed from Ital. *tartuffeli.* (When in the sixteenth century the plant was imported to Italy from Peru, it was named after the truffle.) As in all these examples, it is usually the sound of the unaccented syllable which is modified. Dissimilation is much less prominent in linguistic change than is assimilation.

Dissimilation may also involve the loss of a form segment; this is called **haplology.** As examples we may cite the Modern English adverbs in *-ly* made from adjectives ending in *-le.* In these, one syllable has been lost, as in *gently* rather than **gentlely, simply* rather than **simplely.* Another example is *England* < *Engla lond* 'land of the Angles.' As a phenomenon of change, haplology is relatively infrequent.

Another type of change which apparently results from neural rearrangements rather than muscular is metathesis. By **metathesis** we mean interchange of phonemes. Metathesis was remarkably frequent in late West Saxon, where we find *āxian* 'ask,' *dox* 'dusk,' *flaxe* 'flask,' *waxan* 'wash' and many others. Metathesis of consonant and vowel (to which some scholars restrict the term metathesis) is also frequently attested more generally in Old English, as in *hors* < *hros,* cf. NG *Ross* 'horse,' *ðirda* < *ðridda* 'third,' cf. NG *dritte* and NE *three.* Again complex sounds are most commonly involved, as in the substandard NE *irrevelant*. Moreover, metathesis, like dissimilatory change, is apparently attested only as a sporadic change.

10.22 When we investigate **change by allophones** we find it carried out gradually and over a long period of time. Instances of ME e^2 ($\bar{æ}$), which now rime with $\bar{e}^1$, were for example treated differently in the sixteenth and seventeenth centuries. Dryden rimed *dream* with *shame, sea* with *obey*. Pope rimed *weak* with *take, eat* with *state;* Swift rimed *seat* with *weight, meat* with *say't,* and so on. Much earlier the pronunciation [i:] for $\bar{e}^2$ is attested by grammarians, but not favored by them. We assume it was used by Queen Elizabeth I, for she wrote 'biquived' for *bequeathed*. Although this pronunciation is attested in the sixteenth century, still in 1747 Johnson was troubled about riming *great,* whether with *seat* [i:] or with *state* [e:].

We may ascribe Johnson's perplexity in part to the variation of usage, in part to the gradual and slow carrying out of the shift. For the shift of ME $\bar{e}^2$ and other long vowels must have been similar to the shift of intervocalic *t* in contemporary American English, in which some speakers pronounce *butter* [bədər], others [bəṭər], still others [bətər]. As allophones are modified, their articulation is changed gradually until they reach a new stabilized position in the phonological system, as has *dream* today.

Eventually the higher vowel [i:] for $\bar{e}^2$ was generalized in standard English. Though we have extensive evidence on very few such changes, we can assume that those we have furnish us with a typical picture of sound change by allophones. Further such changes occurring in contemporary languages must now be studied and thoroughly documented.

10.23 For the understanding of sound change attempts have been made to determine its causes and to predict the possible development of given entities. As we have noted above, assumption of change towards ease in articulation is based on a very simple view of language. For what seems easy in one language is difficult in another. German still maintains initial [kn], which has been lost in English; compare *Knie* 'knee,' *Knecht* 'knight,' *Knoten* 'knot,' and so on. Though in Latin there was relative freedom of occurrence of final consonants, in Classical Greek the only final consonants to occur are *n r s*. PIE *-m* in the accusative singular, e.g. Lat. *lupum* 'wolf' shows up as Gk. *-n, lúkon.* Other final consonants were lost, as illustrated by the vocative singular *paî* of *paîs,* gen. *paidós* 'boy'; Lat. *quid* 'what' corresponds to Gk. *tí.*

It is obvious from differences like these in various languages that we can only provide very general statements about sound changes tending towards simplicity.

10.24 We can state somewhat less tentatively that sound systems tend to maintain or develop towards symmetry. When PIE /p/ > PGmc /f/, a similar change to voiceless fricatives affected PIE /t/ and /k/; subsequently the other orders were affected, the Proto-Indo-European voiced aspirates and voiced stops. When ME *ē* was raised, to yield NE /iy/, the other long vowels also were affected, as we have noted above. As in these changes, we can understand the tendency towards maintenance of symmetry by observing that contrasts must be maintained unless the sound system is to become impoverished; moreover, a balance of like sounds assists in controlling the language.

Yet phonological systems are modified toward imbalance adequately often so that we reject overenthusiastic endorsement of development towards symmetry—of therapeutic sound changes which heal holes in the system. Under-exploited contrasts, such as those of PIE *b,* may indeed come to be more fully utilized. In Germanic, many borrowings increased the number of *p,* originally a reflex of PIE *b.* In Slavic, however, *bh* fell together with *b* and one potentially important contrast was lost entirely. When we will have materials available on sound changes in a great variety of languages, we may deal more assuredly with change towards symmetry.

10.25 Gilliéron's view, that one homonym tends to force out another, has also been demonstrated to be exaggerated. English maintains *pair, pear; bear, bare,* (polar) *bear,* etc., though the early NE *let* 'hinder' has survived the competition of *let* 'permit' only in *let ball,* now commonly *net ball.* If on the other hand homonyms are of the same set, morphological or semantic, one of them may be lost. Such modifications are however very minor in a language.

10.26 Somewhat more far-reaching, possibly, is the effect of **taboo,** of avoidance of the unspeakable. Topics which may not be discussed vary from language to language, from clothing, in Japanese, to animal names for hunters, names of excretory functions, death, and divinity for us.

Taboos affect the use of words rather than sounds, though it is strange that among the possible monosyllables **pes, *shet* and **fət* do not exist in English. Similarly in Thai there are sanctions against phonological patterns which may suggest tabooed words.

Although the study of taboo is highly interesting, in linguistic change its effect is limited.

10.27 The influence of individuals on phonological change is also limited. Van Helmont indeed added the word *gas* to his and other languages, yet his proposed *blas* 'emanation from stars' was a failure. George Eastman introduced *Kodak* as a deliberate creation, after he noted the restrictions on the letter *k* in the English writing system; other merchants have followed him in introducing names such as *Kix* for breakfast cereals, *Krax* for crackers, *Klenso* for soaps, yet these have had an effect on external elements rather than on the phonological system. They may have an effect through changing the frequency and distribution of phonological entities, as may any new words, such as names for newly discovered elements: *Curium, Californium.*

Vigorous personalities may exert some effect on the language—poets may look to Latin for models, as did Milton, or to the rustic, as did Wordsworth. The net effect of such innovations is difficult to assess. A poet who has had an extraordinary influence is the Norwegian Ivar Aasen, who in the nineteenth century created a new language, *landsmaal,* from western Norwegian dialects and Old Norse. His creation, adopted as a second standard language by short-sighted politicians, has plagued his countrymen to the present, and will for some time to come, until the two Norwegian languages *nynorsk* and *bokmål* are merged. In spite of Ivar Aasen's success, chiefly with vocabulary but also with the structure of Norwegian, the effect of most would-be linguistic innovators is very minor.

10.28 Nor has it been adequately substantiated whether the interaction of two or more dialects or languages brings about sound changes. Romance historical linguists especially have attempted to account for the separate developments of Spanish, French and other dialects by assuming articulatory modifications carried over by speakers who adopted Latin as their second language. Such supposed underlying influences are referred to as **substrata,** superstrata or adstrata. The French front rounded vowels are, for example, ascribed to a Celtic substratum. The effects of language interaction are determined largely by social conditions. When in some areas non-native speakers acquire a new language, the second generation masters it with rather general adequacy, if the linguistic tradition is well-established. In the United States grandsons of Italians, Germans, Spaniards, Negroes, Irish, Danes speak the English used by their associates without notable differences in linguistic structure.

When substrata have led to modifications of a language, as

of English in India, the linguistic tradition has been less powerful; native speakers may have been outnumbered, or open to modification of their speech. In India relatively few native speakers were available to teach English to speakers who constantly used their native languages.

There is now considerable interest in multilingual communities such as those in India, Africa, and other areas of the world which are predominantly multilingual. The effects on languages involved may be ascertainable after further study, which may permit generalizations about sound changes. If then the linguistic situations of previous times can ever be adequately determined—the proportion of speakers of Latin to speakers of Gaulish, closeness of contact between Gaul and Rome, complete descriptions of the Gaulish and Latin dialects involved—we may also be able to apply the findings from contemporary sociolinguistic study in attempts to describe the development of languages in the past. Until we have such material, we must be cautious in ascribing the development of phonological entities of a language, for example, those of French, to substrata.

10.29 With our present knowledge of sound change, based largely on that in Indo-European dialects, we can make assured statements about its mechanism and processes; about its direction or causes we can only propose hypotheses. Further study is essential to provide information in these spheres comparable to that gathered over the past century and a half on the mechanism and processes of sound change.

SELECTED FURTHER READINGS

Sound change is one of the most widely discussed phenomena in historical linguistics. Bloomfield provides many examples and full discussion in Chapters 20–22, pages 346–403, of *Language*. E. H. Sturtevant's *Linguistic Change* deals with sound change, pages 32–67, and elsewhere, attributing considerable influence to mistakes in speaking; since this suggested influence is disregarded here as negligible, it may be of interest to examine Sturtevant's argument.

In various essays published in *Word,* some of which were later translated and published in *Économie des changements phonétiques,* A. Martinet attempts to make a point for linguistic change in accordance with the principle of least effort. Probably the most eloquent statement of language development in a specific direction is Chapter VII, "Language as a Historical Product: Drift," of Sapir's *Language;* his further chapters must also be noted, especially VIII.

Specific applications of the findings from work on sound change may be found in standard handbooks such as E. Schwyzer's *Griechische Grammatik,* who also discusses theory at some length, or the various grammars of A. Meillet. Further information on sound change may be found in articles, such as Sapir's "Glottalized Continuants in Navaho, Nootka, and Kwakiutl," *Language,* 14.248–78.

Since it is useful to observe as fully as possible the course of a sound change, reports on the voicing of intervocalic *t* in American English are of considerable interest. A phonetician's description of such *t* is provided by R-M. S. Heffner.

An experiment testing the course of the change among selected speakers is reported by V. A. Oswald, "Voiced t—A misnomer," *American Speech,* 18.19–25 (1943).

For additional control over the procedures necessary to understand change in language, and to employ such understanding in historical grammar, students must master Henry M. Hoenigswald's *Language Change and Linguistic Reconstruction.* This also set out to provide terminology for historical linguistics, which was employed to the extent feasible in an introductory text.

11 – Change in Grammatical Systems; Analogical Change

11.1 When we trace the history of NE *brother,* by successive steps we can take it back to PIE /bhrā́tēr/. Between the time of Proto-Indo-European and Modern English the phonemes of /bhrā́tēr/ have undergone various sound changes; by noting these we can derive all the phonemes of NE *brother* from those of its Proto-Indo-European etymon. NE *father,* however, cannot be directly related to PIE and pre-Gmc. *patḗr* in this way. For the Proto-Indo-European medial *t* became PGmc. *þ,* which before the accent became ð; this in turn became OE *d,* so that the Old English form was *fæder,* the Middle English *fader.* Without any further modification, the New English form should have *-d-*. Yet such a modification did occur. Some time after 1400 -ð- was substituted for *-d-,* giving rise to NE *father.* We assume that the substitution was made because the word *father* was associated with the word *brother* and similar words, and remodeled after them.

Similarly we would be unable to derive the preterite participle *swelled* from a Proto-Germanic etymon, or even from an Old English form. The earlier preterite participle was *swollen,* which survives as an adjective; *swelled* was made from *swell* on the pattern of

fell		shell		swell
felled	=	shelled	=	x

and similar forms, and replaced the older *swollen.*

Modifications of this type illustrate the chief mode of change introduced in grammatical systems. By it the members of a grammatical set are increased or reduced in number, and the means involved in marking grammatical categories are extended. Since such changes are carried out in accordance with patterns which already exist in the language, they are referred to as **analogical.** The process itself is called analogy.

11.2 Analogy is a process by which morphs, combinations of morphs or linguistic patterns are modified, or new ones created, in accordance with those present in a language.

We can observe analogy most clearly in the learning of language. Most of us have seen children learning forms such as the plural *cups* to *cup* and applying their discovery to other nouns such as

cat		fork		cap
cats	=	forks	=	caps

if then they see a *jet,* and learn the word, they make a plural *jets;* if they see a new toy in a toystore, they make a plural *sputniks.*

We become especially conscious of such extensions if they produce forms we consider false. Just as children learn to make plurals, they make comparatives, as for

new		old		good
newer	=	older	=	gooder

At this point we object, and supply the preferred form *better.* If we find a further extension from

That's new.		That's fine.		That's fun.
That's newer.	=	That's finer.	=	That's funner.

we may even remark on the cleverness of the child after we correct him. At some time in the past, however, speakers of English were more tolerant of new comparatives, for the form *older* has replaced *elder* (except in restricted usages); *littler, littlest* has replaced *less* and *least* when adjectives, except in stock phrases like *least flycatcher*. In this way irregularities may be removed from grammatical sets. But by far the most important use we make of analogy in language learning is in extending forms and patterns that we have mastered.

If we learn a language like German, we do not memorize separately every inflected form. We learn a model, such as

singen	'sing'
ich singe	'I sing'
er singt	'he sings'

and expect to apply it to *ringen* 'wrestle,' *bringen* 'bring,' and so on. We may assume that native speakers learned their language in much the same way. If on the pattern of the past *ich sang, ich rang* we make a form *ich brang,* we are cautioned, possibly reminded of the irregular cognate of *ich brachte* 'I brought'; we also learn one of the limits of such analogical extension.

We acquire other linguistic patterns similarly. If we master the German syntactic patterns

Wir gehen heute.	'We're going today.'
Heute gehen wir.	'Today we're going.'

we do not need to learn separately every sentence beginning with *heute* or other adverbs to gain control over this type of subject position. If we have under control the normal word order, *Wir reisen heute, Wir lesen morgen,* by pattern practice we train ourselves to say

Heute reisen wir.	'Today we're traveling.'
Morgen lesen wir.	'We'll read tomorrow.'

In this way analogy is constantly applied when we use a language. As in foreign language learning there are limits to its application, some of which we may transgress to the horror of fellow-speakers, others to their mild amusement, others to their admiring imitation. When in a 'new frontier' document the word *focalize* was included, presumably on the basis of *final* : *finalize* :: *focal* : x, the reaction was amusement, at least beyond the corps of new frontiersmen. It is difficult to predict when analogical forms are accepted, when not. We do however know some of the conditions under which analogy operates.

11.3 For the operation of analogy, some linguistic set is necessary. The set may be inflectional, like the English verbs, in which the *t/d* suffix has been replacing internal change, as it has done in *swelled*. The set may be derivational, such as the nouns with *-er* suffix, e.g. *driver;* this suffix, imported from Lat. *-arius,* has come to be used after virtually any verb. The set may also be syntactic. Several English verbs, which formerly took an object in the genitive case, were followed until quite recently by *of* constructions, e.g. *miss, desire, remember, forget, hope, thirst, wait.* Sir Walter Scott wrote: *I remember of detesting the man.* By contrast, the common transitive pattern in English consists of a verb followed immediately by an object; this pattern accordingly was generalized, and extended to the verbs cited above.

Sets may also be semantic, such as the relationship terms *brother, mother, father.* Among such sets are the numerals. In German ordinals, for example, *-te* is used from two to nineteen, e.g. *der zweite, der neunzehnte,* after that *-ste,* e.g. *der zwanzigste,* until the millionth, where formerly *-te* was used; today *der millionste* is being used widely, and promises to replace *millionte.* Numerous examples can be cited from the numerals in the various Indo-European dialects. The spread of Slavic *d-* to 'nine,' cf. NRuss. *d'evyat',* from 'ten,' cf. NRuss. *d'esyat',* is among the clearest.

Such sets are very infrequent at the phonological level, and completely absent among allophones; for allophones are by definition unconscious variants, and accordingly would not be classed into sets, let alone undergo modification in one. An example of analogy at the phonological level is the extension of *-r* before vowels in New England English. Since retroflection was lost before consonants but not before vowels, two forms of such words as *water* exist side by side: *watə was* . . . but *water is* . . . , *watə wheels* . . . , but *water always* . . . . Nouns with final ə fell into this pattern, note *soda, idea,* so that speakers with this variation say: *the idea was* . . . but *the idea-r is* . . . .

A type of analogy limited to literate cultures is purely graphic. ME *rīm,* for example, came to be written *rhyme* because early Modern English writers thought it was connected with *rhythm.* ME *delite* < OFr. *deliter,* Lat. *dēlectāre* came to be written in Modern English as *delight,* because it was considered to be related to *light,* cf. Germ. *Licht.* Again we are most familiar with this type of analogy from language learners—from errors of students and typesetters, or from our own struggles with spelling. We may align *proceed* with *precede,* or vice versa; a part of our schooling is spent differentiating among *to, too, two, their, there,* and like sets. With our contemporary regard for spelling, a great deal of social prestige is involved in producing the standard spelling; we accordingly resist analogical modifications in our spelling system, and maintain the established patterns.

11.4 Essential problems of analogy which require further study include the conditions (1) under which it takes place and (2) by which new patterns get established. We cannot yet provide satisfactory answers. We can however observe effects of analogy in prior stages of languages, especially in inflectional sets.

The history of the strong or irregular verbs in English furnishes us with excellent examples of analogical modification.

The Old English strong verbs are generally divided into seven classes, in accordance with internal vocalic variation. To summarize the possible forms, principal parts are given: (1) the infinitive; (2) the first-third sg. preterite indicative; (3) the preterite indicative plural; (4) the preterite participle. The classes are illustrated with one example for each:

1. drīfan	'drive'	drāf	drifon	drifen
2. cēosan	'choose'	cēas	curon	coren
3. findan	'find'	fand	fundon	funden
4. beran	'bear'	bær	bǣron	boren
5. sprecan	'speak'	spræc	sprǣcon	sprecen
6. standan	'stand'	stōd	stōdon	standen
7. feallan	'fall'	fēoll	fēollon	feallen

In addition to these strong verbs there was a large number of weak or regular verbs in Old English, which continued to expand; for almost every new verb was inflected weak. Weak verbs had three principal parts; the only difference between the preterite singular and the preterite plural consisted in the endings, as for

lufian 'love' lufode lufod

In this situation, with the largest number of verbs making up sets of three forms while a small number made up sets of four, there was reduction of the strong verb set.

In 'drive,' the vowel of the preterite singular was generalized throughout the preterite, to NE *drive, drove, driven.* In *bite,* however, also of class 1, the vowel of the plural was generalized to NE *bite, bit, bitten.* Observing the development of all strong verbs in English, and the basis of selecting either singular or plural vowels in the preterite, would require considerable exposition; here we are primarily interested in demonstrating the analogical reduction to three, or two forms, on the pattern of weak verbs such as *love, loved, loved.*

In *choose,* the vowel of the preterite participle was generalized to the preterite, with *ch* and *z,* the consonants of the present and preterite singular, generalized throughout.

In *find,* the vowel of the preterite plural was generalized; in *bear,* the vowel of the preterite participle. The pattern of class 4 was extended to *speak.*

In *stand,* the vowel of the preterite was generalized to the preterite participle; in *fall,* we find regular developments of the Old English forms, no new forms resulting from analogy.

From the principal parts of the Old English strong verbs then, we may observe thoroughgoing analogical remodeling. When as in *drāf, drifon* or *cēas, curon,* the differences in a set are regularized, we speak of **leveling.**

We may cite further forms of the Old English strong verbs to indicate the interaction between sound change and analogical extension. The present indicative endings in West Saxon with their older forms are as follows:

Present Indicative

1.	sg.	-e < pre-OE -o < -u
2.	sg.	-(e)st < pre-OE -isi (with addition of *-t*)
3.	sg.	-(e)ð < pre-OE -iþi
	pl.	-að < pre-OE -anþi

Since *-i* following *-e-* of the stem syllable occasioned its umlaut to *-i-,* the forms of *beran* in West Saxon were:

1.	sg.	bere	cf. Northumbrian	bero
2.	sg.	bir(e)st		beres
3.	sg.	bir(e)ð		bereð, -es
	pl.	berað		beorað

The pre-Old English sound change of $e > i$ before *i* had taken place regularly. After the change, the stem *bere, birest,* etc., contained two vowels, in contrast with other verbs which had no such interchange, such as *findan, drīfan.* As we know from the forms today, the *e* was extended throughout the present of *bear,* and the difference in vowels was leveled out.

In other ways, the verbs in English have become regularized, so that today they have a maximum of five forms, most of them regular. Similar examples of regularization could be provided from other languages with sets of paradigms.

11.5 In the course of analogical leveling, extensions may be made from inflected, or derived, rather than from base forms. These are known as **back formations.** In Old English, the verbs *flēon* 'flee' and *flēogan* 'fly' were inflected alike in all forms but the infinitive. Like *birest, bireð* the vowels in the second and third singular forms underwent umlaut, and the present indicative was as follows:

1. sg.	flēo
2. sg.	flīehst
3. sg.	flīehð
pl.	flēoþ

The first person singular and the plural, with vowels the same as that of *flēon,* developed to NE *flee*. This should have alternated with *thou fliest, he flies*. Instead, a new infinitive *fly* was produced. In *flee* the base morph was extended throughout the present; in *fly,* an inflected morph was generalized throughout the present, as a back formation.

We may cite further instances of back formations from nouns. When in Middle English *-s* came to be the general plural marker, the singular : plural contrast was based on presence and absence of *s,* on the pattern:

Middle English sg.	fader	=	fō 'foe'
	faders		fōs 'foes'

Some nouns which ended in *s* were mistaken for plurals, and a new singular was produced, e.g., *pes* 'pease' from the Lat. sg. *pisum;* the new singular is now commonly used, though the old has survived in the nursery rime *Pease porridge hot* . . . . Similarly *buriels* < OE *byrgels* 'tomb' was assumed to be plural, and a new singular was produced, which by analogy with *funeral* was spelled with *a, burial.* Other such singulars were made as back formations from *redels* < OE *rǣdels,* compare

Germ. *Rätsel,* and *cheris* < OFr. *cherise,* later reborrowed as *cerise.* In these nouns the base, rather than inflected forms, resulted from analogy.

We may illustrate a further complexity of analogy with West Saxon *eom* 'am.' Like Gothic *im* 'am,' this should have had an *i* in the stem, for it developed from PIE /*ˀés-my*/ > *és-mi,* cf. Skt. *ás-mi.* In Germanic, however, the substantive came to be a composite verb, with forms from the root in *be* and that in *was* as well as that in *is.* From the northern Old English forms such as *bīom, bēom,* we may assume that *eom* is a combination, with the consonant from the root *es* and the vowel from the root *be;* such combinations are called *blends* or *contaminations.*

11.6 The development of blends as well as back formations demonstrates that new, unexpected forms may be produced in a language by analogy. In this way, new suffixes and grammatical markers may result. Examples are the English suffixes *-dom* and *-hood.* In Old English, these were used for compounds: *frēodom* 'freedom' < *frēo* 'free' and *dōm* 'quality,' *cynedom* 'royalty,' *camphad* 'warfare' from *camp* 'battle' and *hād* 'state,' *werhad* 'manhood,' and so on. In the course of time, these second elements of compounds were classed with elements like *-ing* in *cyning* 'king,' *æþeling* 'prince.' They then came to be treated as suffixes and distinguished from the regular forms of *doom* and *hood.*

Separated from the underlying entity, suffixes come to have a development of their own. From forms like *æþeling,* 'improper clipping' was made to produce a suffix *-ling.* From this new words were formed, as *darling,* cf. *dēor* 'dear.' Similarly, *-able* was taken as suffix in such forms as *habitable,* from Lat. *habitabilis,* and used in many new forms, such as *bearable, supportable.*

One such suffix which has enjoyed a wide development is *-burger.* In German, *-er* is commonly used to make adjectives of city names, such as *Berliner, Frankfurter, Wiener.* Some of these adjectives have come to characterize prepared meats. That for *Hamburg* became so completely divorced from the city that *-burger* rather than *-er* was assumed to be the suffix. By chance the first syllable coincided with the name of a meat. It was quite irrelevant that ham was never used in *hamburgers*. One can now buy *fishburgers, cheeseburgers,* or even *burgers* which are labeled for their producer, such as *Mooreburgers*.

By the same process of improper clipping, morphological markers have been produced. One of the characteristic German plural markers is an *-er* suffix. Historically this is a derivational suffix, used to form nouns, as in Skt. *ján-as,* Lat. *gen-us* 'kind, race' from the root PIE *gen-* 'beget.' In pre-Old High German, finals of words had been lost in such a way that *-er* survived in the plural, in contrast with no suffix in the singular, as in *kalb* 'calf' : *kelbir*. It was then taken as a plural marker, and widely extended to many neuter nouns in which the suffix had never been added, such as *Haus* 'house' : *Häuser,* and even to masculines, such as *Mann* 'man' : *Männer*. We find a similar extension in Middle Dutch, virtually none in English, only *child* : *children*.

Only by chance do we have material to determine the source of the *-er* suffix. For *kalb* is the only *er*-plural in Old High German which can be connected with the Indo-European nouns in *-es*. Moreover, the great extension of the *er*-plurals occurred in Old High German and Middle High German times, when we have a fair number of texts. If morphological markers were produced in this way at an earlier stage of the language, we can merely hypothecate their origin and extension. The *-d-* marker for the Germanic preterite, as in Goth. *lagida,* OE *legde,* OHG *legta* 'laid,' with voiceless dental in Goth. *brahta,* OE *brōhte,* OHG *brāhta* 'brought,' may have originated in this way. Similarly the *v* of the Latin perfect, e.g. *amāvi* from *amō* 'love,' the *k* of the Greek perfect, e.g. *pepaídeuka* of *paideúō* 'educate,' and other morphological markers which we find in the early Indo-European dialects. In view of the absence of evidence, our only support of such a hypothesis of their origin lies in general linguistic theory and the possibilities afforded by the structure of the languages after the splitting of Proto-Indo-European.

Possibly of greater amusement than significance in the development of languages are new formations which represent an irresponsible modification, such as Eng. *sirloin.* This is from Fr. *sur-loin,* in which the first element derives from Lat. *super* 'upper,' so that historically the word refers to the upper part of the loin. In English, however, *sur-* was not found in other wide-spread compounds, seemed aberrant, and was modified to the apparently sensible *sirloin,* for the upper part of the loin is a noble piece of meat. Somewhat scornfully, this process has been referred to as **folk etymology.** It does not, however, differ essentially from the analogy by which a contemporary English suffix *-burger* was formed, or an Old English suffix *-ling,* or an Old High German suffix *-er.*

In folk etymology the sportive manipulation of language by individuals may be more evident than it is in less fanciful analogy, as well as the approbation or disapprobation of fellow-speakers; but what is essentially involved is the remodeling of less frequent and less favored patterns in the language in accordance with those more highly favored. When the cognate of Lat. *homo* came to be found in English only in the Old English compound *bryd-guma* 'espoused man,' see Germ. *Bräutigam,* it was modified after the more widespread though illogical *groom* to *bridegroom.* When *pentis* from Fr. *appentis* < Lat. *appendix* was applied to an outgrowth of a large building, it was remodeled to *penthouse.*

Just as folk etymology illustrates the inventiveness of some language users, it may illustrate the conservatism of others. The term *Welsh rabbit* for a cheese dish, like *Cape Cod turkey* for the plainest of piscatorial fare, shows an attempt by the ingenious to make simple food more palatable for the credulous. Their stolid fellow-speakers may however object to this transparent outrage, and insist on *Welsh rarebit,* in much the same way that we today require inventive children to say *men* not *mans, better* not *gooder, went* not *goed,* and to banish *funner* entirely from their speech.

11.7 Repeated attempts have been made to determine when analogy takes place, rather than simply to record instances of analogical remodeling. Among the more recent are those by Kurylowicz and Mańczak. These proceed from completely different bases. Kurylowicz attempts to set up general rules based first on general linguistic principles, then on observation of relationships between forms. Mańczak, on the other hand, after examining a tremendous number of forms which have been remodeled by analogy, has set up general observations which account for those of greatest frequency. Neither permits us to predict when in any given language analogy may take place, or enables us to determine what its direction has been under poorly known situations in the past. Like general statements about other phenomena in historical linguistics, both studies are useful in enabling us to understand analogical developments elsewhere in language and accordingly their conclusions are presented here in part.

Kurylowicz' first rule states that a twofold morphological marker tends to replace one that is single. As example he gives the *-e* plural ending of German nouns, which in some nouns was also associated with umlaut of the stem vowel, for example, *Gast* 'guest' : *Gäste.* This twofold marking has been extended as in *Baum* 'tree' : *Bäume* replacing *baume.* Many further examples for the rule can be found. Yet many instances can also be cited in which it does not apply; note, for instance, the German weak verb *trennen, trennte, getrennt* 'separate,' which has maintained a single marker as opposed to *rennen, rannte, gerannt,* 'run.'

By Kurylowicz' second rule analogy proceeds from the base form to derived forms. While commonly true, as in *sputnik, sputniks,* mentioned earlier, formations such as *pease* to *pea* contravene this rule.

By the third rule, any construction consisting of a constant plus a variable is used as pattern for an isolated entity of the same function. In this way constructions like *wrongly* from *wrong* were used as pattern for remodeling flat adverbs such as *slow* to *slowly.*

In the fourth rule, which deals with the results of analogy, Kurylowicz states that a new analogical form takes over the primary function of a contrast, while the replaced form is used for secondary functions. Thus *brothers* is used for the plural of *brother,* while the replaced *brethren* maintains a peripheral function; similarly *older* versus *elder* and so on. Yet again contrary examples can be provided, such as analogical forms introduced in the German article, *dessen,* which are used today in the relative pronoun, not the article itself. The two other rules are of less interest here.

A set of such general rules would be highly advantageous if they applied to prehistoric languages, such as Proto-Indo-European and pre-Indo-European. Kurylowicz has indeed applied them in this way, especially to problems of Indo-European morphophonemic variation of vowels and to accentual problems. Yet if the rules cannot be established in contemporary languages, their application to earlier periods may be artistic rather than scientific.

Mańczak's first rule, or in his terms hypothesis, at once illustrates the difference between his and Kurylowicz' approach. According to it, long words, except in paradigms, are more often remodeled after short words than vice versa. Thus *bridegroom* was remodeled after *groom,* not *groom* after **bridegoom.* By the second, the alternation of roots is more often abandoned than introduced; the gradual regularization of English strong verbs provides good support. The third rule states that a long inflectional form is more often remodeled after a short (excluding forms of which one has an ending, another none);

the French *chauffer* is from *calefare,* which was built on the present *calfat,* and replaced *calefacere.* By the fourth, zero endings are more often replaced by full endings than not; evidence may be provided from English noun plurals, where *word* : *word* has been replaced by *word* : *words.*

In additional formulae Mańczak indicates that base forms are more often than not the sources of analogy, such as the indicative, the present, common nouns versus geographical terms. Besides his restrained generalizations about analogy, Mańczak has also contributed to analogical theory by suggesting caution in rigid application of the widely used formula a : b :: a′ : x. As in the study of dialect geography it has become quite clear that languages are too complex to permit simple generalizations. Only when we have a complete understanding of all systems and sets in a given language can we suggest when modifications may result from analogy. Our chief aim in comprehending the working of analogy still is to understand its functioning in material we must account for.

11.8 As illustrated by the discussion above, analogy may be viewed as the central process in modifications introduced in grammatical systems. In Chapter 10 it was observed that sound change takes place by phonological sets, with no consideration of their morphological functioning. When it has taken place, however, its effects may be extended analogically, in morphological contrasts.

As examples of sound changes leading to change in grammatical systems we may cite instances from the Germanic languages, such as the pre-Old English umlaut change. When pre-OE *u* and *o* became *y* and *ø* before *i ī y,* a new contrastive marker was possible between many singular and plural forms, for *i ī y* was found especially in the plural. Yet in English this sound change affected the grammatical system only to a minor extent, for we have few plurals of the type *man* : *men, goose* : *geese.* In German on the other hand this sound change was widely extended, to provide one of the prominent plural markers. In this way sound changes may contribute to the possibility of new morphological contrastive devices, which then may be extended by analogy. Such a device has recently been made available by the loss of *-t* in some English final clusters. When *-t* is lost in *slept,* a new contrast *sleep* : *slep* yields new irregular verbs. This phonological change is too recent to predict its results in the morphological system.

As a result of such changes five or more millennia ago, the material was provided for one of the characteristic features of Indo-European languages, ablaut (see pages 104 and 105). Originally a result of sound changes—the loss of *e* in certain forms, for example, *nest* versus *sit,* the change of *e* to *o* > Gmc. *a* in others, *sat* versus *sit*—these contrasts were adapted for marking major morphological categories.

In this way the prime morphological modifications in languages are spread by analogy, though the innovations generalized may be a result of phonological change, or of some other process which has provided a useful characteristic marker for a set, such as borrowing. In the scientific terminology of today, certain entities have been widely spread, with a specific meaning. Thus *-ide* is used for hundreds of chemical compounds such as *chloride, fluoride,* apparently from the term *oxide,* which was borrowed from Fr. *oxide,* a neologism formed from Fr. *oxygène* + *acide*. The suffix *-ate* is found in many names of salts and esters formed from acids with names in *-ic,* for example, *nitrate* from *nitric acid* and so on. The suffix *-eme* has come to be used for entities in linguistics, from *phoneme* to *morpheme* to *grapheme,* and others. Analogy in this way has been useful in expanding and regularizing the derivational system of the greatly expanding vocabularies of contemporary languages as it has served to enlarge and regularize their inflectional and syntactic systems.

The source of the material used in analogy is irrelevant. Any segment of the language may be generalized, whether its origin is in sound change or borrowing, or whether it is simply an extended segment of the language, like OE *-ling,* which seems useful for morphological marking. When new forms are made in a language by analogy, sets of some kind undergo expansion by means of linguistic material which leads to larger sets, and accordingly to greater regularity in the language.

SELECTED FURTHER READINGS

Like sound change, analogy is one of the subjects widely treated in handbooks. Bloomfield's *Language,* pages 404–24, Sturtevant's *An Introduction to Linguistic Science,* pages 96–109, and Paul's *Prinzipien der Sprachgeschichte,* pages 106–20, have well-chosen examples. For a fuller treatment of the relations between sound change and analogy see E. Hermann's *Lautgesetz und Analogie.*

The paper of Kurylowicz referred to, "La nature des procès dits 'analogiques,' " appeared in *Acta Linguistica,* 5.15–37 (1945–49), that of Mańczak, "Tendances generales des changements analogiques," in two issues of *Lingua,* 7.298–325 and 387–420 (1958). For an excellent recent work making extensive use of our understanding of analogy, see O. Szemerényi's *Studies in the Indo-European System of Numerals* (Heidelberg, 1960).

12 – Change in Semantic Systems

12.1 Change of meaning is readily apparent in any language for which we have a series of texts. As example we may cite *persona,* for which a considerable change of meaning can be substantiated in the several millennia over which it and its reflexes are found in Latin and English texts. When we first encounter *persona,* it means 'mask.' In Roman drama, masks were used on the stage, and varied in accordance with roles. Soon *persona* came to mean a 'character indicated by a mask,' thereupon a 'character' as such or a 'role in a play.' From this developed the meaning 'representative of a character,' then a 'representative in general.' For us its central meaning is 'representative of the human race,' except in such expressions as the 'three persons in the trinity,' a usage which has given rise to much discussion. A more restricted usage, 'representative of the church,' has survived in the form *parson,* which was not remodeled in pronunciation after the historical spelling. The word *persona* has accordingly undergone a considerable change, from referring to an article of stage costume through designation for concrete human roles to a general designation for man, all of which can be attested in Latin and subsequent English texts.

Even if we lacked these texts, we could make conjectures about its development of meaning by comparing Modern English usages like 'ten persons were at the meeting,' 'the three persons of the trinity,' and 'he is a parson.' Superseded meanings, as well as the central meaning, may be found in texts produced at one time, and may be used to suggest the change of meaning which a word has undergone. In the Old English *Beowulf,* for example, the etymon of *thank* is attested in a compound with the meaning, 'thought,' line 1060 *fore-þanc* 'forethought.' In *Beowulf* line 379 it means 'satisfaction, pleasure.' On the basis of further examples we can suggest a change of meaning for *thank* from 'thought' to 'favorable thought' to 'satisfaction' to 'expression of satisfaction.' Again numerous examples are available for conjecturing change of meaning in this way from texts for which we have no long succession of predecessors. Such conjectures, however, are much less certain than are conclusions supported by textual references from various periods.

As with *thank,* conjectures on meaning change may be supported by a third procedure, comparison with elements similar in form. It is scarcely hazardous to assume that *thank* is related to *think.* One may therefore suggest for it on the basis of etymology alone the earlier meaning which we find attested in Old English. Such suggestions however require caution, for as we have observed in the two previous chapters forms may be modified in accordance with various sets, not only semantic. If for example we had only the form Germ. *Sündflut* for the flood which Noah survived, we would relate the first element to *Sünde* 'sin' and assume *Sündflut* to be a compound, describing the long flood caused by man's sinfulness. Actually, from older forms we find the analysis wrong; the first component was modified by folk etymology from MHG *sin-*, a cognate of Lat. *senex* 'old man,' and meant the 'long-lasting' flood. Suggesting change of meaning on the basis of etymology or similarity of form may in this way be erroneous. The same caution applies when we attempt to reconstruct change of meaning from forms in related languages. We would have to know considerably more than the fact of their relationship to decide that of the pairs, Eng. *silly* : Germ. *selig* 'blessed,' the German form preserves the earlier meaning, while of the pair Eng. *cup* : Germ. *Kopf* 'head,' the English form does. We can conclude from comparisons of related forms which differ in meaning that change of meaning has indeed taken place. For its exact course, we speak with certainty only when we have texts in which the earlier as well as the later meanings are attested.

In discussing the changes in semantic systems, for convenience we deal with words. Actually, any morphological element may undergo semantic change. We can note it in affixes: *super-* in *superman* differs in meaning from its use as prefix in *superstition* or *superstructure*. On page 185, we noted how the segment *-burger* has changed markedly in meaning. We must make the same assumption for morphemes consisting of suprasegmental material, such as intonation patterns, but with our ignorance of suprasegmental morphemes of the past we cannot provide sure examples. Even though we hold that the principles of semantic change are evident in all morphological entities, for convenience we take examples from words; in discussing some languages, however, like the polysynthetic Eskimo, we would have to deal with morphemes. Yet a brief introduction to change of meaning is sufficiently complex even when we deal with gross and well-established examples, as in the words used for illustration in this chapter.

12.2 One complexity derives from the interest in meaning in fields other than linguistics. Meaning is a prime concern in the study of philosophy, literature, psychology, and similar disciplines. Each brings to the study of meaning its own approach—one which, with the possible exception of the literary student, concerns itself as much with the relation of a word, a linguistic **symbol,** to the object in real life, the **referent,** as to the notion it symbolizes, the **reference.** As a social scientist a linguist may be interested in the relation of symbol, referent and reference. He may for example concern himself with the relation between the symbol *green* and waves of light with a specific length; if he studies Japanese he will learn one counterpart of *green, aoi* for which the referent includes more wave-lengths than does *green.* As a linguist, however, he concerns himself only with the reference of the symbol *green,* with the contexts in which it is found. He must come to terms with compound references like "green roofs," "green dresses," and even that "a person may look green on an unsteady boat" or that "the moon is made of green cheese"—that it has the color of whey. Unless he limits his concern in this way, the study of meaning is the study of culture, a gallant but unlimited undertaking.

Many earlier studies of meaning have dealt with the referent as well as the reference, beginning with Plato's celebrated discussion in his dialogue *Cratylus.* Plato's inquiry whether there is an inherent connection between symbol and referent was unfortunately decided by words like *blackberry* rather than *cranberry.* Even with a correct solution the question is left by the linguist to the philosopher. Since the concern is an important one in learning to think clearly, many introductory treatises on language deal with it, so many that the term semantics seems preempted, and linguists have introduced new terms for the linguistic approach to meaning. Until one of these is established, it seems best to retain the terms *semantics* and *meaning* with the warning that they will have different referents, and references, in some other discussions.

12.3 Linguistically, the meaning of a word is the sum total of contexts in which it appears. Determining the meaning of an apparently uncomplicated word like *house* is a fair undertaking, especially without the help of data-processing equipment. In setting out to define *house* we would compile examples of its use. In

They live in the house over there.

house means a 'structure for human habitation.' To help circumscribe its meaning we attempt to find items that substitute for it, such as *home, cottage, cabin, hut, apartment building,* and so on. Another example may be

Drop in at the house after supper.

Again *house* means a 'structure for human habitation,' but though we might substitute for it *cottage, cabin,* even *hut, home* is an unlikely substitute as is *apartment building*. Apparently *house* has a broader range of contexts than does *home* or *apartment building*. Finding other contexts, such as

Their boy lives in one of the houses at Harvard.
Only the lower house is in session now.
The house roared with laughter.

would be essential in determining the meaning of *house*. One might note that the word is rare in certain technical dialects, such as that of realtors. Or its geographical distribution may be related to difference in frequency; *house* is still probably more frequently used in England than in America. Many speakers may use it only in "plain" contexts, reserving for emotional usage the word *home*. This attitude may even lead to its restriction to contexts of negative connotation. Fixing its range of meaning would include noting these limitations of usage in the various dialects.

Descriptive study, usually undertaken by lexicographers, provides the data by which historical linguists deal with change in meaning. Since words may overlap with others in their possible contexts, as does *house* with *hut, home,* etc., it has proved essential to deal with sets of words, rather than with individual words alone. In such study, based in part on the work of J. Trier, the words which fall into a context or set of contexts have been referred to as an "associative field." When investigating change of meaning, we accordingly do not limit our analysis to single words and their contexts, but rather treat the set of words which may fill a given context or set of contexts; a structural approach is as important in semantic study, as in phonological and grammatical study.

To represent the interrelationships as well as the definitions or meanings of words, we may use sets of circles. For *house* the circle on the one hand would overlap with those for *hut, home,*

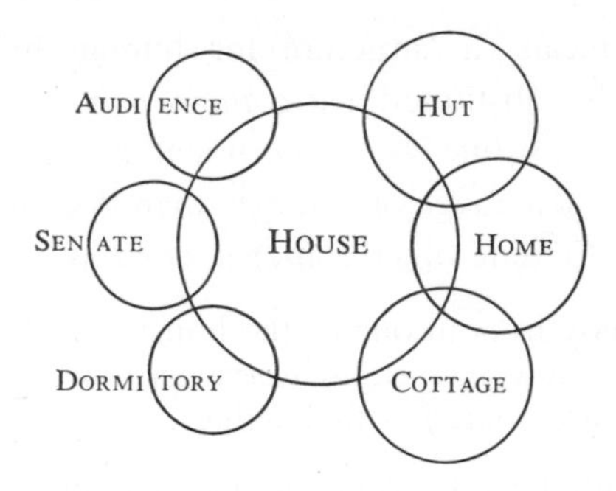

cottage, but also with those for *dormitory, senate, audience*. The right section of the circle represents the meaning of *house* as 'habitation'; sections on the left represent its meanings as 'a building belonging to a university,' 'a governing body,' and 'a group of onlookers,' leaving space for still other meanings. Similar sets of circles could be produced to represent the meanings of various words and fields throughout the language.

Much of the study of meaning in historical linguistics has dealt with attempts to determine reasons for change, rather than to describe the changes themselves.

In a celebrated article, "Comment les mots changent de sens," *Linguistique historique et linguistique générale,* 1.230–271, Meillet proposes three causes for semantic change.

The first of these, changes due to the use of words as contexts change, is also the least productive. An example is the restriction of meaning of French *pas, personne, rien, jamais;* when *ne* was omitted, these came to have a negative meaning.

The second results from change in the reference; an example is the contemporary meaning of *pen* for a writing implement dispensing some kind of fluid ink, no longer a quill. Among such changes Meillet classes those resulting from taboo. One can readily cite circumlocutions for nonfavored objects, such as Gk. *aristerós* 'better' for 'left (hand),' *left,* itself from an Old English word for 'weak,' Lat. *sinister* 'more useful,' itself replaced by *gauche* in French, which too has an unfavorable connotation. The Slavs and Welsh substituted so commonly for 'bear' the circumlocution 'honey-eater,' 'honey-pig,' that the original was lost from their languages. Through enforced disuse of the tetragrammaton JHWH, the Hebrews lost knowledge of its pronunciation.

Many tabooed words are restricted in usage only in certain social situations, so that the word is not totally lost from the language. The attempts to ban *Lady Chatterley's Lover* were determined in part by Lawrence's use of a term tabooed in print; at least from 1939 to 1945, however, and probably since, it has been one of the most widely used words in the language.

With his tremendous interest in language as a social phenomenon, Meillet dealt at greatest length with the third cause he proposed for semantic changes, the interrelations of various social groups. An example is the specialized use of 'elder,' Gk. *presbúteros* by the early Christians; this came to be a part of their technical language and as *presbyter,* later *priest* has retained its specialized meaning, besides leading to a modification of *elder*. In his further examples Meillet was concerned with demonstrating how historical, social and linguistic facts interact to bring about changes of meaning.

The examination of emotive processes in change of meaning, a shortcoming in Meillet's treatment, has been undertaken in many contexts by Hans Sperber. For him the particular emotive connotation of any word is important in bringing about changes of meaning. These are frequent and readily demonstrated especially in areas of strong emotions, such as religion, politics, war. The change of meaning of Germ. *Kopf,* from 'cup' to 'head,' for example, is to be ascribed to the spread of use from a spirited way of referring to head-smashing in battle. While of interest, accounting for changes in meaning is not the historical linguist's first concern. As in historical phonology, our procedure is not to explain why we say *father* rather than *pater,* but rather to relate the two, so in studying semantic change our first task is the relating of same or different words in different stages of a language.

A century ago, the statement

They live in the hogan over there.

may not have been unexpected, in some geographical areas. Now residents of the area are more apt to live in ranch-type houses. A linguist establishes the fact of change, leaving its explanation to the anthropologist. Conversely,

They live in the home over there.

was not likely a century ago. Again, cultural anthropology may concern itself with the reason. For an understanding of language, and the interpretation of different languages, such explanations are not disregarded by historical linguists, but they must first deal with semantic changes as linguistic phenomena, then as facets of culture.

12.4 Regarding our primary concern the change of context of linguistic symbols, we may classify semantic changes under these headings:

1. reduction in contexts (to total loss)
2. expansion in contexts
3. alteration of contexts.

The last is the most complex, for under it we deal with shifts from one geographical, technical or social dialect to another, the most frequent type of meaning change.

12.5 Reduction in context may be illustrated from virtually any segment of the vocabulary, but our first examples will again be taken from the sphere of human habitation. With the favoring of *home* by salesmen who find more profitable the connotation of a fireplace with a happy family than that of a solid, long-lasting structure, *house* has been considerably reduced in context, as has *stable,* and other appurtenances of the happy home of the past. When Lord Atlee was interviewed by a reporter for the *New Yorker,* 3 June 1961, pages 26–7, in a statement interesting in general for its play with changes of meaning, he aroused from his memory a term which is scarcely expected today in this context, the last term of this quotation:

> That's another question Americans are always asking: "How do you like your socialized medicine?" I've no trouble with that one. "How do you like your socialized plumbing?" I ask them. "Or are you still using the old bucket?"

For most contemporary dialects of English, the term *bucket* has virtually been reduced to zero, certainly in the context called up by Lord Atlee.

As the context of words is reduced, they often survive in restricted patterns, or with former peripheral meanings. For the Greeks *myth* meant 'story'; for us it is a special kind of story, whose truth exists largely in the imagination. Formerly in English *ghost* meant 'spirit,' a meaning surviving in the specialized context *Holy Ghost* and evident in the German cognate *Geist.* Similarly *deer* = Germ. *Tier* 'animal' is now restricted in use for one of the commonest wild animals.

Such narrowing may sometimes be ascribed to omission of a modifier. The word 'undertaker' once meant in English 'one who undertakes,' 'an energetic promoter.' One translation of the twenty-third psalm began: 'The Lord is my undertaker.'

A common context in which it was used was that of *funeral undertaker; funeral* then was omitted, and until morticians thought they could sweeten their trade with a new name, the chief context for *undertaker* was for men who assist in the obsequies for the dead. Similarly, *main* came to be used for 'main ocean,' as in *the Spanish Main; mainland* on the other hand was retained as a compound. As restrictions resulting from loss of words we may cite *fall* 'autumn' from 'fall of leaves,' *private* 'lowest-ranking soldier' from 'private soldier.'

Whatever the process leading to restrictions, many further such examples could be cited. The individual course of change would have to be documented for each by observing its own changing contexts and those of the other words in its field.

12.6 Other words may be expanded in possibility of contexts. With proliferation of the 'haves' the term *pool* or *swimming pool* has experienced a broad increase in distribution, as did earlier *garage* at the expense of *stable*. In some regions, *landing strip* is equally favored. Other words referring to transportation by air have risen considerably in number of contexts used. The term *plane* was formerly found largely in modest contexts of scientific materials. Until it is restricted by the knowledgeable younger generation who scorn it in favor of *B–57, 707, DC–8,* and the like, it has a tremendous range and frequency. Other items used in its linguistic environment, *rev up, jet, flame-out* and so on have extended their contexts from near zero.

We can also cite examples of extension in context from the past. A *picture* formerly was something painted; now we can have our *picture taken* with a Brownie kodak. For the Romans, *virtue* was the quality one expected in a *vir* 'man': a compound of bravery, truthfulness, capability with arms, and so on. It then came to be applied generally for moral excellence; to the probably total disbelief of any Roman we today may speak of a 'virtuous woman.' Similarly for the Romans a *street, strata via,* was a 'paved way.' In the course of time it came to represent any passage reasonably capable of progress by vehicle.

Some procedures for such widening of context may be observed today in the expansion of comfortable living. With the increased frequency of little homes in suburbia came increased prestige for linguistic items suggesting life in the hills west of the city. Lots sell rapidly on 'trails' and 'lanes.' While *avenues* were formerly the grand entrances for cities, they may now be the ways on which commercial firms are located, with the former favorable meaning maintained only where some modicum of urban elegance is retained, as on *Fifth Avenue* or *Pennsylvania Avenue.* The formerly humble *trail* and *lane* have in this way outdistanced *avenue* in number of favorable contexts. What entrepreneurs will do in the future when all the haves live on *trails* and the have-mores are in search of suitable housing will provide students of semantic change further examples of expansion in context.

Such expansion may also be noted for entities with a specific meaning which are not words or even morphemes. In English the *fl*-cluster has been extended widely as in *flame, flare, flap, flex, flicker, flounce, flutter,* all of which have the meaning of motion, generally rapid. Further such patterns, such as the consonant doubling found in early German, as in names such as *Anno, Ezzo,* or the present-day pattern for names of endearment using a single syllable plus /iy/, as in *Bobbie, Lucy, Tommie,* are comparable in extension to morphological affixes, but also to words such as *trail, lane;* for like these their extension results from use in favorable reference.

12.7 With the tremendous number of geographical, technical, and social dialects and their interaction in the complex languages of today, semantic change by alteration of context is readily attested. If in the Northeast we hear speakers referring to a cottage for summer relaxation as a *camp,* we may modify our dialect accordingly. If we are in contact with professionals in housing, or even are simply reading ads, we may acquire terms like *split level, Cape Cod bungalow,* or extend our use of *estate* and *ranch* to a plot of an acre or less in a new housing development. Whatever our associations, we are prepared to expand locutions for one uncomfortable but necessary area of habitations, whether *bathroom, dressing room, john, WC,* possibly, but scarcely likely, even *toilet.* We and our fellow-speakers may find more effective means of communication by reaching into the dialects of high prestige, a technical dialect in current favor such as that of rocket specialists, or we may transfer words from a predominantly substandard context to one widely tolerated or even favored.

Of the various contexts which are altered, those of technical dialects are now the most frequent. Intellectual historians may look to meteorology, and speak of a *climate* of opinion. This may undergo a *renaissance,* with *nerves* of communication strengthened, especially for those who are *off center.* The technical dialects of sports have been widely exploited in English. In building a strong group one tries to avoid *bush leaguers* (baseball) or those who might *show the white feather* (cock-fighting) or those with a *bias* (bowling), otherwise one may find himself *out in left field* as far as the competition is concerned. When the former meaning is still the more prominent, we may call such transfers of context **metaphors.** In the course of time, the new meanings may prevail and cause the metaphor to fade. Today we scarcely think of the former meaning of *decide* 'cut off' or *detail* 'cut in pieces' as we *bat around* a topic. The alteration of context is complete.

Often the shift is from a serene to an emotionally active context, which corresponds to the **hyperbole** of literary analysis. *Astonish,* somewhat like *stun,* once meant 'strike by thunder.' In Shakespeare's *King Henry the Fifth,* Act 5, Scene 1, Gower points out to Fluellen that he astonished Pistol when he struck him a second time. Such shifts seem to lead to a less vivid meaning, as may be illustrated by words of strong assent, e.g. *cer-*

tainly, sure, indeed—which today have less force than does *yes*. Similarly, words which indicate degree, especially of behavior or appearance, such as *fine*, which now is scarcely more satisfactory than *superb, grand, perfect, magnificent, great.*

Similar shifts of context are attested for terms of address as for instance the Spanish *don, doña,* from Lat. *dominus, domina* 'lord, mistress.' In French, *domina* gave rise to *dame, madame.* The similar German *Herr,* like Eng. *Mister,* scarcely carries the connotation of mastery today. When generalized, lofty terms come to take on meanings resembling their everyday contexts. Some terms, in shifting from an indication of social to moral inferiority, have undergone even less favorable change. A *villain* was once a worker at a *villa;* other terms for rural work which have developed similarly are *churl* < OE *ceorl* 'common man, farmer' and *boor*—compare the stolid Dutch farmers who settled South Africa. A *knave* as in the *Knave of Hearts* was a boy, see Germ. *Knabe.* Terms for government officials may also suffer, for example, *publican* 'a public servant' or *cheater,* earlier *escheater,* an officer whose duty it was to collect rent.

12.8 Shifts of context which in this way bring about shifts of meaning provide the simplest examples by which we may explain semantic change. When a real estate agent reaches for a term from a different context, such as *broker,* he has brought about a shift in meaning—which may be followed by another if the attitude of the general public towards real estate brokers remains unchanged. Similarly when a stony lake-side lot is widely advertised as an *estate,* brokers undermine with their own status that of a segment of the language.

Some shifts represent general cultural or geographical changes, rather than those introduced by a class of imaginative speakers. When people from Britain settled America they gave a red-breasted thrush the name of their *robin,* a much smaller bird with similar coloring. A *holiday* is not merely a sacred festival day any longer, but rather any day in which one engages in more than usually vigorous activities.

Other shifts follow general attitudes of the speakers. When members of a society consider it essential to use a circumlocution for a tabooed term, it may change entirely to the new meaning. *Bear* is scarcely 'the brown one' for any speaker of English today. Various words were changed in meaning as they were introduced for the tabooed names for *hand, left, right* in Indo-European languages, as we may illustrate from the panoply of Indo-European words for *hand*—OE *folm,* Skt. *hastas,* Gk. *kheír,* Lat. *manus,* Lith. *rankà,* Goth. *handus*. As we have already noted, words are more commonly restricted through taboo to certain contexts than led to extinction.

Other shifts merely indicate overpowering linguistic sets. NE *demean* simply resembles *mean* too closely for speakers to retain the use 'comport oneself.' NE *presently* in much the same way looks like the adverb for *present* rather than a word meaning 'in the future.'

From these examples we may note that the same forces are at work in semantic change as in phonological change: the position of words in a set, or field; the effect of homonyms, of social attitudes such as taboos, of innovating individuals, of contacts with other languages or dialects. Change of meaning is more complex than is sound change, however, for sets based on either the linguistic symbol or its reference are involved. We then find that the various forces may have a twofold effect: either through the symbol, as in *demean,* or through the reference, as in *publican,* or both sets may be involved in a composite effect, as in *hamburger*.

As with sound change, a distinction must be made between the shift itself and its dissemination. Every small group of speakers is familiar with shifts in meaning for certain words, often tabooed words for which a child's aberrant usage or mispronunciation has provided the material, but few of these are widely disseminated. Some organs of our culture may do such service: toilet equipment for babies may be sold as *toidy seats;* retailers of pet supplies would probably scandalize Oriental potentates by selling *dog divans.* Other such terms, mercifully, scarcely survive a generation. To understand any such shifts in meaning one must know the context in which they first appear, and the conditions which assure their continuation. With the greater energy devoted to language study today, examples are commonly available, as in the journal *American Speech.*

12.9 When semantic shifts have taken place, relics of former meanings may survive in restricted usages, such as *ghost* 'spirit' in *Holy Ghost, meat* 'food' in *nut-meats,* and so on. These assist us to a limited extent in reconstructing earlier features of a culture; they are scarcely useful for this purpose except for linguistic groups of which the only certain surviving segment of culture is the language, for instance the Indo-European community. Archeology has yielded materials from the time of this community, but in the absence of literacy we cannot relate artifacts to speech, or determine which archeological findings are to be associated with given linguistic groups. The linguistic possibilities we have for reconstructing the culture of the Indo-European community have been exploited by study known as **linguistic palaeontology.** With the uncertain bases available in a reconstructed language for reconstructing a culture there have been many disputes over its conclusions, especially since they have often been modified by modern nationalism. For some palaeontologists it has been important that the "home of the Indo-Europeans" be located on German territory, for others on Polish, or elsewhere for still others whose nationalism outweighs their scholarly capabilities. In spite of these problems, the possible contributions of linguistic palaeontology for prehistory are so important that its techniques must be noted; for through archeological finds we cannot now predict we may at some time be able to relate some of the prehistoric communities of Europe and Asia with the Indo-Europeans, and in this way improve our knowledge of the history of a part of mankind—thereupon applying established techniques to other prehistoric communities.

By linguistic analysis we reconstruct for Proto-Indo-European many items which tell us little about the culture of its speakers—grammatical markers, verbs like 'go, bear, taste, know,' nouns like 'eye, water, tree, father.' But besides these are words which give us such information. When we find terms for 'father, mother, brother, sister, son, daughter, daughter-in-law,' and others which indicate a close relationship with the son's wife but not between a man and his in-laws, we conclude that in the Indo-European community the family was not matriarchal. The term for the father of the wife in Greek, *pentherós*—from the root in our word *bind*—by indicating the secondary relationship between the wife's family and the husband's, supports this conclusion.

Proceeding to more complex social groups, in Skt. *dámpatis* = Gk. *despótēs* 'head of the *dam* = *domus* "house"' there is evidence for a social organization governed by a petty chieftain. Similarly, from Lith. *viẽšpats,* Skt. *viśpatis* 'head of the dwellings,' see Gk. *oîkos*. But the absence of general terms for leaders of larger social groups requires us to conclude that social organizations in the Indo-European community were restricted in size. A word for 'ruler,' related to the Latin verb *regere* 'guide' is found in Lat. *rēx,* Ir. *rī,* Skt. *rā́j-,* but other dialects have different terms, such as Gk. *basileús,* OE *cyning,* OCS *cěsar'i* from the Lat. *Caesar* and late OCS *kral'i* from the later widely known ruler Carolus, i.e., *Charlemagne*. Accordingly we may posit for the Indo-European community a well-developed family system, but no higher social or political organization.

Proceeding to the everyday life of the Indo-European community we find terms for 'herd, cow, sheep, goat, pig, dog, horse, wolf, bear—goose, duck, bee—oak, beech, willow, grain.' The lack of specific terms for grains or vegetables indicates a heavy reliance on animals for food.

The terms for 'beech, bee, salmon' and others have been used for the additional purpose of attempting to pinpoint the original home of the Indo-European speech community, with varying results. One problem involved may be illustrated by a word considered among the most reliable evidence, that for 'beech,' for it may have undergone shifts in meaning—Gk. *phēgós,* cognate with *beech,* means 'oak.' Yet the restricted range of the beech to north and central Europe has been widely used in locating the home of the Indo-Europeans. Another problem may be illustrated by the word, Germ. *Lachs,* which some scholars ascribe to the Indo-European vocabulary, concluding further that the salmon concerned is *Salmo salar,* which is found in the waters of northern Europe, though a similar fish exists in the waters flowing into the Caspian. Such possibilities of interpreting variously the words, and their meaning in prehistoric times illustrates the problems involved in attempting to determine the home of the Indo-Europeans.

The time during which the Indo-European community flourished has been subject to less dispute. When we attempt to reconstruct words for metals, we can ascribe to the Indo-European vocabulary no words even for 'silver' or 'gold,' let alone 'iron,' and scarcely even a general term for 'metal, bronze, copper,' Lat. *aes,* OE *ār*, NE *ore,* Skt. *ayas.* On the basis of such vocabulary, we put the Indo-European community at the end of the Neolithic period.

Adequate procedures to deal with meaning change are then of interest not only for our understanding of language and its historical development, but may yield additional results. Since meaning is at once the most complex and least satisfactorily investigated area of language, we can scarcely expect the study of semantic change to have achieved the goals we expect for it. We may however consider the techniques for determining semantic change well developed. When they are applied to the quantities of language data which can now be processed, we will be able to deal more confidently with the bases for semantic change.

SELECTED FURTHER READINGS

For a reliable introduction to change of meaning, see S. Ullmann, *The Principles of Semantics,* especially pages 171–257. Ullmann gives a thorough discussion of previous work, in addition to an approach of his own and a lengthy bibliography. Further discussion of the principles involved in the study of meaning may be found in *Einführung in die Bedeutungslehre* by Hans Sperber, one of the scholars who has devoted much time to its problems. In a long article, "Language, Society and Culture," *Norsk Tidsskrift for Sprogvidenskap,* 17.5–81, Alf Sommerfelt deals with meaning in its social setting.

J. B. Greenough and G. L. Kittredge, *Words and Their Ways in English Speech* provides an interesting discussion of various types of meaning change in English; its prime interest today is for its examples, some of which were used here, rather than their analysis.

Any student interested in linguistics has probably made thorough use of the data available in his dictionary, whether Webster's *Collegiate* or another desk dictionary. Historical linguists should also acquire the standard etymological dictionaries for their fields of specialty, Skeat for English, Kluge for German and so on. Because of the price, they probably will be restricted to library use of the *Oxford English Dictionary* and C. D. Buck's *A Dictionary of Selected Synonyms in the Principal Indo-European Languages,* a copious source for the study of semantic change, as well as a good portion of the Indo-European vocabulary—with sober comments on the conclusions which may be drawn about Indo-European culture.

13 – Borrowing: Influence of One Language or Dialect on Another

13.1 When we examine virtually any material in English, we find segments varying in origin. In the passage from Shakespeare's poetry, quoted in sections 1.1, we noted that some words were native Germanic, others introduced from outside the Germanic branch of Indo-European. A further example, *poet,* was imported into Middle English from OFr. *poete* < Lat. *poēta* < Gk. *poiētḗs* 'maker,' compare Gk. *poieîn* 'make.' The Proto-Indo-European root *k^wey-,* from which the Greek forms developed, gives us secure evidence that *poet* cannot be a native Germanic word, that it could scarcely be anything but a Greek development from Proto-Indo-European. For the Proto-Indo-European labiovelars, such as *k^w,* would have yielded velars in Germanic, but in Greek before *a* and *o* they characteristically yielded labials. On the other hand, *word* can be taken back to OE *word,* compare OHG *wort,* ON *orð,* Goth. *waurd.* It cannot be an importation from likely neighboring languages; in Latin the final consonant of the stem, PIE *-dh-,* shows up as *b* in *verbum;* in some dialects of Greek the initial *w* would have been lost, as in the probable cognate *eírein* 'speak.'

The vocabulary and grammatical patterns of a language can in this way be separated into two categories: **native elements,** which we can take back to the earliest known stages of a language, and **borrowed elements,** which were imported at some time from a different language.

Native words we deal with in accordance with the findings discussed in the last three chapters. As items in the stock of the language they are subject to phonological, morphological and semantic change. Borrowed forms are also subject to such change, but differ from native forms in their mode of entry into a language. This may be of various types, just as the types of contact between languages may differ. That between English and French differs appreciably from that between English and Arabic, even though Arabic words as well as French words have been borrowed into English. The influence of French on English, however, is immeasurably greater than is that of Arabic. Similarly the types of contact between any two dialects, whether geographical, social or technical, may differ, and as a result have different effects. In dealing with borrowings, then, we must examine the types of contact which have been common between languages and note the results in them, with inferences we can make generally about the types of contact between two or more languages or dialects.

Any linguistic item may therefore be identified either as native or borrowed. We find borrowings more common at the higher levels of a language. At the phonological and morphological levels virtually all elements of any language are native. Borrowings of vocabulary are especially likely, next those of syntactic patterns; morphological patterns are rarely borrowed, and phonological patterns even less commonly. Borrowings may, however, have an effect on the phonological structure of a language, as /ž/ in English, or even be instrumental in introducing phonemes, as for example Skt. /ṭ ṭh ḍ ḍh/. In dealing with borrowings it is of interest to note the various types, and to attempt to understand the processes by which borrowings are made into any given language.

13.2 We may classify borrowings by the type of reproduction of entities from a second language. Some borrowings, known as **loanwords,** mirror the phonemes of the foreign language. In Eng. *poet,* for example, the French phonemes were reproduced almost exactly in English. Most recent borrowings are of this type, though they may be based on written forms; words like *oxygen, hydrogen, telephone* are made up of entities borrowed from Greek.

Borrowings of a different type reproduce the morphemes of a foreign language, using native material. An example in English is *gospel* 'good story' in which the Greek components *eü* and *aggélion* are reproduced by translation. These are known as **loan-shifts, loan translations,** or as **calques.** In German, loan-shifts are particularly prominent; instead of taking over the Greek components for 'acid' and 'material' as did English in *oxygen,* German translated them to form the loan-shift *Sauerstoff.* Similarly *Wasserstoff* is a loan-shift for 'hydrogen,' *Fernsprecher* for 'telephone,' and so on.

In a further type of borrowing, only the meaning of a linguistic entity may be changed. OE *eorl* 'earl' meant 'brave warrior': the present meaning was taken over from Old Norse, where it was a rank of nobility. Similarly, OE *dwellan* meant 'lead astray' but was modified in meaning by ON *dvelja* 'abide' to present-day 'dwell.' Changes in meaning under the influence of a foreign language are known as **extensions.**

13.3 To understand borrowings of various types we must know the degree of command which speakers have of the languages in question. For the extent of reproduction is often determined by the extent of control which speakers have acquired of a second language, especially before conventions of borrowing have been established.

We may illustrate possible modifications by noting how English words are treated in Japanese. The English word *violin* is reproduced variously depending on the speaker's command over English. Educated speakers may use a very similar form when they speak Japanese, i.e. *vaiorin,* even though their own language does not contain a /v/. Less educated speakers substitute for English *v* either /w/ or /b/, to say *waiorin* or *baiorin.* Both sets of speakers reproduce *l* as *r*. But especially among noneducated speakers, borrowings show substitution of phonemic, not phonetic, entities.

The role of phonemic structure in borrowings may be illustrated through the treatment of English *t* in Japanese. The stop [t] occurs in Japanese only before [e a o]; before [u] we find the affricate [ts], before [i y] the affricate [tš]. If a word like *tank* is borrowed into Japanese, the result is *tanku,* different only in the mandatory final vowel. For *touring* the Japanese form is *tsuringu,* for *team* and *tube, tšiimu* and *tšyuubu.* [t ts tš] are in complementary distribution in Japanese, by one analysis members of the same phoneme. Naive speakers automatically substitute any of the allophones of /t/ in accordance with their distribution before following vowels.

To illustrate a different treatment we may note the forms of *jet* in Japanese. Like [tš], [dž] may occur in Japanese only before [i] and [y]; *jib* is then taken over with the similar pronunciation [džibu]. Before [e a o], on the other hand, [z] is found, in complementary distribution with [dž]. With these limitations of the Japanese phonological structure, the word *jet* has been borrowed in two forms: [džietto] and [zetto]. In the first the initial consonant is similar to that of English, with vowel modification; in the second the vowel is unchanged but the initial consonant has been altered.

For the examples cited, knowledge of the phonological structure of Japanese and English is necessary to explain the Japanese forms. One must know the allophones of the English phonemes, and their possible Japanese counterparts. The English words have undergone modifications determined largely by the possibilities in Japanese.

Morphological modifications are similarly brought about by the structure of the borrowing language, for borrowings generally take on the patterns of native elements. When, for example, *bask* was borrowed into Old English from Old Norse *báða sik* 'bathe oneself' and *busk* from Old Norse *búa sik* 'ready oneself,' they were treated like simple verbs in English. For reflexives were not combined with verbs in English, and accordingly the speakers failed to recognize the final pronouns. To be sure, foreign inflections may occasionally be maintained, especially by sophisticated speakers. Many nouns were imported into English with their Latin or Greek plural inflections, such as *datum* : *data, colon* : *cola, skeleton* : *skeleta, maximum* : *maxima,* and so on. Except in learned contexts, these now make their plurals in *-s,* with the exception of the first, *data,* which is being fitted differently into the English pattern. It is increasingly treated as a singular: *the data is . . .* ; in this way it, too, is fitted into the English grammatical structure.

Similarly in Japanese, borrowings are equipped with the Japanese morphological markers. Words borrowed into Japanese from Chinese such as *kenkyuu* 'study' were treated as verbs with the addition of *suru* 'do,' *shita* 'did,' e.g., *kenkyuu shita* 'studied.' When English words were borrowed into Japanese, they, too, followed this pattern. The loanword *purosesu* 'process' may be accompanied by forms of *suru,* as is *taipu* 'type' and many others. The large number of borrowings into Japanese from Chinese and English in this way was provided with inflections though no new morphological markers were introduced.

Further, syntactic expressions borrowed from another language are difficult to maintain. English *marriage of convenience* < Fr. *mariage de convenance* 'marriage for advantage' when used today is generally cited with an indication of its original meaning, to avoid misunderstanding. The phrase *it goes without saying* < Fr. *aller sans dire* has apparently become established among some speakers. Yet neither of these expressions has affected the language deeply. A more widespread example of syntactic borrowing may be the German favoring of highly complicated sentence patterns, a result of the influence of Latin syntax. As with other supposed borrowings of syntactic patterns, such as the introduction of numerary adjuncts into Japanese from Chinese, the evidence is not conclusive. As in the examples cited above, the clearest instances of borrowing are in the lexical and semantic sphere.

13.4 We may view borrowings as instances of cultural diffusion and acculturation. In doing so, we must attempt to determine the conditions under which they are made. Various situations in the history of English provide us with good examples; for various types of language contact can be attested for English, with differing effects on the language.

The first of these was contact with Celtic speakers. When English was brought to the British Isles in the fifth century A.D., presumably there was a preponderance of Celtic speakers, a minority of Germanic invaders. Yet English survived and ousted Celtic. Moreover, it adopted very few words from Celtic, a few common nouns like *bannock* 'cake' and *brock* 'badger,' and numerous place-names, such as *London, Thames, Dover*. The resulting linguistic situation is much like that of American English vis-à-vis the American Indian languages. A few nouns from American Indian languages were borrowed: *tomahawk, skunk,* and numerous place-names, such as *Chicago, Mississippi, Kentucky*. The two linguistic situations had much in common; from them, with the support of other parallels, we can suggest the typical situation in which few borrowings are made.

When speakers learn a new prestige language, they are under social pressure to acquire it without flaws. They speak the acquired language as accurately as possible and avoid carrying over into it items from their native language. Examples may be taken from America in the nineteenth century. Immigrants who came to this country attempted to learn accurate English, though their own language was grossly modified, often with importations from English. In the German area of Chicago a mixed German was referred to as *die schönste lengevitsch.* It consisted in great part of German structures filled with borrowings from English. On the basis of this situation, and those just cited, we may conclude that speakers modify the language they are certain of much more readily than they do a language which they know imperfectly and attempt to use without loss of prestige.

As a further well-documented example we may cite Germany in the eighteenth century. At the courts French was the language of prestige, German that of everyday communication. Frederick the Great of Prussia considered German a language fit for peasants. He often wrote French; when he did, he avoided German importations. His German letters on the other hand abound with French loanwords.

From these and other examples we may view the English–Celtic relationship as a typical situation in the contact of languages. Old English was regarded as the language of cultural prestige. Though they may have been preponderant numerically, native Celtic speakers set out to learn English, gradually abandoning their native language. In the course of time an English resulted with few importations. Apart from place-names—which had a healthy rate of survival before modern political revolutions—only those items were borrowed from the receding into the dominant language for which the dominant language had no readily available terms. Such replacement represents one of the least complex situations of language contact.

Although we have no contemporary evidence for this type of language interrelationship in many prehistoric situations, from the results we may assume it for other areas. It is especially relevant in the spread of Indo-European languages: of

Hittite into Anatolia, of Greek into the Hellenic peninsula, of Italic into Italy, even of Indic into India, although in India there was considerable phonological modification resulting from the borrowing of cacuminals. This situation applied also for the spread of Arabic, which was adopted from Iraq to Morocco with little change in structure. Except for special situations discussed below, it also applied for the spread in recent centuries of two of the most widely spoken languages today: Russian and English.

13.5 A second typical situation, English in the eleventh century, at first glance parallels that of the fifth century. A relatively small group of invaders took over political control of an established population and continued as the ruling class. Yet the results were quite different. In the centuries after 1066 Norman French was used by a small segment of the population, but eventually ousted by English.

We explain the different result by noting that the type of contact was completely different from that in the fifth century. During the eleventh and subsequent centuries the indigenous speakers adopted words for only those cultural spheres in which they maintained contact with the ruling classes. For everyday communication they used their own language. We may illustrate this restriction of contact by noting the spheres of borrowing.

One notable sphere of borrowing was government and administration. A great number of English words in these areas was borrowed from French, for examples *council, country, crown, government, minister, nation, parliament, people, state*. For titles, *prince, duke, marquis, viscount, baron* were borrowed; only the native *earl* was kept, but the earl's wife is a *countess*, and *count* is the equivalent rank for foreign nobles. In the related area of heraldry, many French terms were taken over, including those for colors such as *sable, gules, vert*. Moreover, military words were borrowed: *armor, army, banner, navy, siege, war;* similarly, such legal terms as *court, crime, defendant, judge, jury, justice, plaintiff*. In the sphere of legal terminology, some oddities were introduced and maintained, presumably because of the extended period of French influence. Although English became the official language in 1362, legal French was not given up in courts of justice until 1731. The phrase *puis né* 'later born, inferior' was borrowed as an adjective, surviving in *puisne judge,* and more widely as *puny*. Moreover, some syntactic phrases, with adjective following noun, have been maintained: *attorney general, malice aforethought.*

The difference in social status of the two languages may be illustrated in contrasting words: for a small crime the English *theft* is used, for a serious one the French *larceny.*

Today, foods are still commonly said to reflect the social relation between the Norman French and their English subjects. English terms are used for animals in the field: *cow, calf, ox, sheep, boar, swine,* French for animals on the table: *beef, veal, mutton, bacon, pork*. Moreover, the humble meal, *breakfast,* has an English name, the more elegant *dinner* and *supper,* at which *jelly* and *pastry* may be served, have French names. The social relationship is further reflected in words for *sport* < *desport,* the *chase, falconry, cards* and *dice,* where even words for numbers were taken over: *ace, deuce, tray*. As with foods, names for artisans in the lower groups are English: *baker, fisherman, miller, shepherd, shoemaker, smith,* those in contact with upper classes are Norman French in origin: *carpenter, mason, painter, tailor.*

The general situation is clear. A few upper-class invaders maintained positions of prestige for some time, but gradually were replaced by speakers of English, or they themselves learned English. We conclude that the language of lesser prestige maintained itself because of the numerical, and eventually political, preponderance of its speakers. Yet the language of greater prestige has left a great effect on certain segments of the vocabulary.

Again we find this situation in other areas as well. The Dravidian languages of India have been maintained, though with numerous borrowings from Indic languages. In early Mesopotamia Akkadian ousted Sumerian, though it took over many words from the earlier language of prestige. When the Japanese became aware of the higher culture of China in the second half of the first millennium after Christ, they sent emissaries to China who imported with the higher culture a tremendous number of borrowings; but Japanese was maintained as the national language.

To a certain extent this type of contact exists today wherever western civilization and science are being imitated or adopted. Words like *electricity, telephone, airplane* are being introduced as loanwords or loan-shifts, though the structure of the native language is being maintained. We find a variety of parallels to the English-French contact, in which the invading language leaves a marked effect in the native language, without replacing it.

13.6 A third typical situation is the contact between English and Scandinavian, in the ninth to eleventh centuries. Both languages existed side by side for some time, until eventually Scandinavian was lost. But unlike Celtic several centuries earlier, it left a considerable imprint on English. This imprint, on the other hand, was not in higher segments of culture, as was the later Norman French influence, but extended through much of the everyday vocabulary. To be sure there were various martial and legal terms of Scandinavian origin in early English, but few of these have persisted; one that has remained, *bylaw* (by = village), has merely a vestige of its original sense.

The Scandinavian borrowings show no specific areas of cultural superiority. The term for a possible architectural improvement, *window* (wind-eye), merely replaced an older *eagþyrel* (eye-hole); it did not accompany a cultural innovation. Little more can be claimed for the borrowed *steak* and *knife*. Unlike

French, Scandinavian furnished many elements of the common vocabulary: *gift, husband, root, skill, skin, sky, wing; happy, loose, low, same, wrong; addle, call, die, drown, gape, get, give, hit, screech, take, want.* Still others may have been borrowed but cannot be identified, for many words were alike in tenth-century Old English and Old Norse.

Most interesting are grammatical elements: *they, them, their* have taken the place of older *hie, heom, heora.* In these borrowings the central core of the vocabulary was affected. On a much greater change in the language, the loss of grammatical distinctions in the inflections of English nouns and verbs, we can only speculate whether or not it was furthered by the contact between the two linguistic groups. We can tentatively suggest, however, that the type of contact existing between English and Scandinavian may have been one force in the morphological simplification of English.

This was a contrast between two languages of equal prestige. We are not certain to what extent the two were mutually intelligible; this question may also lack pertinence. For the significant point may be that the two languages were used for communication on an everyday level. The language with the larger number of speakers was maintained, though with simplification of structure.

Even further simplification is evident when speakers communicate only on simple cultural levels. A readily attested example may be found in baby-talk. In using it speakers may avoid lexical items that border on the grammatical, such as pronouns: *baby like candy?* In even less unabashed utterances, such as *baby go seepee,* we find phonological as well as morphological simplification. Such simplification, used not only to infants when attempting to convey affection, is very similar to that found in the so-called pidgin languages or creolized languages.

Pidgins (apparently a simplification of *business:* Chinese *p* = Eng. *b, ž* = *z,* yielding [pižinz] < [biznis]) have arisen in areas where men communicated on a very simple level. On the Chinese coast intercommunication was carried on in English for commerce; in the Pacific islands it was carried on for the direction of work. In South America, descendants of slaves evolved a simple common language called *taki-taki*. When as in Haiti such simplified languages are the sole languages of a community, they are referred to as **creolized languages.** To illustrate the changes which may take place when speakers are in contact on a low-cultural level interesting examples may be found in *Melanesian Pidgin English,* a study by Robert A. Hall, Jr.

Melanesian Pidgin is not learned as first language by any speaker except possibly by children of parents who cannot understand each other's language. It is spoken by speakers with a Melanesian or Papuan background, and by Europeans. When spoken, it is not uniform. Speakers carry over their native speech habits. Melanesians, for example, may pronounce voiced stops with prenasalization; *nəbawt* 'about' may be [nə^{m}bawt]. Germans may use *tæsɔl* 'but' like German aber, which corresponds to Eng. but and however.

In Melanesian Pidgin, the sound system of English was considerably simplified. There are no /θ ð z ž/; for instance, *this* is [dis], *nose* is [nos]. Further, in speaking Melanesian Pidgin English, Melanesians generally substitute the following:

[p] for [f v]: [pinis] = [finiš] 'already';
[æp] = [hæf] 'piece'
[s] for [š č]: [masin] = [mašin]
[š] or [tš] for [dž] as in [pičin]

[h] is omitted, as in [bi ajn] 'later.' Moreover, consonant clusters may be simplified by intercalating vowels, as in [gəris] for [gris] 'pig.'

In morphology, none of the bound forms of English are attested. There are however characteristic bound forms. The suffix *-felə* is used as an adjective suffix for monosyllables, and also for numerals, for example:

disfelə haws i-bigfelə	'this house is large'
tufelə pikinini	'two children'
nədərfelə səmtiŋ	'another thing'

It is also added to first and second person pronouns to indicate plurals:

mi	'I, me'	mifelə	'we, us'
ju	'you'	jufelə	'you'

Characteristic affixes are also used with verbs. *-im* is used as objective suffix for most verbs when transitive, as in

ju faytim pig 'you strike the pig'

A predicate marker is used as prefix, unless the subject is *mi, mifelə, ju, jufelə, jumi,* for example:

mašin i-bəgərəp finiš 'the machine is ruined.'

The syntax too is simple, with sequences of coordinated clauses.

In Melanesian and other pidgins, then, we see an extreme effect of language contact. A language is stripped down for the essentials of communication, with resulting phonological and morphological simplification. How often such processes of simplification took place in the past we do not know; whether the Assyrian merchants in Asia Minor used simplified forms of communication during the second millennium B.C.—or the Romans in Gaul—the Hittites in Asia Minor—the Phoenecians in their wanderings. Observing the simplification of structure in contemporary pidgin languages, we may wonder whether a somewhat similar situation may not have led to the form of English we find spoken after the tenth century, with its progressive loss of inflections, and to other, similar reductions of complexity in language structure.

13.7 In discussing these three types of contact we have dealt only with the relations of languages to each other. We must assume, however, similar types of contact between all different forms of speech: geographical dialects, social dialects, technical dialects and even idiolects. Borrowings are made from any such subtype to any other, from all of them into the general language. Illustrations could be given in abundance. For 'edible corn on the cob' the northern American *sweet corn* seems to be becoming the standard term rather than the southern *roasting ears*. With the interest in jazz many terms have been adopted into the standard language from uneducated speech, such as *the blues, reefers* for marijuana cigarettes, and so on. Technical dialects of the present have introduced so many new terms that we may forget the strong influence of those in the past. We are quite aware of the time of introduction of *x-ray, radium, irradiate, isotope*. Other sources in earlier times were from the technical terms of the ecclesiastical vocabulary. Our *noon* is from OE *nōn,* Lat. *nōna hōra* 'ninth hour,' the time of the nones, a service held originally at 3 P.M. but later shifted to 12 noon.

The extent to which these have been modified may be illustrated by our use of legal terms. For us, *subpoena,* originally a phrase meaning 'under penalty' can be used as a verb. *Affidavit,* on the other hand, a Latin verb form meaning 'he has pledged his faith' can today be a noun, as can *alibi,* 'elsewhere' in origin a Latin adverb.

Though genetics has changed our views on biological inheritance we still maintain the technical language of medieval science. We may excuse a failing by saying 'it's in my blood.' Our disposition we still refer to as our 'liquid,' OFr. *humor,* for according to medieval science there were four important liquids in man: blood, phlegm, bile, black bile. If one had too much blood he was *sanguine,* too much bile, *bilious,* too much phlegm, *phlegmatic,* too much black bile or melancholy, *melancholic*. If the liquids are in balance, one is *good-humored*. His *temperament* is also evident in the 'weaving together' of humors, and indicated on his face by his *complection,* now *complexion*.

Like those in medieval and modern English, borrowings

adopted in technical dialects are generally based on a learned language. In Arabic-speaking countries Classical Arabic is used as a source, in India, Sanskrit. In the languages of Western Europe, Latin and Greek are plundered for technical terms. Since European technology and science have been spread throughout the world, the influence of Latin and Greek has not been confined to Indo-European languages. Names of elements provide examples. The word for 'hydrogen' in Japanese is *suiso* 'water-substance,' the word for 'nitrogen' *chisso* 'suffocating substance,' and so on.

Often the translation or adaptation is not literal. In Chinese and Japanese the morph for 'electricity' is extended from the meaning 'lightning'; 'electricity' in Japanese is *denki* 'lightning spirit,' 'telephone' *denwa* 'lightning speech,' 'telegraph' *dempoo* 'lightning report,' and so on.

Moreover, the adaptations may fail to follow forms of the model. In linguistic terminology, for example, the proper Classical suffix for terms ending in *-eme* would be *-ematic; phonematic* would then be the Classical adjective for phoneme rather than *phonemic,* and so on. Yet the adjectival suffix *-ic* is so common, e.g. *base basic,* that it is applied to terms ending in *-eme* contrary to Classical practice. The complexities of such formations, and the attitudes of speakers towards them, are subjects of interest which have been inadequately explored.

In the multilayered contemporary languages we may find results of borrowings made at different times from the same ultimate source. In this way *frail,* ME *freyl,* was borrowed from OFr. *fraile,* which is from Lat. *fragilis,* the source of our *fragile; male* is from Fr. *mâle,* OFr. *masle,* which is from Lat. *masculus;* a derivative *masculīnus* is the source of *masculine,* and so on. Such related words are known as **doublets.**

13.8 Another contemporary source for adaptations is the written language. Abbreviations, such as *Prof.,* may be used as full words. With the expansion of government agencies many such terms have been incorporated into everyday speech; /yənéskòw/, UNESCO, from United Nations Economic, Social and Cultural Organization, may be as widely used today as /nəbískòw/, Nabisco, from National Biscuit Company, /yûw ès ès ár/, USSR, or in the Soviet Union, /és ès ès ér/. The written language has become such an important source for borrowings of this kind that new names for organizations are generally contrived so that they will provide suitable abbreviations.

Written languages have furnished other modifications for spoken languages. A slight novelty is the odd form of *ye* for the English definite article in the name *Ye olde gifte shoppe;* this arose from the use of *y* for *þ* when printing was introduced into England in the fifteenth century. If the form /yiy/ is only jocular and hardly more general than this context, the pronunciations /əšúwm/ or /əsyúwm/ for *assume,* /súwət/ or /syúwət/ for *suet* exemplify deeper modifications from the written language. The historically modified /š/ < /sy/ has been maintained only in *sure, assure, sugar,* and to some extent in *sumac,* while imitation of the written form has brought about change in pronunciation in *assume, consume, ensue, suet,* and others.

Influences from the written language indicate a socially favorable attitude of speakers towards it; the written language enjoys a higher prestige than does the spoken language. Spelling pronunciations, such as /índiyən índyən/ for *Indian* (compare Injun Joe in *Huckleberry Finn* and the British pronunciation /ínǰə/ for India) and /níygròw/ for *Negro* are considered to confer a dignity on the objects of the appellation which they may lack in the eyes of the speaker or other benighted users of the language.

When such influences are exerted, the effect of individual speakers may be as significant as is that of varying dialects. With the development of widespread education the idiolects of school teachers, for example, have exerted a considerable effect during the last few centuries on languages. Modifications such as those in *assume* may serve as one illustration. Virtually anyone can supply examples from his own schooling. A favorite target in some American schools was *aunt*. It was frequently considered undignified to label such a distinguished relative with a homonym for an insect. The spelling contributes a possible distinctive pronunciation, /áhnt/ /ɔhnt/ or the like. Another is *buoy;* it apparently wouldn't do to suggest that a youth was floating in the water directing traffic. Again the spelling furnishes a solution for the linguistically insecure.

Teachers and the bureaucracies supporting them may be responsible for even greater modifications in the language. Since the high front offglide used in parts of New York instead of retroflection in words like *bird* and *earl* has come to seem substandard, the whole weight of the New York school system has been thrown behind an effort to restore retroflection. School teachers are also undoubtedly responsible for depriving American English speakers of a negative in the first person of the auxiliary *be* parallel to *isn't, aren't, wasn't, weren't;* again /éynt/ has seemed undignified for products of a widespread educational system.

Such exertions have given rise to **hyperforms** in contemporary languages of culture. This term is used for forms which are attempted corrections, extended erroneously. Brooklyn children taught to modify /bəyd/ to /bərd/ in *bird* may extend their new learning to /bɔyd/ in *Boyd* or to /ɔyl/ in *oil,* and pronounce these something like *bird* and *earl*. German children, speaking dialects with unrounded vowels, may round vowels in which rounding is not present in the standard language; taught to change from [fílə] to [fýlə] in *Fülle* 'abundance,' they may also change the vowel in *bilden* 'cultivate' and speak 'gebüldetes Deutsch.' Such modifications may be introduced without aid from a teacher or a school system, merely in an attempt to speak like the folks in the city; they are therefore also known as **hyperurbanisms.**

Besides illustrating conflicting influences which result from differing dialects, hyperforms are examples of the effects of analogy. If one is taught to substitute *I* for *me* in contexts like *It wasn't me,* one may be led also to say 'with Mary and I.'

13.9 Whether spontaneous or induced, borrowing is one of the important influences on speech. In using speech one of our aims is adequate communication. To achieve the readiest communication, we constantly modify our phonological and grammatical systems and our vocabulary to the speech of our associates. If we wish to impress a fellow-speaker we may borrow a word of his, or imitate a pattern in his grammar. If he prefers a plural verb form after *data,* we may say 'the data are.' If he prefers the spelling pronunciations /lítəratyùwr néytyùwr/, we may adopt these. We may consider ourselves squares unless we adopt new extensions of meaning.

Whenever language is used, it is used for contact with others. Their different systems may bring about interference with ours, leading to changes in idiolect, dialect or language. The various types of individual contact and modifications are a part of general cultural contacts and their results. Effects on language structure vary with our patterns of culture. The problems involved in language contact, interference and modification are accordingly complex. Like other cultural problems they are now receiving serious attention, from which historical linguistics will profit. For the results will be highly useful for our understanding of language change.

Attempts, many of them oversimplifications, have been made in the past to account for language change through contact. Instead of dealing with the tremendous variety of relationships involved in language contact, linguists concerned themselves with the phonological habits of speakers, assuming that these persisted in the adoption of a new language. We now hold that articulatory habits are not inflexible; while the articulatory habits of adults may be difficult to modify, children learn with ease the language of their surroundings. Adult Gaulish speakers may have adopted Latin imperfectly; their children, however, could have learned it with the same mastery as that exhibited by their Latin playmates. Yet if two languages are spoken side by side over an extended period, either or both may be modified, as English has been in India. We can account through borrowing for many linguistic changes, especially in vocabulary.

13.10 Understanding of contact phenomena is important for historical linguistics as a diagnostic tool as well as the means to interpret the non-native segments of a language. For when items are introduced into a new language, they undergo different influences from those of their original language. By proper interpretation we may therefore gain information both about the imported language and the source language at a given time. For example, the [w] of Eng. *wine,* imported into the Germanic languages around the beginning of our era from Lat. *vinum,* informs us that at this time Latin *v* was pronounced [w]; when imported into English later from French, the pronunciation of *v* had changed to that of a labio-dental, as illustrated by *vine,* a doublet of *wine*.

Such information may be important in giving us means of describing a language at any given time. We have for example no contemporary description of Gothic, merely materials from the fifth and sixth centuries, most of which were produced by earlier translations. Apart from the alphabetic system, which was based on the Greek alphabet and therefore transparent in part, our best source of information about Gothic pronunciation is the set of words taken into Gothic from Greek and Latin, and into them from Gothic. Most of these are names. When for example our Gothic texts transcribe 'Ephesus' as *Aifaiso,* we may infer that the combination *ai* represented a sound something like [ɛ]. Since we know less about the spoken Greek encountered by the Gothic fourth-century translator than we would like, and about the exact sources of the Gothic alphabet, we cannot solve all of our problems about Gothic pronunciation; the importations into Gothic, however, give us some basis for proposing a solution.

Similar procedures have been applied in a variety of languages. For determining the pronunciation of early Chinese, our primary materials are importations into Japanese. Chinese riming dictionaries help us with the ends of morphs; for the beginnings we would be hard pressed if we could not compare the thousands of importations taken at different times from different Chinese dialects into Japanese.

Another use of borrowings for the dating of language contacts, and beyond that of language changes through analysis of the forms of importations, is highly delicate, almost treacherous. As an illustration we may consider the attempts at dating completion of the sound change [θ] > [d] in German, as illustrated by Germ. *dank* vis-à-vis Eng. *thank*. We associate this change with the change of obstruents in High German, though it was further extended into Low German territory than was the change of [t] to [s]. An attempted source for dating is the name of the missionary who came to Iceland from North Germany shortly before 1000 A.D. Icelandic sources give his name as *þangbrandr;* in High German of the time it would have been *Dankbrand*. It is concluded that the Low German form of the name must still have been *Thankbrand,* and that [θ] was still maintained in Low German around 1000 A.D. We cannot however be completely certain of either conclusion, for if Icelanders heard the name even after the sound change, they might have substituted their own form of it, morph by morph. Because of such complexities, dating of linguistic changes with the help of borrowings involves consideration of many possible complications, and even so must be regarded with caution.

Study of importations, however, enables us to draw conclusions about the interrelationships of dialects and languages, the prestige accorded them by speakers, and with care to draw inferences about the language of previous periods and even the time of linguistic changes.

SELECTED FURTHER READINGS

For a thorough statement on borrowing, see Bloomfield's *Language,* pages 444–95. Otto Jespersen, who was much interested in the influence of one language on another, deals at some length with borrowings in English in his widely read book, *The Growth and Structure of the English Language.* It, like many introductory histories of languages, deals especially with the external history of the language. Jespersen's views expressed more generally may be found in *Mankind, Nation, and Individual from a Linguistic Point of View.* Greenough and Kittredge, *Words and Their Ways,* also have interesting sections on borrowings from technical dialects in the history of English.

A full treatment of a Pidgin language is available in Robert A. Hall, Jr., *Melanesian Pidgin English; Grammar, Texts, Vocabulary.* Einar Haugen's *The Norwegian language in America: a study in bilingual behavior* deals with theory as well as the changes which Norwegian underwent in this country.

General study of the intereffects of languages can start best from Uriel Weinreich's *Languages in Contact: Findings and Problems,* which deals with the synchronic problems concisely and gives an extensive bibliography.

Ω

14 – Conclusion

14.1 When we deal with individual changes in language, changes in sound, in form, or in meaning, it is difficult to avoid the impression that entities in a language are neatly undergoing change of only one type at one time. We fail to observe that as phonological changes are taking place, morphological or semantic changes may be going on at the same time, and also that importations may be introduced; moreover, that none of these changes may be related to one another.

Further, when we deal with any problem we generally use a single method among those established in historical linguistics. To secure our data for Old English strong verbs we simply master the writing system of Old English and compile the essential material. If we wish to deal with Proto-Germanic strong verbs we use the comparative method. In attempting to find an explanation for the vowel variation in Germanic strong verbs and related forms in other languages, which is already present in the reconstructed Proto-Indo-European, we use the method of internal reconstruction. Again, however, we cannot divorce method from method. Especially if we are dealing with the history of a language rather than an isolated problem, we must be prepared to use at one time all the methods developed in historical linguistics. Even when we deal with an isolated problem, our explanation may be inadequate if we rely solely on one method. The interlocking of the various changes and our use of all possible methods may be illustrated with virtually any linguistic material. Let us use some of the developments which the English verbs *write* and *shrive* have undergone.

14.2 OE *wrītan* and *scrīfan* belong in the class with *drīfan* and *bītan,* having the principal parts:

wrītan	wrāt	writon	writen
scrīfan	scrāf	scrifon	scrifen

Between Old English and contemporary English the *ī* of the first principal part underwent the same sound change to NE /ay/ as did accented *ī* in words of whatever class, nouns, e.g. *life,* pronouns, e.g. *I,* adjectives, e.g. *blind,* and so on. See section 10.5. Still other sound changes affected the forms of these verbs, such as the loss of *w* before *r,* the rounding of *ā* to *ō,* compare NE *home* < OE *hām,* and others. Through sound changes which modified their forms, but did not affect their morphological contrasts, the Old English forms of *write* and *shrive* developed to the forms we know today: *write, wrote, written.*

14.3 At the same time changes were taking place which affected the morphological system in which they belong. If the Old English forms had been continued with the intervening sound changes, we today would say *I wrote* but *we writ.* This complication of distinguishing the preterite plural from the singular through internal vowel differentiation was absent in the numerous weak verbs, and in classes six and seven of strong verbs; in classes four and five of strong verbs it was essentially a contrast of quantity, which was eliminated in Middle English (see section 10.19) as in OE *bær* 'I carried' : *bǣron* 'we carried.' Accordingly only the first three classes of strong verbs indicated the distinction; they were regularized in keeping with the predominant pattern. This morphological, or analogical change, was wholly unconnected with contemporary sound changes. We have noted earlier, section 11.4, that in the morphological rearrangement the plural vowel was generalized in *bite, bit,* whereas in *write, wrote* like *drive, drove,* the singular vowel came to be used throughout the past.

Other morphological changes are directly connected with sound change. The Old English first singular present *wrīte* became a monosyllable as final vowels were lost, falling together with the imperative. Moreover, the infinitive ending, OE *-an,* became *-en, -e* and was finally lost.

The plural of the present underwent further changes which we cannot account for without drawing information from study of the English dialects. The Old English plural ending *-aþ,* as in *wrītaþ* 'we, you, they write,' should have been maintained as some sort of final dental today. But as noted in section 9.3, contemporary standard English is not a direct continuation of the Old English in which most texts survived, rather a reflex of the Midland dialects. Even in Middle English the Midland dialects generalized the subjunctive plural ending *-en* to the indicative. Chaucer, for example, who used the Midland dialect of London, says in the Prologue to the *Canterbury Tales,* line 12: *thanne longen folk to goon on pilgrimages*. Like the infinitive ending, the plural *-en* was gradually lost, surviving however to the time of Shakespeare. Through the sound changes affecting final *-e* and *-an/-en,* the morphological system was greatly modified. These sound changes are partially responsible for the reduction to a small number of forms in the contemporary English verb system.

At the same time syntactic changes were taking place. When the first singular was distinguished from the second and third singular, and the plural by endings, pronouns were not essential. In the *Beowulf* verbs may be used, as in Latin and Greek, with no pronoun specifying the subject. Today a telegraphic statement like *wrote* is quite ambiguous, for the subject could be singular or plural, first or third person, possibly even second.

14.4 As these and other shifts were taking place in the phonological and grammatical systems, entities in the semantic system were being modified. When the Germanic peoples came into contact with the Romans, they learned new activities, such as writing. With the process they took over the name, borrowing Lat. *scrībere.* Their early writing was done on wood, bone, even stone. Accordingly a native term, the etymon of *write,* meaning 'scratch' was modified and extended as a synonym for the borrowed form of *scrībere.* In New High German its cognate *reissen* still means 'tear,' earlier 'scratch,' though compounds like *Reissbrett* 'drawing board' exemplify the meaning 'write.' NHG *schreiben,* a reflex of the borrowing from Latin, is the general term for 'write.' In English, however, *shrive* came to be restricted more and more to the technical dialect of ecclesiastics, with the meaning of 'hear confessions, and give absolution.' The related *Shrove* was used primarily for the Sunday, Monday and Tuesday preceding Ash Wednesday, when one confessed in preparation for Lent. This was the time of carnival, Med. Lat. *carne vale* 'farewell, oh flesh!' With growing abandonment of confession, *shrive* and *Shrove* have virtually passed out of use; but nonecclesiastics may still give offenders *short shrift.* On the other hand *carnival* has somewhat ironically been transferred from ecclesiastical to secular contexts, and has come to mean a time when one gives the flesh full rein.

14.5 *Shrive* as loanword and *write* as extension illustrate changes which may result from contact with a foreign language. In their development both illustrate the interplay of technical dialects. One such dialect was that associated with the production of runes, which commonly were inscribed on *beech* tablets, as we know today from the modification of meaning in *book* < OE *bōc* 'book, beech-tree.' The technical dialect subsequently involved was that of the church. At the same time forms of *shrive* and *write* were changed by the contacts between northern and southern English geographical dialects. Without a readiness to admit variables introduced in the development of a set of forms by borrowing, which (noted in the analysis of *shrive* and *write*) may be superposed on changes in the phonological, grammatical and semantic systems, we would be unable to account for many phenomena in language.

14.6 Although for simplicity we are restricting our discussion here primarily to two words, we cannot account for their development if we isolate them from the structural sets to which they belong. Both *write* and *shrive* belonged in Old English to a phonological set in which the initial consonantal segment was a cluster composed of consonant plus *r*. Morphologically their roots fell into a set with roots like *bītan,* in which the initial consonantal element was followed by *ī* plus consonant. This structure characterizes strong verbs of the first class; as a result of its coinciding with this structure, the borrowed Latin *scrībere* was taken over as a strong verb. To understand both phonological and grammatical changes, we must deal with entities in their structures. Historical linguistics, to be adequate must be structural.

In semantic study as well, we must deal with words in their semantic fields. Unless we dealt with OE *wrītan* and *scrīfan* as members of a semantic set which were used for writing and related activities, explaining their shifts of meaning would be difficult. It may be an oversimplification to ascribe the shift of meaning found in *shrive* to its presence in a semantic set with *write;* we find this shift, however, in the Germanic area in which the term used especially for production of runes was generalized for all kinds of writing.

14.7 Besides achieving mastery of the changes which elements of a language undergo, each in its several systems, we must be able to manipulate the techniques which give us our information. Through control over the Old English writing system as it was developed from the Roman, with modifications because of strong Irish influence, we learn to know our basic Old English material. Unless we bring to the study of Old English a mastery of the lessons taught by the study of dialect geography, our understanding of it and its changes to the Middle English and the Modern English periods will be poor. We have noted complexities in the development of the English verb paradigm. More such are involved in the development of the third singular present ending *-s*. Its etymon is found in northern texts in Old English times, but the reflex of Old English *-eþ* persists in southern dialects; Chaucer still uses it, e.g. *hath*. In the fifteenth and sixteenth centuries there is increasing evidence for *-s* in the speech of London, but in literary texts *-th* is still used, as in the Authorized Version of the Bible. In the course of time *-s* replaced *-th,* through influences on which scholars are not yet commonly agreed. An influence besides the northern *-s* forms may be the third singular ending in the frequent *is*.

14.8 Since English is well attested, we rely almost entirely on written texts for information on its development. When however we wish to deal with the grammar of Proto-Germanic, in the absence of texts we must use the comparative method to determine our materials. Comparing OE *wrītan,* OS *wrītan,* OHG *rīzan,* the Runic ON *wrait* 'wrote' and Goth. *writs* 'stroke,' plus other forms, we reconstruct the Proto-Germanic verb forms. With the help of the comparative method, we can assume for Proto-Germanic a strong verb system in which roots show a variation which for the etymon of *write* would be:

wreyt-, wrayt- < wroyt-, writ-, writ-

We apply the comparative method further to our reconstructed

Proto-Germanic forms and cognates in other dialects, such as Gk. *rhī́nē* 'file,' reconstructing Proto-Indo-European in the same way as we reconstruct Proto-Germanic.

Understanding of Proto-Indo-European and its dialects is deepened in various ways, by study of texts that are available, by applying the comparative method, by using the techniques of lexicostatistics, by applying whatever findings may have been provided by typological studies. But, since Proto-Indo-European has no known cognates, these methods do not permit us to carry our investigations of language farther back in time.

14.9 The method of internal reconstruction enables us to analyze Proto-Indo-European itself, and to make inferences about segments of it at an earlier time. Section 6.5 indicated the application which we may make of the method of internal reconstruction to the vowel alternations found in Germanic strong verbs. This method has led us to conclude that the various forms of the vocalic nucleus can ultimately be related, through sound changes which we may indicate in a simplified manner as

e > o (in the form we know as preterite singular)
e > ø (in the forms we know as preterite plural and the preterite participle)

We have also observed, section 6.3, how with the method of internal reconstruction Saussure posited for pre-Indo-European laryngeal consonants for which distinct reflexes were later discovered in Hittite.

14.10 The methods developed in historical linguistics have in this way enabled us to push our knowledge of one language family back to 3000 B.C. and earlier. The same methods can be applied to other language families, the Finno-Ugric, Afro-Asiatic, Sino-Tibetan, even to families in which we have only contemporary materials and accordingly must rely very heavily on the method of internal reconstruction. After we have in this way reconstructed proto-languages for each of the language families from which materials are available, we may find relations between some of them. The brave attempts in the past to relate Indo-European with Hamito-Semitic will scarcely provide much information for such future work. Yet even after we reconstruct proto-languages other than Proto-Indo-European, we may find the differences between them so great that they cannot be interrelated. It is quite possible that the near relatives of Proto-Indo-European were all lost and that it alone was widely carried into areas where it displaced other quite unrelated languages, such as the Hattic language superseded by Hittite and numerous totally unknown languages in Europe.

14.11 Historical linguistics in this way takes us back along a route which we know to be much longer, the development of human language, from its ultimate origin. Although this is one of the questions which in the past encouraged historical linguists to continue arduous analyses, it has been demonstrated to be so complex and the origin of human speech so remote that it is now considered quite outside the sphere of historical linguistics, a part of the study of early man. Here it is sufficient to warn of naive theories which have gained wide circulation, such as the bow-wow theory that language is in origin like animal cries, the ding-dong theory, that imitation of natural noises sparked the first speech, and so on. The essence of language is its use by a social group as a system with a definite structure. We may speculate how such a system was first evolved, but we have even less information to support such speculation than we do on the origin of cave paintings.

14.12 Yet though historical linguists may regard the problem of the origin of language beyond the techniques which they control, there is no shortage of activities in store for them. Problems still remain in the most widely analyzed language family, the Indo-European. Indo-Europeanists have scarcely been able to assimilate the contributions resulting from the newly accessible Mycenaean Greek, nor even the additional texts found almost annually. The new perspectives produced by the discovery that Greek was the language of a brilliant civilization from 1450 B.C. have brought about a revision in our view of the Indo-European languages in the second millennium. These revised views must be applied in a re-evaluation of the ancient inscriptions found elsewhere, in Italy, particularly those in Asia Minor, where vigorous archeological work promises further clarification of the language interrelationships through the second and first millennia B.C. Even without new data, our study of Proto-Indo-European must deal with suprasegmental phenomena, and must bring previous analyses into accord with the structural approach that provides a clearer account than that available in past works on historical linguistics.

Outside the Indo-European family, historical linguistics has tremendous opportunities, and obligations. Historical grammars of individual languages, of language families, and their branches are almost universally needed, as are studies in dialect geography, vocabulary and etymology. Even in a set of languages so well known as the Arabic, historical grammars must now be produced on the basis of the descriptive grammars which are becoming available for its various dialects. When we have an adequate historical grammar of Arabic, we hope that the other West Semitic branches will be similarly equipped. Then a historical analysis of West Semitic will be possible, followed by comparison with East Semitic to yield a Proto-Semitic grammar. With this an Afro-Asiatic historical grammar will be possible, if in the meantime Egyptian, Berber, Chad and Cushitic have been equally well studied.

Afro-Asiatic is only one of the language families which in this way needs a series of studies on which syntheses will be based. As they are being produced new insights, techniques or discoveries may be developed by which some of the further problems of historical linguistics will be solved, such as the decipherment of Linear A or the Mohenjo-Daro inscriptions, the discovery of cognate languages for Sumerian, demonstration of relationship between American Indian languages and those of Asia—all of which would permit us to expand our knowledge of linguistic conditions to the third millennium B.C. and earlier, in much the same way as work in the first half of this century has expanded our information on the second millennium.

As we work to extend our knowledge of early languages, careful control of linguistic techniques is increasingly important. This can be derived only from mastery of the techniques applied to well-known languages. Initial mastery of the principles of historical linguistics can best be obtained through control of the historical analysis of one's native language. For this reason it is essential that historical grammars of one's own and other languages be available which incorporate the current techniques of historical linguistics. On their pattern grammars will be produced when adequate data and interest are available regarding any language.

SELECTED FURTHER READINGS

Probably the best historical grammar available for a language family is A. Meillet's *Introduction à l'étude comparative des langues indo-européennes,* though essentially it has been unchanged since 1934. Two monographs in which historical grammars are undertaken for languages with no long series of texts are Robert E. Longacre's *Proto-Mixtecan* and Sarah C. Gudschinsky's *Proto-Popotecan:* A comparative study of Popolocan and Mixtecan.

The publication on the origin of speech is tremendous. Alf Sommerfelt's essay, "The Origin of Language: Theories and Hypotheses," *Journal of World History,* 1.885–902 (1954) gives a concise and sober statement of the problem, and recent concern with it. A more vivid presentation is Charles F. Hockett's "The Origin of Speech," *Scientific American,* 203.88–96 (1960), with scant bibliography, page 276.

ANNOTATED BIBLIOGRAPHY

A welcome number of excellent articles and books may be found for the various facets of historical linguistics, enough to bewilder students entering the field unless they are given some initial guidance. Their chief aim should be to become thoroughly acquainted with a small number of publications from which they can move to other materials, preferably with suggestions from instructors. Fortunately, historical linguistic methodology has not been widely diverse in the various countries in which it has developed, so that students may master it from works published in their own language, especially when these are studied with a structural approach. Beginning students should be selective even about the small number of works cited here. For these reasons this bibliography has been highly restricted and briefly annotated rather than swelled to proportions that may be more impressive than useful.

Atwood, E. Bagby. *A Survey of Verb Forms in the Eastern United States*. Ann Arbor, 1953.

An excellent illustration of the diversity of usage among a population with great mobility.

Bach, Adolf. *Deutsche Mundartforschung*. Heidelberg, 1950.

A book illustrating the tremendous energy which has been expended on dialect geography, especially in German-speaking areas.

Bloomfield, Leonard. *Language*. New York, 1933.

A remarkably thorough introduction to linguistic study, reflecting however historical linguistic theory developed by the neogrammarians and accordingly somewhat confining.

Borgstrøm, Carl Hj. *Innføring i Sprogvidenskap*. Oslo, 1958.

A brief, capable introduction for Norwegian students.

Buck, Carl Darling. *A Dictionary of Selected Synonyms in the Principal Indo-European Languages*. Chicago, 1949.

The preface, and the dictionary itself, can be read with the interest and profit one may derive from a carefully composed work.

Buck, Carl Darling. *Comparative Grammar of Greek and Latin*. Chicago, 1933.

A brief, clear introduction to historical linguistics, pages 30–67, and a concise, factual, though somewhat dated treatment of Greek and Latin historical grammar.

Dauzat, A. *La géographie linguistique*. Paris, 1944.

A good introduction to dialect geography as carried on in France.

Diringer, D. *The Alphabet*. Second edition. New York, 1948.

A general introduction to writing.

Encyclopaedia Britannica.

With other encyclopedias it may be an excellent source of information on linguistic groups. Sapir's widely known article on the Indian languages of North America appeared in volume 5, pages 138–141, of the fourteenth edition (1929). In using this and other encyclopedias, whatever the edition, the name of the author and the bibliography for any article should be checked.

Finck, F. N. *Die Haupttypen des Sprachbaus*. Berlin and Leipzig, 1909.

A brief, clear treatise illustrating typological classification as developed in the nineteenth century.

Francis, W. Nelson. *The Structure of American English*. New York, 1958.

A good elementary statement of English grammar, with

information on recent work in English. Chapter 9, "The Dialects of American English," by Raven I. McDavid, Jr., is the best summary available on dialect geography in the United States.

Gelb, I. J. *A Study of Writing: the foundations of grammatology*. Chicago, 1952.

An introduction to the structural analysis of writing systems.

Gleason, H. A., Jr. *An Introduction to Descriptive Linguistics*. Revised edition. New York, 1961.

A sober statement of the descriptive procedures essential for capable historical study. Accompanied by a fine workbook.

Gray, Louis H. *Foundations of Language*. New York, 1939.

Useful now primarily for its discussion, with bibliography, of language families. The severe review by Z. S. Harris, *Language* 16, pages 216–231, followed by the bibliographical comments of D. C. Swanson, pages 231–235, should be read for its criticism of pre-structural historical linguistics.

Greenberg, J. *Studies on African Linguistic Classification*. New Haven, 1955.

A reclassification of the African languages which has become the basis for further study.

Greenough, J. B. and G. L. Kittredge. *Words and their Ways in English Speech*. New York, 1902.

A pleasant discussion including many examples from literature, with the musty flavor of New England at the turn of the century. Reprinted as Macmillan Paperback 65. New York, 1961.

Hall, Robert A., Jr. *Melanesian Pidgin English:* grammar, texts, vocabulary. Baltimore, 1943.

Though a serious scholarly work, this is a book which can be read with great enjoyment.

Heffner, R-M. S. *General Phonetics*. Madison, 1949.

A comprehensive statement especially on articulatory phonetics.

Hermann, E. *Lautgesetz und Analogie*. Berlin, 1931.

A useful monograph dealing with the relations between sound change and analogical modification.

Hockett, Charles F. *A Course in Modern Linguistics*. New York, 1958.

An introduction to contemporary linguistic theory, including historical techniques; interesting but often personal.

Hockett, Charles F. *A Manual of Phonology*. Baltimore, 1955.

Of interest for its typological statements.

Hoenigswald, Henry M. *Language Change and Linguistic Reconstruction*. Chicago, 1960.

A rigorous presentation especially of the comparative method and the method of internal reconstruction; not an elementary text.

International Journal of American Linguistics 26.3. July, 1960.

Contains important articles on typological classification.

Jakobson, Roman, and Morris Halle. *Fundamentals of Language*. 's-Gravenhage, 1956.

Essays on selected subjects in general linguistics which illustrate some of the contributions emanating from the Prague circle; here of interest for its statements on distinctive features.

Jensen, Hans. *Die Schrift in Vergangenheit und Gegenwart*. Second edition. Berlin, 1958.

A handsome, well-illustrated text on writing.

Jespersen, Otto. *The Growth and Structure of the English Language*. Ninth edition. Oxford, 1946.

A well-written account of the external history of English, which reflects however the author's view of evolution in language development.

Jespersen, Otto. *Language, its Nature, Development and Origin*. London, 1922.

Pertinent especially for its concise history of linguistics, pages 19–99.

Kurath, Hans. *A Word Geography of the Eastern United States*. Ann Arbor, 1949.

A fundamental study of the dialect groupings in the longest settled part of the United States.

Kurath, Hans, Marcus L. Hansen, Julia Bloch, Bernard Bloch. *Handbook of the Linguistic Geography of New England.* Providence, 1939.

Probably the best handbook from which to learn the complexities of undertakings in dialect geography. In addition to the findings it presents on the dialect situation in New England, it is of interest for its chapter on settlement history, for its discussion of the phonetic alphabet, and for its sketches of the individual informants.

Malmberg, Bertil. *Nya Väger inom Språkforskningen.* Stockholm, 1959.

A discussion for Swedish students of various recent linguistic theories, of interest for the perspectives provided by a careful observer.

Martinet, A. *Économie des changements phonétiques.* Berne, 1955.

Essays on the role of structure in historical linguistics, with study of sound change as taking place in accordance with the principle of least effort.

Martinet, A. *Éléments de linguistique générale.* Paris, 1960.

A personal view of language which may be interesting for its contrasts, and similarities, with views more widely held.

Meillet, Antoine. *Introduction à l'étude comparative des langues indo-européennes.* Paris, 1937. Eighth edition, subsequently reprinted.

Though dated, still the best introduction to Indo-European historical grammar, with a concise statement on the principles of historical linguistics.

Meillet, Antoine. *La méthode comparative en linguistique historique.* Oslo, 1925.

Still one of the best introductions to the comparative method.

Meillet, Antoine. *Linguistique historique et linguistique générale.* Paris. I, 1926, II, 1938.

Collected essays on a variety of subjects from one of the

most lucid writers in linguistics, and the most influential historical linguist in the decades before his death in 1936.

Meillet, Antoine and Marcel Cohen. *Les langues du monde.* Second edition. Paris, 1952.

Summaries of language families prepared by various scholars, with maps and a useful bibliography.

Mitzka, Walther. *Handbuch zum Deutschen Sprachatlas.* Marburg, 1952.

A good statement of dialect undertakings in German-speaking areas.

Paul, Hermann. *Prinzipien der Sprachgeschichte.* Fifth edition. Halle, 1920.

The last edition of a treatise on language, especially historical linguistics, by one of the most eminent neogrammarians. Now useful largely as an example of an eminent intellectual achievement.

Pedersen, Holger. *Linguistic Science in the Nineteenth Century.* Translated by John Spargo. Cambridge, 1931.

A readable discussion with numerous illustrations of the principles of historical linguistics as they were evolved in the course of the nineteenth century.

Pop, Sever. *La Dialectologie. Aperçu historique et méthodes d'enquêtes linguistiques.* I. *Dialectologie romane.* II. *Dialectologie non romane.* Louvain, 1950.

An authoritative introduction to projects in dialect geography throughout the world.

Pulgram, Ernst. *The Tongues of Italy: Prehistory and History.* Cambridge, 1958.

A review of the Italian linguistic area from the earliest recoverable time, in relation to the peoples of the peninsula.

Sapir, Edward. *Language.* New York, 1921.

Important in historical linguistics especially for its discussion of typology, and of change in language.

Schmidt, Pater W. *Die Sprachfamilien und Sprachenkreise der Erde.* Heidelberg, 1926. See especially the useful atlas.

Schwyzer, E. *Griechische Grammatik.* Three volumes. München, 1939–53.

One of the most comprehensive historical grammars available; a lengthy introduction deals with linguistic theory.

Sethe, Kurt. *Der Ursprung des Alphabets*. Berlin, 1916.
An excellent early discussion of the origin of the alphabet.

Sperber, Hans. *Einführung in die Bedeutungslehre*. Second edition. Leipzig, 1930.
An introduction by one of the important contributors to semantic theory.

Stern, G. *Meaning and change of meaning, with special reference to the English language*. Göteborg, 1931.
Useful for its thorough discussion, with excellent examples drawn from English.

Sturtevant, E. H. *An Introduction to Linguistic Science*. New Haven, 1949.
Interesting primarily because it reflects the views of an outstanding historical linguist; not a comprehensive handbook.

Sturtevant, E. H. *Linguistic Change*. Chicago, 1917.
An elementary introduction to various types of change. Now reprinted as a paperback by the Chicago University Press.

Thomas, L. L. *The Linguistic Theories of N. Ja. Marr*. Berkeley and Los Angeles, 1957.
An exposition of one of the most notable perversions in linguistic study.

Trubetzkoy, N. S. *Grundzüge der Phonologie*. Prague, 1939. French translation: *Principes de phonologie*. Paris, 1949.
Of primary importance in descriptive linguistics, but valuable for its typological statements also in historical work.

Ullmann, Stephen. *The Principles of Semantics*. Second edition. Glasgow, 1957.
Useful especially in summarizing various theories, and in providing a comprehensive bibliography. Observe especially the supplement on recent developments in semantics, which includes discussions on works published to 1957, including handbooks like H. Kronasser's *Handbuch der Semasiologie* and more original theoretical work like

Wittgenstein's *Philosophical Investigations.* Further readings in the subject may be selected from the numerous works cited.

Wartburg, Walther von. *Einführung in Problematik und Methodik der Sprachwissenschaft.* Halle, 1943. Translated: *Problèmes et méthodes de la linguistique.* Paris, 1946.
Of interest as an introduction by one of the great Romance linguists.

Weinreich, Uriel. *Languages in Contact: Findings and Problems.* New York, 1953.
An attempt to provide a rigorous framework for studying the interrelationships of languages, with an extensive bibliography.

From the first, students should become acquainted with journals in the field, not least for reviews of new publications. The *Bibliographie Linguistique,* published annually, has a full list of relevant journals, as well as works throughout linguistics. As with bibliography, one will soon learn which are the profitable sources for further investigation.

Bibliographie Linguistique. Paris. Annual bibliography of linguistic publications, beginning with 1939. Volume I appeared in 1949. (Abbreviated: BL)

Bulletin de la Société de Linguistique de Paris. Useful for the views of French linguists, especially in the annual volume of reviews. (BSL)

Bulletin of the School of Oriental and African Studies. London. Useful for reviews and articles covering the area indicated by the title. (BSOAS)

Indogermanische Forschungen. Berlin. One of the leading German journals, giving views primarily on Indo-European studies. (IF)

International Journal of American Linguistics. Baltimore. (IJAL)

Journal of the American Oriental Society. New Haven. Especially for the languages of Asia. (JAOS)

Language. Baltimore. Journal of the Linguistic Society of America. A general journal, reflecting the views of American linguists. (Lg.)

Lingua. Amsterdam. International Review of General Linguistics. Somewhat comparable to *Language,* with European scholars represented.

Norsk Tidsskrift for Sprogvidenskap. Oslo. Contains views of the vigorous Norwegian group of linguists, often of great value for reviews. (NTS)

Voprosy jazykoznanija. Moscow. Journal presenting the views of Russian linguists. (VJa)

Word. Journal of the Linguistic Circle of New York. In aim similar to *Language*.

SYMBOLS, TECHNICAL TERMS, AND ABBREVIATIONS

Symbols:

- a hyphen, with other symbols indicates their relative position:

  t- indicates a *t* in initial position;
  -t- indicates a *t* in medial position;
  -t indicates a *t* in final position

> indicates "developed to, became"

< indicates "developed from"

= indicates "corresponds to"

* indicates a nonattested, usually a reconstructed form; placed after a form it indicates that the form is nonattested, but that we can be reasonably certain of it from similar forms or from other inflected forms of the same paradigm, e.g.

OHG	*drīe*	>	NHG	*drei*			
NHG	*drei*	<	OHG	*drīe*	<	IE	**treys*
OHG	*drīe*	=	Skt.	*tráyas*	=	Goth.	*þreis**

[ ] enclose material in phonetic transcription

/ / enclose material in phonemic transcription

' ' enclose glosses; note that glosses are given for identification of cited forms, not to provide the central meaning

Italics are used to indicate a citation

Bold-face is used to point up a term when it is defined in the surrounding text.

Technical terms:

Technical terms are defined in the text and are better learned from continuous discussions than from lists, but a few common terms are given here for convenience.

Dialect is used for a subdivision of a language or of a language family, e.g. English is an Indo-European dialect. The Midland dialect is used across a central portion of the United States. For a contrast with the term *language,* cf. pages 3 and 35.

Etymon is the form from which another developed, e.g. PIE *treys* is the etymon of NHG *drei.*

Reflex is a form which has developed from an earlier form, e.g. NHG *drei* is a reflex of PIE *treys.*

Gloss is a word used to identify or define another word, e.g. Skt. *tráyas* 'three.'

Abbreviations for grammatical terms:

acc.	accusative
f., fem.	feminine
indic., ind.	indicative
m., masc.	masculine
nom.	nominative
nt.	neuter
pl.	plural
pres.	present
pret.	preterite

ptc.	participle; pret. ptc. preterite participle
sg.	singular
suff.	suffix

Abbreviations used in dating (cf. pp. 18–19, 36)

M = Middle, e.g. ME Middle English
N = New, Modern, e.g. NE Modern English
O = Old, e.g. OE Old English
P = Proto-, only for reconstructed languages, e.g. PGmc. Proto-Germanic
pre- = a prior stage, e.g. pre-OE, pre-Old English

Symbols used for geographical subdivisions

E = East   S = South
N = North   W = West, e.g. WGmc., West Germanic

Abbreviations

Languages:

Arab.	= Arabic
Arm.	= Armenian
Av.	= Avestan
Chin.	= Chinese
Crim. Goth.	= Crimean Gothic
CS	= Church Slavic
E	= English
Egypt.	= Egyptian
Fr.	= French
Franc.	= Franconian
Fris.	= Frisian
Germ., G	= German

Gk.	=	Greek
Gmc.	=	Germanic
Goth.	=	Gothic
Heb.	=	Hebrew
HG	=	High German
Hitt.	=	Hittite
Icel.	=	Icelandic
IE	=	Indo-European
IIr.	=	Indo-Iranian
Ir.	=	Irish
Ital.	=	Italian
Jap.	=	Japanese
Lat.	=	Latin
LG	=	Low German
Lith.	=	Lithuanian
Myc. Gk.	=	Mycenaean Greek
N	=	Norse
Pers.	=	Persian
Port.	=	Portuguese
Rum.	=	Rumanian
Russ.	=	Russian
Sax.	=	Saxon
Skt.	=	Sanskrit
Span.	=	Spanish
Sum.	=	Sumerian
Turk.	=	Turkish

INDEX

The index is arranged in accordance with the Latin alphabet; differing pronunciations are disregarded, so that Sanskrit *c* is alphabetized with English *c;* moreover, diacritics are disregarded, so that *č* is treated like *c*. Thorn, *þ*, and edh, ð, are treated like *th*. English items are unmarked.

D

I

S

W